Monitoring School Performance
A Guide for Educators

by

J. Douglas Willms

Centre for Policy Studies in Education
University of British Columbia
and
Centre for Educational Sociology
University of Edinburgh

 The Falmer Press

(A member of the Taylor & Francis Group)
Washington, D.C. • London

USA   The Falmer Press, Taylor & Francis Inc., 1900 Frost Road, Suite 101,
             Bristol, PA 19007
UK   The Falmer Press, 4 John Street, London WC1N 2ET

© J. Douglas Willms 1992

First published 1992

A catalogue record for this book is available from the British Library

ISBN 1 85000 970 8 cased
ISBN 1 85000 971 6 paperback

**Library of Congress Cataloging-in-Publication Data are available on
request**

Cover design by Caroline Archer
Typeset in 10/11pt Times by
Graphicraft Typesetters Ltd., Hong Kong

*Printed in Great Britain by Burgess Science Press, Basingstoke
on paper which has a specified pH value on final paper
manufacture of not less than 7·5 and is therefore 'acid free'.*

Contents

List of Tables and Figures

Preface

This book is intended as a practical guide for teachers and administrators who are developing systems for monitoring school performance, either at the school level, or at the education authority, district, or state level. It endeavours to contribute to the promotion of better monitoring systems, and to serve as a general reference for those conducting educational evaluations. However, the book is more than a 'how-to' manual in that it also discusses the theories underlying monitoring systems, reviews the literature on various aspects of monitoring, and examines the potential uses and misuses of data describing the schooling process. The book also discusses the inherent tensions of monitoring related to accountability and the professional autonomy of teachers. Much of this discussion, and the examples given throughout the book, pertain to monitoring in Canada, the US, and the UK. However, the book establishes general guidelines for developing monitoring systems that would apply elsewhere.

A central theme of the book is that the estimation of school effects is not an exact science. The processes of schooling are complex and interactive. For over two decades researchers have been trying to answer questions about the extent to which schools differ in their results and why some schools seem to perform better than others. Their work is being furthered considerably by recent improvements in tests and survey instruments, statistical methods, and research design. While the attempts to answer these questions are helping us to understand better how schools work, they are also revealing the complexity of schooling. If anything, the research has shown us that monitoring systems by themselves are inadequate for diagnosing the causes of poor school performance and prescribing corresponding remedies. However, monitoring systems can provide useful feedback about the strengths and weaknesses of a schooling system. They can enable us to gauge whether inequities in academic achievement are increasing or waning. They can serve to assess whether a school or district reform is having a significant impact. They can help us learn why some schools are performing better than others, and thereby raise critical questions about educational policy.

The misuse of data describing school performance has created mistrust and scepticism amongst many educators, particularly principals and teachers who fear they may be judged unfairly. Observed differences between schools in their outcomes may be attributable to unmeasured differences between pupils upon intake, to wider social and economic factors, or to measurement and sampling error. Because of poorly conducted analyses which did not take these factors into account, and because of the widespread misinterpretation of achievement data, some researchers have called for the abandonment of school comparisons (Research for Better Schools, 1990). I believe this is an extreme position. School comparisons can enable us to identify schools that are consistently performing above average; these schools can help us understand the effects of certain policies and practices. School comparisons also enable us to judge whether a particular school's standards are inconsistent with those set by other schools. This book describes some of the methods for making school comparisons, and examines the limitations of these methods. In this respect, I hope it will prove useful to principals and teachers who seek a better understanding of the validity of assessments derived from monitoring systems.

Many of the ideas for this book grew out of research derived from a long-term collaborative relationship between Fife Regional Education Authority and the Centre for Educational Sociology (CES) at the University of Edinburgh. For more than a decade Fife has been testing its pupils in reading and verbal ability at the end of primary 3 and primary 7. At the same time, Andrew McPherson, David Raffe and their colleagues at CES have been conducting biennially the Scottish Young People's Survey (SYPS). The SYPS is based on a questionnaire mailed to pupils nine months after they leave secondary school. The questionnaire covers a wide range of topics pertaining to pupils' family background, secondary schooling, and experiences upon entering the labour market and further education. The Director of Education in Fife, Magnus More, and the Deputy Director, David McNeill, saw the value in supporting CES to conduct a program of basic research that used their data in conjunction with data from the SYPS. Accordingly, the CES increased its coverage of pupils in Fife from 40 per cent to 50 per cent in 1980, and from 10 per cent to 100 per cent in 1984.

During the early years of the relationship between Fife and CES, one would have characterized the research program as 'basic' or 'pure' research, rather than 'policy' or 'applied' research. The work was supported not only by the Fife Regional Educational Authority, but also by the UK Economic and Social Research Council, the Social Sciences and Humanities Research Council of Canada, the Scottish Education Department, and the US Spencer Foundation. The emphasis of the program was on examining the overall relationships between class, gender, ability, and examination attainment, and on determining whether the aggregate characteristics of a school's intake had an effect on pupil attainment over and above the effects of pupils' individual family backgrounds. This work led to the testing of different statistical models of school effectiveness, and to assessing whether schools were stable in their effects. The relevance of the work to school policy did not become fully apparent until 1988, when the UK government announced its plans to establish a national testing program for pupils of various ages, and to require head teachers to make regular reports of their pupil attainment to local school boards or school governors.

The examples used in this guide are based mainly on data describing pupils who entered Fife's secondary schools in 1980, and completed their secondary schooling between 1984 and 1986. These data describe an entire cohort of pupils and include information on pre-entry ability and a number of family background variables. Because of this, they are better than many other sets of data for examining particular questions about school effects and for demonstrating a number of different types of analyses.

Some of the examples are based on data describing pupils' achievement scores for a set of pupils from one Canadian school district. These data were collected as part of a study on kindergarten screening and pupils' growth in mathematics which Suzanne Jacobsen and I conducted between 1987 and 1990. Our study included annual measures of academic achievement for a large cohort of pupils taken while they were progressing through their intermediate years. The data are useful for monitoring performance because they provide estimates of pupils' rates of growth in academic achievement, in addition to their status at particular times.

Recently, there has been considerable discussion and debate in the professional literature about what is meant by the term 'school effects', how accurately school effects can be estimated, and what data are required for their accurate estimation. The recent development of statistical models for analyzing multilevel data has played an important role in this debate. In this regard, the work in developing multilevel methods by Murray Aitkin (Tel Aviv University), Tony Bryk (University of Chicago), Harvey Goldstein (London Institute of Education), Nick Longford (Education Testing Service), and Stephen Raudenbush (Michigan State University) is central to many of the ideas in this book. Much is owing to Raudenbush, in particular, for the time and energy he has devoted to the work at CES; many of his ideas are embodied in the CES research on school effects.

The book draws heavily on research that was conducted at the Centre for Educational Sociology (University of Edinburgh) and the Center for Policy Studies in Education (University of British Columbia). The work has been supported generously by grants from the UK Economic and Social Research Council, the Scottish Education Department, Fife Regional Council, the Social Sciences and Humanities Research Council of Canada, and the Spencer Foundation. I am grateful for their support.

I also wish to thank the many colleagues who contributed to this effort. At the Centre for Educational Sociology, Andrew McPherson, David Raffe, Lindsay Paterson, and Stephen Raudenbush made many helpful suggestions on how to improve a report I wrote for the Fife Regional Educational Authority. Their suggestions and support encouraged me to write this book for a more general audience. Andrew McPherson was very helpful later, too, when he provided detailed feedback on the opening chapters. Several colleagues at the Center for Policy Studies in Education gave helpful advice on drafts of various chapters. I thank Bill Day, Frank Echols, Donald Fisher, and Kjell Rubensen for their encouragement and advice. Murray Ross read the entire manuscript, and offered many helpful suggestions. He helped me to see more clearly the views of those who oppose monitoring.

I was fortunate also to receive assistance from Martin Turner and Robin van Heck. Martin provided expertise in data analysis, and helped produce most of the figures. Robin edited the manuscript with very careful attention to detail.

Last, I thank my wife, Ann. She regularly listened to readings of lines, paragraphs, and pages. She provided a teacher's perspective which served to balance my zeal for research. Most of all, she understands the troubles and joys that the creative process entails, and thus was a constant support and companion throughout the period of research and writing.

Chapter 1

Introduction

Educators and administrators have dramatically increased their efforts to collect data describing the performance of their educational systems. Many countries are establishing programs to collect 'indicators' of school quality for monitoring performance at national, regional, and local levels. The quest for more and better data is widespread. Nearly every country in Europe is developing a monitoring system based on performance indicators. The UK Government established a national curriculum of core and foundation subjects, and mounted an ambitious testing program to assess pupils' attainment of the curricular objectives. The US Department of Education, through its Center for Education Statistics, collects a variety of indicators describing the 'health' of the elementary and secondary schooling systems. From these data, it publishes the Secretary of Education's 'wall chart', which includes state-by-state comparisons for a number of performance indicators (Smith, 1988). Currently the National Governors' Association Panel to Monitor the National Education Goals is developing a 'national report card' for monitoring progress towards the national educational goals recently established by President Bush and the Governors (Lewis, 1991; Pipho, 1991). Most states have established monitoring systems based on performance indicators (Selden, 1988), and many school districts are following their lead.

An 'indicator' is simply a statistic describing some feature of the schooling system associated with its performance, such as the average test score of a school, the proportion of drop-outs, or the pupil-teacher ratio. Like most statistics, an indicator derives its meaning from its trend over time, from its variation within a sample, or from comparison to some standard. The standard can be the average value for a set of schools, a predefined goal, or a socially determined standard (Oakes, 1986; Shavelson, McDonnell, Oakes, Carey and Picus, 1987).

The collection of performance indicators is not a new phenomenon. There is a long history of using national data to monitor long-term trends in educational performance; to examine inequalities in attainment between racial, ethnic, and social-class groups; to make inter-regional comparisons; and to assess the impact of major educational reforms (Chartered Institute of Public Finance Accounts, 1986; Koretz, 1986; McPherson and Willms, 1987; Murnane, 1987; Powell and Steelman, 1984; Stern, 1986; Welch, 1987).

Schools and school districts[1] have collected data for planning and decision-making, for assessing strengths and weaknesses in various curricular areas, and for selecting and allocating pupils to different types of programs.

What distinguishes the current work on indicators from earlier evaluation efforts is the amount and kind of data that are being collected, and the way data collection is being institutionalized at all levels. Previously, programs to monitor performance included easy-to-measure indicators, such as graduation rates, pupil-teacher ratios, and achievement test scores. Now administrators are acquiring information on a much wider range of outcomes, including not only cognitive measures, but also affective measures such as self-concept and attitudes to school and work. Many programs include measures describing pupils' family background, and various indicators of school 'processes' believed to be related to schooling outcomes. Before the recent interest in performance indicators, data of this kind were collected only in evaluations or research studies addressing particular questions. Many school districts now collect and analyze these data as part of an institutionalized routine. The routine includes the production of annual reports to school boards, parents, teachers, and administrators.

The Impetus for Monitoring Systems

School boards, administrators, and teachers rely heavily on their working knowledge to make decisions (Sproull and Zubrow, 1981; Williams and Bank, 1984). The 'working knowledge' of decision-makers includes the large body of facts, principles, and perceptions that determine their particular view of the world. It is influenced by their values, attitudes, and beliefs, and by the steady stream of information gathered from friends, colleagues, clients, and the public. But decision-makers often view their working knowledge as inadequate for confronting certain issues: it is too subjective or shallow, or biased because it does not represent the opinions of a wide constituency. Thus they regularly seek 'specific knowledge'. They appoint committees, hire consultants, conduct evaluations, commission research, and attend courses to obtain information focused on specific problems or activities. Although specific knowledge is often more objective and relevant, obtaining it requires time and resources. Also, specific knowledge is sometimes at odds with working knowledge, and does not always fulfil decision-makers' needs (Husen and Kogen, 1984).

Monitoring information can fill some of the gaps between working and specific knowledge. If data are collected routinely from a variety of sources, then many regular information needs can be met more quickly. Monitoring data on some topics can be more objective than those obtained through in-

---

[1] The administrative units for governing schools at the regional level are generally called local education authorities (LEAs) in England and Wales, education authorities (EAs) in Scotland, and school districts in North America. For sake of brevity I use the term 'school districts' to cover all of these, unless I am referring specifically to administrative units in the UK.

formal observations and conversations. Monitoring data tend to cover a wider variety of topics than those obtained through evaluations, consultancies, or commissioned research. In some cases monitoring information is insufficient for addressing particular problems, but it can provide a basis for the kind of specific knowledge required.

The collection of monitoring data also can serve several functions directly pertinent to improving schooling and reducing inequities. The information can be used to identify problem areas in the schooling system, so that corrective action can be taken. It can assist administrators in determining the best allocation of resources. It can be used to diagnose strengths and weaknesses in pupils' mastery of curricular objectives, and therefore guide curriculum and instruction. It can be used to assess the effects of interventions implemented at the state, district, or school level. It can stimulate discussion about the goals of schooling, and give rise to new ideas that affect policy and practice.

Monitoring data can also motivate administrators and teachers to improve performance and reduce inequities. This function is not necessarily achieved through top-down accountability tactics. In many cases the provision of information itself stimulates the self-regulatory mechanisms already existing in most schools. Research on school and teacher effectiveness suggests that effective schools generally have some system for monitoring performance (e.g., Cohen, 1981; Odden, 1982; Purkey and Smith, 1983), and that effective teachers frequently test their pupils and conduct weekly and monthly reviews (Rosenshine and Stevens, 1986).

However, the movement to collect performance indicators is driven not just by a desire for better information. Many educators believe that the explicit intention of monitoring systems is to make schools accountable through market forces. Throughout Europe and North America a faith in market mechanisms pervades government offices. One of its doctrines is that publicly funded organizations should be held accountable by having to report regularly on their performance. In some public services, such as transportation, postal services, media services, and public utilities, performance is equated with profits or losses. Balance sheets of the public services are compared to those of private companies offering comparable services. Public services that are unprofitable become candidates for closure or privatization. But in areas such as education, health, social welfare, corrections, and the environment, the outcomes are less tangible. Value for money is more difficult, perhaps impossible, to ascertain. In these areas the push has been towards measuring performance on a number of criteria, and comparing results across organizations. The belief is that such comparisons will stimulate competition and motivate organizations to provide higher levels of service.

Some administrators and educators believe that the introduction of market mechanisms to education will significantly improve schooling. The view is that inter-school or inter-regional comparisons will bring pressures to bear on schools, particularly those performing below the average. These pressures will induce schools to perform better, and if not, the data will constitute objective grounds for closing schools or appointing new staff. Also, if indicators can be used to accurately and fairly assess the performance of individual teachers or principals, then they might be used as an objective basis on which to decide promotions, merit pay, and dismissals. Indicators of school performance have been used in school award programs in California, Florida, and South Carolina (Mandeville and Anderson, 1987; Wynne, 1984). A few states have proposed that teachers be awarded cash bonuses for superior results based on indicator data.

Educators do not unanimously accept the view that market mechanisms will improve the education system. Landsberger, Carlson, and Campbell (1988) surveyed approximately 6000 administrators in England and Wales, West Germany, and the US to determine the most important policy issues facing educational administrators. The primary concern of these administrators was whether 'market mechanisms' should be built into the educational system. Opponents to monitoring argue that there is not consensus about the goals of education, the characteristics of an effective school or teacher, or the nature of educational achievement. They believe that monitoring restricts what is taught in schools, displaces valuable teaching time, and reduces the autonomy of teachers.

Even if administrators do not intend to use monitoring data explicitly for purposes of accountability, the collection of data by itself unleashes subtle and indirect market forces. For example, the results of inter-school comparisons might be used only to supplement other evaluative data, and to support schools in their self-evaluations. But schools directly or indirectly compete for the best teachers and pupils, and monitoring results affect schools' reputations, which eventually influence teachers' decisions about where to teach, and parents' decisions about the best area in which to live. These market forces are supported by policies that promote greater choice and diversity in schooling, such as open enrolment plans that allow parents to choose schools outside their designated catchment areas. Parents sometimes use monitoring results to exert pressures through their locally elected school boards. The pressure can be considerable in areas with declining enrolments, where some schools are threatened with closure.

Some of the impetus for monitoring has come from the fear that monitoring data collected at national or state levels are inadequate or will be used inappropriately. Smith (1988) suggested that the widespread interest in performance monitoring in the US stemmed from the discontent of analysts and policy-makers with existing national data, and a determination on the part of the federal government to use performance indicators for purposes of accountability. The government's intention to continue publishing its 'wall chart' of state-by-state comparisons, and the criticism the document received from some of the states, induced the Council of Chief State School Officers (CCSSO) to develop a more comprehensive and valid system for monitoring performance at the state level. In turn, some school districts have created monitoring systems as a means of protection against criticisms that might stem from state assessments on a narrow set of schooling outcomes.

Finally, the collection of indicator data is consistent with a more general trend amongst governments and other administrative bodies to amass extensive amounts of data and to compile descriptive statistics. This trend has been supported by rapid advances in the technology for collecting, storing, and analyzing data. These activities serve not only an administrative function, but also a political one. Statistics describing the health of education systems can be used to demonstrate the need for reform arising from the poor management of a previous administration, or to demonstrate improvements stemming from reforms of the administration in power. Some critics contend that analysts choose to report, depending on their political purposes, statistics describing absolute levels of performance, changes in levels of performance, levels or changes for a particular subsample of the population, or comparisons with other districts, states, or countries. Porter (1988) argues that performance indicators are merely a political tool designed to strengthen the hand of those favouring centralized control of the process and products of teaching.

Purpose of the Book

This book is intended to guide the many decisions entailed in developing a monitoring system. Its purpose is to specify the kind of data that might be routinely collected by a school district or by individual schools, and to describe appropriate methods for analyzing and reporting data. No single design for a monitoring system could be appropriate across all districts or schools, and a district-level design would not necessarily serve the requirements for individual schools. The guide begins therefore with a more general discussion of the main issues pertaining to performance monitoring, and sets forth some general principles concerning the design of a monitoring system.

The guide does not describe qualitative approaches to educational evaluation, such as those proposed by Eisner (1985), Fetterman (1988), Hammersley and Atkinson (1983), Lincoln and Guba (1985), and Patton (1980). This decision was not intended to disparage these methods; it was made simply to limit the scope of the book. The multilevel models and methods proposed in this book provide a framework for describing the variability in schooling outcomes between and within schools. This framework is potentially useful for guiding qualitative study in that it invites one to think about how policies and practices at different levels of the system affect schooling outcomes, and whether their effect varies for pupils with differing backgrounds. The framework also serves to contextualize the findings of qualitative studies (e.g., see Raffe and Willms, 1989).

The development of a system for monitoring school or district performance is not an easy task. If a monitoring system is to be useful for planning and decision-making, it must be based on a sound theory about how schools achieve their effects, and it must have a clearly defined purpose which is understood by educators and policy-makers at all levels of the schooling system. It must cover a wide range of educational goals, and be responsive to changes in the educational system. Yet it cannot be too costly in terms of pupil, teacher, or administrative resources.

Several technical issues concerning the measurement of schooling outcomes and the assessment of school effects also must be addressed. Perhaps the most difficult issue concerns the identification of goals that are common across schools in a system. This is complicated by the fact that schools often have different goals for pupils with differing interests and levels of ability. In addition, test developers find it difficult to construct measures that span the entire range of achievement for pupils at a particular grade level, particularly in the later years of schooling, and yet cover the curriculum in enough detail to be useful for diagnostic purposes.

Even with adequate solutions to the measurement problems, the task of separating the effects of school practices and policies from factors that lie outside the school is complicated and requires extensive data. Research on school effectiveness at the Centre for Educational Sociology (University of Edinburgh) showed that pupil attainment at the secondary level is related to pupils' socioeconomic status (SES), their prior level of ability, the composition of their family, the type of neighbourhood they live in, the overall ability and socioeconomic composition of their school, and the level and structure of local employment (Garner and Raudenbush, 1991, McPherson and Willms, 1986; Raffe and Willms, 1989; Willms, 1986). The multilevel modelling techniques discussed later in this book allow one to make statistical adjustments to the school means on an outcome measure to take account of factors that lie outside the school. Estimates of the adjusted means provide a better basis for making comparisons between schools; however, the accuracy of the estimates depends on the amount and type of data available. The accuracy depends also on the assumptions made about the relationships between outcome measures, policy and practice variables, and measures describing outside influences.

All of these theoretical, administrative, and technical issues are inextricably tied to political issues concerning the professional autonomy of teachers, the nature of the curriculum, and the control of resources. The development of a monitoring system requires hundreds of little decisions about what kind of data should be collected, how data will be analyzed, who will have access to data, and what actions will be taken on the basis of findings. These decisions are affected by how those developing the system view the purposes of monitoring, and the amount of resources that can be devoted to the enterprise. If a guide is to establish a standard for performance monitoring, it must either attempt to take the competing interests of several groups into account, or set forth its own biases.

Initial Premises

One could feasibly write an entire volume discussing the political issues concerning performance monitoring. This is not my purpose. However, I will not skirt the central issue of whether such a book should be written at all. Those who decry monitoring may view the book as an attempt to accelerate it. They oppose its acceleration because they believe monitoring may curb educators from questioning the purposes of schooling, and from critically examining what they teach and how they teach it. They would argue also that monitoring systems help institutionalize organizational structures and practices aimed at goals that have not been justified or accepted by the educational community. The opponents of monitoring include hundreds of teachers and administrators who feel that monitoring places unrealistic demands on their time and resources, and that ultimately it will reduce their authority and be used against them.

Advocates of monitoring would counter that both administrators and teachers need objective information to make sound educational decisions. They would argue that market mechanisms have a positive effect on schooling, or at least that monitoring motivates teachers and administrators. They would point to Gallup Poll results for the US that suggest over 80 per cent of parents with children in school want standardized national testing programs to measure the academic achievement of pupils attending public schools in their community (Elam and Gallup, 1989). The advocates of monitoring might concede that data derived from standardized tests and questionnaires have limitations, but would maintain that such data are better than no data at all.

The debate in the UK has taken a different turn. The Government strived to involve teachers in setting standards and constructing tests. The standardization of the tests has been based on teachers' judgements of what a child should be able to accomplish at various stages, rather than on statistical criteria pertaining to how well test items discriminate amongst pupils. The tests also incorporate several different types of assessment tasks, including performance-based tasks that require pupils to use higher-order thinking skills. Thus, in many respects, the national testing program increases the professional autonomy of teachers. Despite these efforts, however, the pilot testing of the national tests has met with widespread resistance. Many teachers are unhappy because the Government has not made it clear how the results will be used. In particular, it has not specified whether school comparisons will be made, and if so, on what basis. A number of parents are sceptical too. They are unsure whether they want their children tested because they fear the results may be used to make decisions about the type of school program suitable for their children. More generally, there is mistrust of the Government's political agenda connected with national tests and monitoring.

My own position on monitoring is that the benefits *can* outweigh any negative consequences. I believe also that some of the dangers of monitoring can be avoided, or at least minimized. This position has several antecedents. First, it is derived from my interest in studying the causes and consequences of inequities in schooling. Through my research on public and private schools in the US (Willms, 1985a), and my research with McPherson on the effects of comprehensive schooling in Scotland (McPherson and Willms, 1987), I saw the potential for using systematically collected data for examining questions about equity between racial, ethnic, and social-class groups, and between the sexes. I also learned about some of the limitations of monitoring data. If educators are to argue for equality of outcomes, they must be prepared to specify and defend some set of outcomes. My position on monitoring stems as well from having witnessed inappropriate uses of performance indicators. In many cases comparisons between schools are made without making statistical adjustments for the types of pupils entering schools. Thus, the findings frequently suggest that the best-performing schools are those with the most favourable pupil intakes. These conclusions are often unwarranted. The third antecedent to my position on monitoring is a genuine curiosity about how schools work. As an educational researcher I see great potential in using monitoring data to further our understanding about the relationships between schooling processes and pupil outcomes.

Monitoring systems have acquired some momentum; to a large extent I take them as a *fait accompli*. I hope that this guide will help administrators and teachers use indicator data more fairly, and remind them of the limitations of performance indicators. I believe that monitoring can further our understanding of the effects of educational policies and practices on schooling outcomes, and can help determine whether particular educational interventions have a desirable effect.

However, my endorsement of monitoring is not without qualifications. I also make some assumptions about what could be, even though its realization in practice is difficult. To begin, therefore, I am setting out a list of premises as a means to clarify my position. They are presented in the spirit of Cronbach *et al.*'s ninety-five theses of evaluation (Cronbach *et al.*, 1980); that is, I hope they will provoke further discussion of the issues:

- Monitoring systems can contribute to the working knowledge of both teachers and administrators. They can serve a number of functions relevant to improving schooling and reducing inequities.
- Monitoring data are not a substitute for other kinds of data. Monitoring data should be used in conjunction with data collected both from discussions with staff and pupils, and through detailed observations of school and teacher practice.
- Monitoring systems can induce debate about school policies and practices. Their usefulness in raising questions can be as great as it is in answering them.
- Monitoring systems will not turn the social control and management of schools into a technology. The fear that this will occur presumes that administrators are ignorant of the complexities of schooling and the limitations of monitoring data, and that teachers and pupils are fully submissive to administrative authority.
- One of the dangers of monitoring is that it can restrict the goals of education to a set of objectives defined centrally rather than locally. This can be alleviated by devolving the design and control of most aspects of monitoring to the level at which decisions about policy and instruction are made.
- Administrators must make decisions concerning accountability, such as decisions about school closures, the dismissal of teachers, or staff promotion. If monitoring data are available, they will inevitably be used, either formally or informally, in these decisions. Some of the anxiety concerning accountability can be lessened if administrators use monitoring data to provide constructive feedback about policy and practice. Those monitoring school performance need to specify clearly how monitoring data will be used in summative decisions — what analyses will be undertaken, how findings will be reported, and who will have access to the findings.

In writing this book I continually encountered two difficulties. I wanted to describe what I consider to be *best practice* of monitoring school performance, rather than describe the benefits of monitoring or belabour its pitfalls as it is currently practiced. The problem is that the degree to which best practice can be accomplished is always circumscribed by political considerations, and these tended to temper my view of the ideal. Thus, I was continually caught in having to decide between what constitutes ideal practice and what may be practical. Generally, I attempted to prescribe standards for the ideal and discuss attendant practical considerations — rather than attempting to assess what may be practical in most situations, and discussing limitations because the practical was less than ideal. The second difficulty, related to the first, is that even the best practice of monitoring has limitations. In attempting to set a standard for good practice I wanted also to delineate the shortcomings of monitoring. However, the requirements for best practice may be overwhelming to administrators wanting to get started, such that they decide monitoring is too costly given their resources. There is the danger too that by providing detailed descriptions of the shortcomings of monitoring, I would give the impression that there are so many problems with it that it may be best not to do it at all. I chose to present an optimistic picture of what could be accomplished through monitoring, but have not ignored the many limitations. I hope that the reader will view the work as simply a guide for better assessment, and not prematurely judge the benefits or limitations of monitoring.

Overview of the Book

The next chapter examines the above premises in the light of current reforms and policy initiatives in the UK and the US. The two systems are very different, especially at the secondary level, in part because of the long history of national examinations in the UK. These examinations to a large extent drive the curriculum, and ensure a degree of uniformity. The US curriculum is characterized by diversity more than uniformity, which poses special problems for the development of monitoring programs. In both schooling systems there is an explicit agenda to develop indicators for purposes of accountability.

Chapter 3 describes the input-process-output model, the theoretical model on which systems of monitoring performance are based. It also discusses how three different types of monitoring systems, defined by their purposes, are related to this model. I suggest three ways in which the model can be strengthened. These concepts underlie many of the arguments in the chapters that follow regarding the kind of data to be collected and the approach to analysis.

Chapter 4 describes four ways that researchers and educators use the term 'school effects'. Using the definition relevant to the comparison of schools, I suggest there are two types of school effects that should be considered. These are defined and a model for their estimation is presented. I also discuss some of the technical issues raised by the estimation of school effects and the comparison of schools.

Chapters 5, 6 and 7 outline the substantive and technical issues concerning the measurement of schooling inputs, processes, and outcomes, respectively. In the first two of these chapters I distinguish between schooling inputs and processes. 'Schooling inputs' is used to refer to factors exogenous to the schooling system; that is, factors associated with pupils' family backgrounds, and the social, economic, and political factors that affect schooling outcomes but lie outside the control of teachers and educational administrators. 'Schooling processes' is used to refer to factors directly related to school policies and practices. This distinction is not always a comfortable one because many factors are related to school policy and practice and are influenced also by forces outside of schooling. The distinction is important mainly for the statist-ical modelling of school effects; Chapters 5 and 6 discuss the reasons for this distinction in detail.

The purpose of Chapter 5 is to discuss the role of input measures in analysis and to make recommendations for their measurement. I accomplish this to some degree by employing data describing pupils' family backgrounds, cognitive abilities, and schooling outcomes for a large sample of pupils that attended primary and secondary schools in Fife. The chapter also discusses strategies for handling missing data.

Chapter 6 attempts to specify a 'best set' of process indicators. But here I attempt to accomplish this by reviewing the literature and proposing some criteria associated with their coverage of the domain, their usefulness, and their measurability. The measurement of schooling processes is in many ways more difficult than the measurement of inputs or outcomes, and therefore the chapter includes considerable discussion about the problems entailed in meas-uring and interpreting school process data.

Chapter 7 describes some of the outcome measures that can be included in a monitoring system. I argue that monitoring systems should be based on a wide range of outcome measures. The chapter discusses issues concerning the identification of the goals of schooling, and outlines the major considerations in selecting appropriate tests and constructing indicators. One important issue concerns whether indicators emphasize *equity* or *excellence* in schooling. For example, an indicator of the percentage of pupils that achieved some min-imum level of competency underscores the importance of equity more than an indicator of the percentage of pupils that achieved outstanding results on a statewide achievement test. A discussion of validity and reliability of outcome measures is included here. Readers unfamiliar with these terms may wish to read Chapter 7 before Chapters 5 and 6.

The discussion in Chapters 4 to 7 suggests that it is impossible to specify a set of definitive principles on how to develop a system for monitoring school or district performance. The development of a system requires many inter-related decisions, most of which have political ramifications. At the end of each of these chapters I offer a set of guidelines for the development of a monitoring system. These should be considered guidelines, not definitive principles.

Chapter 8 presents a design of a system for monitoring schools at the district or EA level. This design is based on earlier designs set out for a school district in Canada and an educational authority in Scotland. Variants of this design are now being implemented in these settings. The purpose of the chap-ter is not to present a fully comprehensive design, but rather to provide some starting points for a school district or education authority beginning the process. The chapter proposes the kind of data to be collected at various levels, and discusses the problem of confidentiality. It also specifies the stages for developing a system and a time line.

Chapter 9 does two things. It delineates the types of analyses that could be included in an annual report, and describes the statistical and graphical techniques connected with each type of analysis. These techniques could be used for describing the performance of individual schools or entire school districts. Most of the analyses can be done with commercially available statistical software packages such as SPSS/PC or SYSTAT, and graphical packages such as Harvard Graphics.

Chapter 10 discusses how information from a monitoring program can be used to develop a district-level research program aimed at answering research questions relevant to a district's needs. I begin by specifying four basic questions that pertain to nearly all research on school effectiveness. These questions provide a framework for discussing the strengths and limitations of various designs. The first type of design discussed requires only cross-sectional data; it could be employed after the first year of operation of a program. After two or three years of operating a monitoring system, longitudinal data could be used to assess the effects of particular interventions, or to examine whether certain policies or practices improve outcomes or reduce inequalities between high- and low-status groups. The chapter includes examples from the research programs in Scotland and Canada. This is the most technically demanding chapter. I have strived to make it easier for the reader who prefers words over equations by moving the technical description of multilevel modelling to an appendix.

The final chapter provides an executive summary of the material covered in the first ten chapters. It also suggests how administrators and policy-makers might tackle some of the political issues concerning accountability, reduction of the curriculum, and teachers' professional autonomy.

Chapter 2

The Social and Political Context of Monitoring Systems

One view of monitoring systems is that they provide an orderly, objective means to identify effective and ineffective schools, and to determine what factors affect school performance. The belief is that subjective judgements about the schooling process can be replaced with objective facts, which can be used to make rational decisions about the problems facing educators. Torgerson (1986) called this the positivist's dream, where knowledge replaces politics. He referred to it as the first face of policy analysis:

> It is a dream of the abolition of politics — of putting an end to the strife and confusion of human society in favour of an orderly adminis- tration of things based upon objective knowledge. (p. 34)

The opposite view is that monitoring school performance is itself a polit- ical activity: those doing it wish to control the operation of schooling and use 'objective knowledge' to silence opposition. Those holding this view would argue that the knowledge derived from monitoring lacks scientific objectivity. It depends on the design of a monitoring system, and the design cannot be separated from the social and political context of the schooling system. This argument is not without merit. The monitors of school performance must decide when to collect data, which grade levels to monitor, which outcome measures to use, what aspects of school policies and teacher behaviors are important, and how best to analyze and report data. These decisions are ultimately subjective because there is no consensus amongst educators or parents on the goals of schooling, nor is there an uncontested model of school or teacher effectiveness. Decisions about design and implementation neces- sarily have favourable consequences for some groups in a schooling system, and unfavourable consequences for others. Thus the view that monitoring can be a politically neutral administrative tool is naive. The extreme position, that monitoring is entirely a political tool, is consistent with Torgerson's (1986) second face of policy analysis, where it appears as 'the domination of politics over knowledge' (p. 37; see also Carr and Kemmis, 1986; Gaskell, 1988).

The goal of this chapter is to describe the social and political context of monitoring systems in the UK and the US, and to discuss the tensions inherent in monitoring in both contexts. The first chapter listed some of the wider forces that spurred interest in performance monitoring. This chapter deals with recent and current events that influence how monitoring systems are being developed, and tries to identify sources of tension between competing groups. Its intent is to provoke the question of whether monitoring systems can appear as Torgerson's third face of policy analysis, where 'politics and knowledge are no longer deadly antagonists' (p. 39).

Central to the discussion is the issue of accountability. I use the term in the sense defined by Kogan (1986):

> a condition in which individual role holders are liable for review and the application of sanctions if their actions fail to satisfy those with whom they are in an accountability relationship. (p. 25)

Kogan's definition is more restrictive than popular usage of the term in that it requires a judgement or evaluation followed by some reward or formal sanction administered by an authority with a legitimated right to affect the behavior of others. Many researchers, such as Becher, Eraut and Knight (1981), use the term more broadly to include also the sense of moral and professional responsibility workers feel towards their clients and colleagues. The distinction is useful for considering how agents at one level of the education hierarchy use indicators to affect the behavior of those below them.

The UK Context

One of the salient features of schooling in the UK is that there are national systems of certificate examinations. Pupils must attend school to age 16. In England and Wales, pupils in their final compulsory year may elect to sit General Certificate of Secondary Examinations (GCSEs) in a wide range of academic and vocational subjects. Although the structure of secondary schooling and the certification process in Scotland differs from that of England and Wales, pupils also sit national examinations at the end of their final compulsory year. The analogous examination in Scotland is the Standard Grade (SG). Nothern Ireland has yet another structure of secondary schooling, but its examination system is similar to the system in England and Wales. Success in these examinations is valued by prospective employers and by colleges of further and higher education (Raffe, 1984). Slightly more than half of the pupils in Scotland, and about 40 per cent of the pupils in England and Wales, remain in school beyond the compulsory period for one or two years. During that time pupils prepare for more specialized, advanced-level (A-levels or Highers) examinations. Universities and other institutions of higher education specify their entry requirements to various programs in terms of the number and achieved grades in examinations relevant to each program. Thus, these formal, summative examinations substantially influence pupils' life chances, and despite the differences in the form and structure of certificate examinations, the secondary systems in all countries are strongly influenced by their importance.

Administrators have used examination results to monitor school and EA performance. Until 1980, this was done informally: they typically compared results from year to year, or examined overall trends in subject areas. They placed little emphasis on inter-school or inter-authority comparisons. Many educators felt that success in certificate examinations was not necessarily an appropriate goal for all schools, especially for those in working-class areas.

Market Forces

The 1980 Education Acts gave parents the statutory right to make 'placing requests' for schools outside their designated catchment areas, and required education authorities to take these requests into account.[1] The Acts also changed the rules on the number of pupils that schools were required to admit. At this time, education authorities were coping with severe budget cuts stemming from a prolonged period of falling rolls which began in the mid-seventies. The new rules allowed authorities to fix the admission limit for a school up to 20 per cent below the standards based on 1979–80 entry (Maclure, 1988). Together, these changes meant that provision in popular schools could be maintained at 1979–80 levels despite falling rolls, while less popular schools would lose disproportionately more pupils and become candidates for closure or amalgamation.

The 1980 Acts therefore provided a decentralized means for reducing expenditures and effecting contraction (Stillman and Maychell, 1986). They also gave parents considerable power to influence the schooling system through their right to 'vote with their feet'. But these results were not the Government's sole agenda: implicit in its intentions was greater account-ability, although not necessarily in the formal (Kogan) sense of the word. Many believed that the market forces unleashed through open enrolment would improve the education system by increasing competition. The assumption was that unpopular schools were less effective, and therefore their clos-ure or merger with more popular schools would strengthen the system. Also, the prospect of closure for some schools, gauged by dwindling admissions, would encourage teachers to produce better outcomes, or at least be more responsive to parents' demands.

The validity of the Government's assumptions, however, depended in part on the extent to which parents exercised choice based on informed judgements. To foster informed choice, the 1980 Education Acts also required schools to publish their examination results. Publication generally took the form of 'league tables' that showed schools' pass rates in each subject area and the percentages of pupils with higher grades on five or more of the first-level examinations.

However, the first studies of parental choice following the 1980 Acts suggested that parents who chose schools outside their catchment areas did so mainly for pragmatic reasons, such as the proximity of the school (Adler and Raab, 1988), or because they perceived their child would be happier at the

---

[1] See Adler, Petch, and Tweedie (1989) for a discussion of the Acts passed in Scotland and in England and Wales.

school (Petch, 1986). The reputation of the teachers or the methods they used were less important.

Examination performance may be more important at the secondary level than at the primary level, but for parents who might choose a secondary school on the basis of examination performance, league tables are of little use. One reason is that the format of league tables renders comparisons between schools difficult. They allow comparisons between schools in the pass rates of pupils who took particular courses. But these can be misleading because schools vary considerably in the proportions of pupils taking courses in each subject, and because examination standards vary across subjects (Kelly, 1976). Also, schools vary in their policies for presenting pupils for examinations. Some schools present only those pupils likely to succeed, while other schools have more liberal presentation policies. A school with a relatively selective presentation policy would likely have better pass rates and therefore better league table results than a school with comparable pupils that was less selective in its presentation policy. Many parents know too that the social-class intake of a school makes a difference, and league tables do not take the intake of schools into consideration. Thus league tables are a crude form of monitoring. As a means to increase accountability through market forces, they have little value.

Many education authorities use league tables to compare schools, but have not established formal accountability procedures. This does not mean that league table results have never precipitated meetings between a Head Teacher and the Director of Education (or the Chief Education Officer) about a school's performance, or that they have not played a role in backroom decisions concerning closures or reorganization. But on the whole educators appreciate their limitations.

At the national level administrators have given aggregate examination results more credence. The Department of Education and Science (DES) annually publishes *Statistics of Education*, which compares examination results across education authorities. The DES has made a few attempts to examine the relationship between education authority spending and examination performance (DES, 1983, 1984; see also Lord, 1984). The findings suggested the relationship between exam results and expenditures were very weak. The Government used this result to exert pressure on authorities to achieve better results with less money, arguing that consumers in some areas were not getting 'value for money'. However, the analyses were inadequate on many counts, especially because they failed to take account of the types of pupils served by different education authorities (Gray, Jesson, and Jones, 1984; Willms, 1987; Woodhouse and Goldstein, 1988).

National Curriculum and Assessment

The Education Reform Act of 1988 further strengthened the Government's power over teachers and educational administrators. Maclure (1988) called it:

> the most important and far-reaching piece of educational law-making for England and Wales since the Education Act of 1944 ... because it altered the basic power structure of the education system. (p. ix)

The Act weakened local education authorities and gave the Secretary of State authority to introduce a national curriculum and to specify programs of study and assessment arrangements. The Act also increased the rights of parents by making provision for schools to 'opt out' of local authority control. Authorities were required to devolve fiscal management to the schools, thereby increasing the power of school governing boards (see Coopers and Lybrand, 1988).[2]

Section 4 of the 1988 Education Reform Act states that:

(1)   It shall be the duty of the Secretary of State ...

    (a)   to establish a complete National Curriculum as soon as is reasonably practicable (taking first the core subjects and then the other foundation subjects); and

    (b)   to revise that Curriculum whenever he considers it necessary or expedient to do so.

(2)   The Secretary of State may by order specify in relation to each of the foundation subjects —

    (a)   such attainment targets;

    (b)   such programmes of study; and

    (c)   such assessment arrangements;

as he considers appropriate for that subject.

The core subjects specified by the Act are English, mathematics, and science, and in Welsh-speaking schools, Welsh. Foundation subjects include history, geography, technology, music, art, physical education, and, at the secondary level, one modern language. In non-Welsh-speaking schools in Wales, Welsh is also a foundation subject. Sections 6 to 12 of the Act set out requirements for religious education, including the requirement for daily collective worship.

The Act specifies programs of study and attainment targets for pupils aged 7, 11, 14, and 16. The Act was not specific in its prescription for assessment, except that nationally prescribed tests were to be taken by all pupils. The prospect of Government assessment based on national tests angered many teachers (*Observer*, 5 June 1988). They believed that comparisons between schools would be unfair, because like the league table comparisons, they would not take account of pupil intake. At the time of writing, the tests are being piloted in Scotland and England. Many parents and teachers continue to object to the examinations because the issue of how the results are to be used has not been resolved.

The Secretary of State for Education commissioned a Task Group on Assessment and Testing (TGAT), headed by Professor Paul Black, to advise

---

[2] The Act covers only England and Wales; however, the Department of Education in Northern Ireland (DENI) introduced reforms with the same objectives. In Scotland, education to the secondary level is governed by the Secretary of State for Scotland. An act with a similar agenda was also passed in Scotland.

the Government on practical considerations for the development of a national assessment scheme. The TGAT report (DES and the Welsh Office, 1987) recommended that the assessment scheme should emphasize *criterion-referenced*, *formative* assessment, based on a *progression of skills* related to pupils' expected rate of educational development. The aim of criterion-referenced assessment is to describe tasks that pupils can perform, and to compare their performance to a clearly specified achievement domain, rather than to the performance of other pupils (Gronlund, 1982). This type of assessment typically requires several tests, each covering a limited domain of learning tasks that are tied closely to the content of the curriculum. Often criterion-referenced tests (CRTs) are developed locally by teachers, or are provided in teachers' guides which accompany classroom textbooks. Teachers tend to favour CRTs over standardized, norm-referenced tests (NRTs) because CRTs identify areas requiring further teaching, and provide information on whether specific pupils have mastered a particular lesson. CRTs contribute to the formative assessment of pupils, and when used well, can motivate pupils.

NRTs typically cover a large domain of learning tasks, but have relatively few items covering the skills related to any specific objective. Items are selected on the basis of their difficulty, so that the tests serve to discriminate amongst individuals. Often they are used, like the GCSE and A-level examinations, for summative assessment of achievement at the end of a program of study. The results of NRTs are usually expressed as a grade level, a percentile, or a rank in the norm-referencing group. Many parents want this kind of information to judge their child's standing against pupils in the same age group. Also, because NRTs cover a wider domain of skills than CRTs, and because they are designed to detect individual differences in achievement, NRTs are generally better suited for making comparisons between schools or education authorities, and for assessing the impact of national or regional reforms. Thus NRTs generally serve the administrative and accountability purposes of administrators better than CRTs.

The Government's requirements for national assessment would be best fulfilled by a well-constructed set of NRTs. The problem with locally-developed CRTs is that norms vary across schools and authorities because teachers' expectations are naturally conditioned by factors such as parents' and pupils' aspirations, the school's intake, and the performance of prior cohorts of pupils. But the use of NRTs is inevitably met with resistance from teachers. The TGAT recognized this inherent tension. It recommended that criterion-referenced assessment should be calibrated or *moderated* through group discussions of teachers and other professionals. The moderation activities would aim to bring individual teachers' judgements in line with national standards, and therefore allow for the development of what TGAT called 'standard assessment tasks'. On the whole, the scheme proposed by the TGAT accommodated the needs of teachers more than it did the Government's desire for an accountability mechanism.

The Government's plan, delivered through an answer in Parliament (*Hansard*, 7 June 1988), adopted many of the TGAT recommendations, but maintained a summative, norm-referenced element:

the results of tests and other assessments should be used both *formatively* to help better teaching and to inform decisions about next steps for a pupil, and *summatively* at ages 7, 11, 14, and 16 to inform parents about their child's progress.

In many respects the national tests that are being developed could be characterized as criterion-referenced: the standard assessment tasks are closely tied to the curriculum and represent a broader range of testing formats than is typically found in NRTs. However, the national tests resemble NRTs in that they are constructed through sampling from a large pool of assessment tasks. Thus they are limited in the depth of their coverage, and therefore do not adequately fulfil the formative and diagnostic functions associated with CRTs. The Government's plan also stated that results of the assessments would be given in full to parents, and that aggregate results of the tests given at ages 11, 14, and 16 would be published so that the wider public could make 'informed judgements about attainment in a school or LEA'. The Government was unwilling to leave assessment and reporting to the professional judgement of teachers.

The status of national examinations in the UK is uncertain. As previously mentioned, pilot tests are now being conducted in Scotland and in some areas of England and Wales. For those administering the examination system, it seems overly complicated and cumbersome. For teachers, it entails vast amounts of work, with little direct return. One question, therefore, is to what extent can the system be simplified and still remain faithful to the TGAT aims. The other pertinent issue concerns the reporting of results. At what level will results be aggregated, and in what form will they be reported?

Selective Schooling: The Hidden Agenda?

The policies established by the Education Reform Act of 1988 may inhibit or even reverse the trends towards equalization and improvement that stemmed from the reorganization of schooling during the last two decades (see McPherson and Willms, 1987). Schooling was made compulsory in England and Wales by the 1944 Education Act, and in Scotland by the 1945 Education (Scotland) Act. For the next two decades, most education authorities operated a two- or three-tier selective system, whereby pupils were channelled into grammar, technical, or secondary modern schools. Selection was based on pupil attainment in primary school and teachers' estimates of their ability. In 1965 the Labour Government announced its plan for the reorganization of secondary schooling along comprehensive lines. The intention of the reform was to postpone differentiation at least until the latter stages of compulsory schooling, and to establish 'comprehensive' schools that served all pupils in designated catchment areas. The designers of the reform believed that young people would benefit in both their personal and social development by spending their early adolescence in schools that served a full cross section of the community (e.g., Scottish Education Department, 1965, p. 2). Many believed also that by eliminating the 'creaming' of able pupils from one school to another, reorganization would reduce the association of attainment with social class (see McPherson and Willms, 1987 for a detailed account of the goals of comprehensive reorganization in Scotland).

Comprehensive schooling received bad press, even during its early development:

> By the early 1970s, fuelled by press and television 'horror stories', the level of 'public concern' about the state of the nation's schooling had reached the level of a moral panic. (Ball, 1984, p. 6)

Many middle-class parents, whose children might otherwise have gone to a grammar school, saw reorganization as the demise of the schooling system. Research in the eighties in England and Wales did not support comprehensives: two large-scale national evaluations (Marks, Cox, and Pomian-Srzednicki, 1983; Steedman, 1983) that attempted to compare comprehensive and selective schools in their examination results did not show educationally significant advantages for either type of system. Heath, who wrote in defence of comprehensive schools (Heath, 1984), later concluded that the attainment gap between children from middle- and working-class backgrounds had not changed dramatically since the war (Heath, 1987, 1990).

McPherson and I contend that Heath's conclusion that comprehensive reorganization had little impact on reducing social-class inequalities is incorrect (McPherson and Willms, 1989). We believe that Heath's study lacked sufficient power to detect the effects of reorganization, and that many of the effects occurred after the period covered by his data. However, if Heath *is* correct, at least for England and Wales, it may be because reorganization was slow and incomplete: more than half of the LEAs retained some form of selective schooling (see Gray, Jesson, and Jones, 1984). In Scotland, reorganization was swift and more complete. By 1981 over 95 per cent of Scottish pupils entered non-selective schools. McPherson and I used data from the Scottish School Leavers' Survey to examine changes in school performance during the latter stages of reorganization (McPherson and Willms, 1987). Because some communities had been more selective in 1965, and were slower than others to reorganize, we could compare the effects of reorganization on pupil attainment in communities that were undergoing reorganization with those in communities that were substantially comprehensive by 1965. We found that reorganization had effected a small but important increase in pupil attainment. More significant is that reorganization substantially reduced social-class inequalities in attainment. We concluded that the pessimism in England and Wales about the effects of reorganization may have been premature.

Northern Ireland did not begin reorganization in 1965, and still maintains a selective system of grammar and secondary modern schools. Consequently, schools differ markedly in their levels of attainment. The overall distribution of attainment is even more heterogeneous than that of England; for example, 19.8 per cent of school-leavers in Northern Ireland attained two or more A-level passes in 1986, compared with 13.7 per cent in England, but 19.3 per cent of the pupils in Northern Ireland left school without qualifications, which is approximately double the statistic for England (DENI, 1988; DES, 1988).

The Scottish research on comprehensive schooling, and on the effects of the school segregation along social-class lines (Willms, 1986), suggests that the degree of selectivity of a schooling system may not be strongly related to over-all levels of attainment. However, the gap in attainment between high- and low-status pupils may be greater in selective systems. The heterogeneous attainment pattern in Northern Ireland supports the thesis that the gap in attainment between pupils from working- and middle-class backgrounds is greater in selective schooling systems.

One of the dangers in the Government's proposal for national assess-ment is that comparisons between schools will be biased in favour of schools with high social-class or ability intakes. The proposal does not include a procedure for making statistical adjustments to school means to take account of pupil intake. Therefore, schools with high social-class or ability intakes, other factors being equal, will appear to be performing better than schools with low social-class or ability intakes. The same will be true of comparisons between education authorities. If parents choose schools on the basis of unadjusted results, without at least mentally adjusting for pupil intake, they will be more likely to choose high social-class schools. And if those exercising their right to choose are disproportionately represented by middle-class parents, the reform will tend to increase social-class segregation between schools, making the system less comprehensive. A study of the first cohort of Scottish secondary pupils whose parents were eligible to make placing requests confirmed this fear: high social-class parents were more likely to choose schools outside their catchment area, and they more often chose high social-class schools and older schools (Echols, McPherson, and Willms, 1990).

Another danger of unadjusted comparisons is that inter-authority com-parisons will be biased in favour of education authorities that have retained selection. Gray, Jesson, and Jones (1984) pointed out that English authorities that have retained selective arrangements, on average have lower proportions of pupils from working-class backgrounds. These authorities will inevitably rank higher on unadjusted comparisons, incorrectly suggesting that selective systems produce higher levels of attainment. If the Government's agenda is to diminish the reputation of comprehensive schooling, thereby setting the stage for a return to selective schooling, a national monitoring system with unadjusted comparisons between schools and LEAs will advance that agenda.

The US Context

Schooling in the US has been characterized as a loosely coupled system (March and Olsen, 1976; Weick, 1976). This means that units in the schooling system are responsive to each other, but each unit preserves its own identity and autonomy. Teachers and principals, for example, are loosely coupled. They are coupled by the official line of authority, and by mutual goals and responsibilities. But a principal's authority entails few formal regulations, inspection is infrequent, and the means to accomplish school goals are largely at a teacher's discretion. In the same way, pupils and teachers, principals and superintendents, superintendents and school boards, and school boards and state officials have loosely coupled relationships. The attachments are circumscribed, infrequent, and weak in their mutual effects (Weick, 1976).

Loose-coupling refers also to the links between events or other elements of the schooling process, such as intention and action, attitudes and behaviour, processes and products, teaching and curriculum.

The US schooling system could be viewed as a number of small- to medium-sized firms, rather than as a large state industry. Within each district, parents act as shareholders who elect a board of directors. The board appoints a chief executive officer — the superintendent — who is charged with managing school affairs. The superintendent delegates much of the authority and responsibility to school principals. Although most links are loosely coupled, those between parents and the board often are not, at least compared with analogous relationships in the UK. Parents in the US are quick to voice concerns to their elected boards, and boards are usually quick to respond.

The result is greater diversity in types of school offerings. In most districts, parents can choose from a number of schools that are distinctive in their philosophy, organization, curriculum, and extra-curricular activities. Magnet schools, designed to draw pupils to particular areas for specialized programs, are common. Schools offering special training in the fine and performing arts are particularly popular. Schools with bilingual or 'immersion' programs also draw pupils from outside their catchment areas. Choice is actively encouraged in many districts, not only as a means to promote desegregation, but also because choice is seen as a parent's right. Many teachers welcome choice: it increases their autonomy and gives them the opportunity to offer specialized programs in their subject areas. Some educators believe it is the only way to escape the mediocrity of the 'old authoritarian school system' (Clinchy, 1989, p. 289).

The US system is diverse also in the quality of school provision. Variation in funding is part of the explanation. Federal and state contributions to schooling, which amount to about 10 and 20 per cent, respectively, of the average school district's budget, are relatively uniform across districts. But the majority of funding comes from local taxes, levied at rates determined by local school boards. These differ markedly across school districts. Residential segregation along racial, ethnic, and social-class lines also accounts for some of the diversity. Schools in the poorest areas find it difficult to attract and keep the best pupils and teachers.

Glenn (1989) argues that the diversity in school quality and types of offerings increases the need for consumer protection (p. 296). Parents choosing schools want to be sure that their children are not being short-changed in their academic, personal, or social development. But in most educational institutions there is little coordination or control of instruction or standards (Dornbusch and Scott, 1975; Lortie, 1973). Meyer and Rowan (1988) contend that the coordination and control comes from an elaborate system of institutionalized rules and regulations. These define acceptable education. Their view is that there is an implicit agreement between teachers and administrators: teachers participate in the 'ritual classifications of education' in return for freedom from close inspection.

Links at higher levels of the system that might ensure accountability are also loose or decoupled. An observer from the UK would find the link between the state and school districts particularly slack. State school acts would appear to constitute rough guidelines for district policy, instead of statutory regulations. The curriculum of the schools would seem vague and haphazard. But what would be particularly disturbing to the UK observer is the lack of a national or state examination system. Most schools in the US base assessment on teachers' observations, locally produced tests, or commercial tests that accompany textbooks. Prospective employers rely mainly on their own assessments; often they care little about grades and are content if pupils have completed a requisite number of years of formal schooling. Colleges and universities rely on the schools' internal assessments, or on standardized achievement scores from tests such as the Scholastic Achievement Test. Unlike the English A-levels or Scottish Highers examinations, tests like the Scholastic Achievement Test have relatively little to do with what is taught and learned in school.

Monitoring for Tighter Coupling

Performance monitoring provides a means to tighten the organizational links between national, state, and district goals, and what teachers actually do in the classroom. The national monitoring system, embodied in the Secretary of Education's wall chart, includes indicators pertaining to broad educational goals, such as high school completion rates, levels of proficiency in particular subject areas, and Scholastic Achievement Test scores. State-by-state comparisons of wall-chart indicators reach the popular press, arming parents with data with which to confront politicians if their state system is not faring well. State politicians and educational administrators are sensitive to the state scores, and use them in arguments supporting their political agenda. Many of them question the validity of the comparisons, however, on the grounds that they do not take account of local economic and social circumstances, and because the indicators do not adequately reflect state goals. Dissatisfaction with the national monitoring system resulted in the Chief State School Officers developing their own monitoring system (Smith, 1988), which includes not only indicators of schooling outcomes but also indicators of schooling inputs, and teaching and organizational practices (Selden, 1988).

At the district level monitoring is rapidly becoming institutionalized. In response to the report *A Nation at Risk*, by the National Commission on Excellence in Education, many state legislatures mounted ambitious programs of reform during the mid-eighties. These programs set out to revamp teacher education programs, standardize the curricula, and establish state-wide examinations (Futrell, 1989). Many states issued mandates and directives towards these ends. District responses to this 'official version of reform' varied because of differing political agendas and capacities to act at the district level (Timar and Kirp, 1989, p. 507). Nevertheless, several districts embraced the top-down management strategies advocated by the states. Participation by some districts entailed the setting of state goals, and the development of monitoring programs. A number of districts hired consultants to provide schools with technical assistance that would help them boost scores on standardized tests. Some provided in-service training for teachers to teach them strategies congruent with high test results. A few districts established formal systems to reward schools with above-average performance (e.g., see Mandeville and Anderson, 1987; Wynne, 1984).

The Inherent Tensions of Performance Monitoring

The centralization and bureaucratization of teaching has met with considerable resistance, in both the UK and the US. The general secretary of the UK National Association of Head Teachers, Dr David Hart, was quoted:

> I don't believe this attempt to find acceptable performance indicators is going to work unless teachers are first consulted. It will be regarded by the profession as attempt to put teachers through the hoop and schools into league tables. Teachers will withdraw into their shells and be defensive, because once again they are under attack. (*Observer*, 5 June 1988, p. 8)

Three years later, judging from the reactions of teachers to the pilot testing of the national examinations, we can say that Hart's predictions have proven correct.

Mary Futrell, President of the US National Education Association between 1983 and 1986, called on researchers to reform the reforms:

> Every attempt at reform that dilutes the authority of the classroom teacher dilutes the quality of instruction in our nation's classrooms.... Teachers cannot hope to ready students for responsibility within a participatory democracy if they themselves are condemned to an autocratic bureaucracy. (Futrell, 1986, as cited in Futrell, 1989, p. 11)

Arthur Wise, Director of Rand Corporation's Center for the Study of Teaching, also wrote passionately about what he saw as the problems inherent in the state's attempt to regulate the quality of education:

> By mandating educational outcomes through standardized tests, content through curriculum alignment, and teaching methods through teacher evaluation criteria, states set in motion a chain of events that alter educational ends and means. In effect, mandates say to many elementary school teachers: don't teach everything, just teach the basics; don't teach children to read, just teach reading skills; don't teach children to write, just teach them to fill in the blanks; don't teach them to think, just teach them to give the right answers. (Wise, 1988, p. 330)

Thus, educators' concerns have not been limited to issues pertaining to accountability. These are important, but teachers are concerned also that monitoring will restrict their work and devalue their professional role. A number of teachers also argue that monitoring is too costly in terms of the time devoted to testing and administration.

Accountability

The problems of accountability necessarily present tensions in the development of a monitoring system. Several questions need to be addressed: Who will design the system? What data will be collected? By whom? At what level? Who will have access to the data? How will the data be analyzed? By whom? Will schools be compared? If so, will schools' intake characteristics be taken into account? How will the data be reported? To whom? What rewards or sanctions are implicitly or explicitly linked to the findings? (e.g., see US Department of Education, 1988).

Actors at different levels of the schooling system differ in their goals for performance monitoring. Those at higher levels of the system want information pertaining to overall trends in performance, and want to assess whether particular schools or districts are consistently performing below standard. In some cases, they use monitoring data to examine inequalities in attainment, or to assess the impact of particular reforms. Principals and teachers want the kind of information that is useful for informing school policy and practice, especially as it relates to instruction. The differing reasons for monitoring is the source of many of the tensions.

Administrators at the district or state level tend to want indicators that pertain to universal criteria, such as graduation rates and levels of literacy and numeracy. They want relatively simple measures that can be easily administered and scored, yet will be credible to the public. Standardized NRTs are preferable to CRTs because they facilitate comparisons between schools. They want measures that are valid in the sense that they reflect the curriculum, but reliability is less of a concern because most of their analyses entail aggregate scores, which can be reasonably reliable even when individual scores are not. (See Chapter 3 for a discussion of validity and reliability.) Overall, the evaluations at higher levels of the system tend to be more summative than formative.

Teachers, on the other hand, are interested also in indicators of specific, detailed criteria, such as proficiency in certain reading skills, or mastery of content in a subject area. Tests can be longer and more complex. Criterion-referenced tests that identify specific strengths and weaknesses are better suited to most of their needs. Both validity and reliability are a concern, because in many instances they use the data to make diagnostic or selection decisions about individual pupils.

The Professional Autonomy of Teachers

A number of educators contend that monitoring can lead to an over-emphasis on examination success, and, as Wise warned, to the delimitation of classroom instruction to test-relevant topics. Over time, teachers who are attempting to become accountable in terms of success on norm-referenced, standardized measures, will try to achieve a congruence between textbooks, classroom activity, instruction, and the tests. In essence, the tests will define the curriculum.

McNeil (1988) takes the argument further. She contends that central control over curriculum and assessment fundamentally undermines teachers' discretion about what pupils need to know and how they can best be taught. For her, monitoring is a recipe for boring, mechanical teaching that produces disaffected and uninterested pupils. Her detailed ethnography of several US high schools (McNeil, 1986) suggests that teachers who strive to comply with external standards lapse into teaching that is teacher-centred, devoted to lists and outlines, unchallenging, and impersonal. Eventually they lose interest; they distance themselves from their subject and sometimes their pupils. The message to pupils is that education has only instrumental rewards, and these seem infrequent, transient, and given only to a chosen few. Pupils also find school boring, and distance themselves from course content, classroom interactions, and their teachers.

Several arguments can be made against McNeil's position. One is that state or district testing does not necessarily lead to the delimitation of classroom instruction. Teachers in the UK constructed large pools of standard assessment tasks for the national tests. The tasks cover a broad range of topics in each subject area. Each test comprises only a sample of tasks from the relevant pool. Few of the tasks are multiple-choice questions; the tasks include essay questions and performance-based assessments that evaluate pupils' ability to solve problems, organize data, and present ideas. Because teachers constructed the tasks, and because of the broad coverage of the tests, 'teaching to the test' is synonymous with teaching the content of the curriculum.

Another argument is that there is little empirical evidence that central control over curriculum and assessment leads to boring, mechanical teaching, or to disaffection amongst teachers and pupils. McNeil's analysis assumes that achieving high scores on state or district examinations can be best accomplished through teacher-centred, impersonal, and unchallenging teaching, or at least that many teachers perceive this to be the case. But teachers who provide rich and challenging experiences for their pupils are more likely to generate better test results, and therefore more likely to view testing in a favourable light. The UK Task Group on Assessment and Teaching (DES, 1988) argued that when testing is carefully aligned to the curriculum, it can build enthusiasm and enhance learning. One of the critical questions is whether a testing program provides clear and attainable goals for the majority of pupils.

A further argument relevant to the struggle over autonomy is that in any profession there is considerable variability in commitment, standards, and performance. Teaching is a demanding profession, and maintaining enthusiasm and commitment over the long term is difficult. Those advocating monitoring systems at the state or district level could argue that monitoring helps identify the small number of schools and teachers that consistently perform below standards. The advocates of monitoring would contend, therefore, that the 'consumer protection' value of monitoring outweighs any detrimental effects such as a perceived loss of autonomy by some teachers. They could argue also that testing and comparing scores to an external standard serves another function: it safeguards against the possibility that schools will become complacent about standards and performance. A school's history, its intake characteristics, and its social and political context in the community shape its goals and expectations. As a result, a school's norms can differ markedly from district or state norms. Monitoring can identify discrepancies between a school's norms and those of the district and the state.

The Costs of Monitoring

Performance monitoring is expensive. There are considerable direct costs for constructing tests and questionnaires, collecting data, coding and entering data, analysis, producing reports, and disseminating findings. The indirect costs can also be considerable: establishing a monitoring system requires a number of meetings with participation from administrators and educators at all levels. Once a system is in place teachers and principals inevitably are involved in the administration of tests and questionnaires, and in the dissemination of findings. Pupils also pay a price in terms of lost teaching time devoted to testing and filling in forms and questionnaires. An important question is whether monitoring diverts administrative resources away from efforts to reform schools, or teacher and pupil resources away from activities that directly affect pupil outcomes.

David (1988) argues that the costs will outweigh the benefits unless educators make a conscious effort to collect the right kind of data, and create conditions that increase the likelihood that data will be used for planning and decision-making. Indicator systems are more likely to improve the quality of schooling if the indicators are closely linked to specific policies and practices that teachers and administrators can act upon. David maintains that teacher involvement in the design of a monitoring system is one critical requirement. Another is the commitment from district administrators to gather information and provide the necessary resources to help teachers improve their practice.

Knowledge and Politics as Spirited Rivals

Can monitoring systems appear as Torgerson's (1986) third face of policy analysis, where knowledge and politics are not deadly antagonists? The experiences with monitoring in both the US and the UK indicate that knowledge and politics may never be the best of friends, but they might appear as spirited rivals. Some administrators have suggested that monitoring necessarily entails a subtle form of 'horse-trading', whereby teachers comply with monitoring activities in return for better working conditions, better pay, or other favors. While I agree there needs to be negotiation, it does not need to occur at the bargaining table. There is leeway to create monitoring systems that provide information of value to both teachers and administrators.

Events in the UK have shown that teacher involvement is a critical requirement. Teachers need to be involved in the construction of tests and other assessment instruments, and in the design and implementation of the monitoring system. Teacher involvement increases the likelihood that performance indicators will inform school policy and practice. But the implications of teacher involvement go beyond the question of better information. It also fosters higher status for the profession. If the design of monitoring systems is left to administrators, and the construction of tests to the test-publishing companies, then the real questions about the purposes of schooling, what is taught and how, will not receive the debate they deserve. Porter (1988) makes the point also that teacher involvement increases the *authority* of performance indicators. Teachers are more likely to value and respect the findings from a monitoring system designed by expert teachers, than from one designed by persons outside the profession. Feasibly, monitoring systems could offer an opportunity for teachers to acquire greater autonomy in setting and regulating standards for their profession. If teachers take control of monitoring, performance indicators are more likely to be used as a first filter in decisions about dismissal of teachers or school closures, rather than as an authoritative tool. Finally, teacher involvement in monitoring may spur interest in classroom- and school-based research. Monitoring systems could provide an opportunity for action-based research programs or collaborative research programs between schools and universities.

Another critical requirement of monitoring is that the procedures pertaining to the use of indicators for accountability need to be well specified. If monitoring is to be more than a political activity, teachers and administrators must state clearly how data will be collected, who will have control of data, what analyses will be conducted, in what form results will be presented, and who will have access to reports. The time spent debating whether or not to collect monitoring data could be better spent determining procedures for their use.

The third requirement is high standards. Scientific objectivity is a matter of degree. The validity of assessments based on performance monitoring depends on the standards of data collection, design, analysis, and reporting. Validity depends also on the social and political context, but this does not mean that monitoring is devoid of scientific objectivity. When standards are high there is less cause for knowledge and politics to be at odds.

Chapter 3

Monitoring Systems and the Input-Output Model

Monitoring systems are based on a theory about how schooling 'inputs' cause schooling 'outputs'. The theory presumes that pupil outcomes are largely determined by family influences and pupils' experiences at school, and that the latter are shaped by the organizational structure and practices of the classroom, school, and school district. Researchers have conducted a number of large studies to explore the relationship between schooling inputs, such as pupil, teacher, and school resources, and schooling outputs, such as pupils' examination results and their overall examination attainment. The goal of the research was to determine the effects of various teacher and school factors on pupil outcomes by controlling statistically for pupils' entry-level ability and for factors associated with their family background. In general the findings have been contradictory and suggest weak organizational effects (e.g., Bridge, Judd, and Moock, 1979; Glasman and Biniaminov, 1981; Murnane, 1981; Rutter, 1983).

Researchers have found it difficult to determine the effects of teacher and school factors on schooling outcomes because many policies and practices do not vary much across schools, and because schools that are advantaged in some respects tend to be disadvantaged in others. For example, class size may be an important determinant of academic achievement, but in most schooling systems average class size does not vary substantially across schools. In systems where there is sufficient variation, schools with small class sizes tend to be advantaged also in terms of the experience and training of their teachers (e.g., Rumberger and Willms, 1991). Although it may be easy to show that schools with small class sizes have superior academic achievement it is difficult to discern whether it is class size or teacher characteristics causing the desired effect. Another difficulty is that the variation between schools in their outcomes is usually small compared with the variation within schools (Gray, 1988). Even though a school or teacher variable may have an important effect on schooling outcomes, its effect may be small compared with the effects of all of the other factors influencing pupil outcomes.

Research based on the 'input-output' model attempted to overcome these difficulties, but its success was limited for several reasons. One is that it failed to specify how policies and practices at one level of the system influence events taking place at other levels (Barr and Dreeben, 1983; Meyer, 1980).

Until recently, studies of school effects used data describing either pupils, schools, or school districts. The data were analyzed at only one level because appropriate multilevel statistical techniques were not available (Raudenbush and Willms, 1991). Also, the research examined only the lowest 'levels' of the schooling system – pupils, classrooms, and schools. It did not take into account the wider social, cultural, and economic factors associated with the community settings and larger systems in which schools operate. The research had limited success also because it emphasized factors that were easy to define and measure. Many of the processes that affect schooling outcomes are difficult to define, and even more difficult to measure. Researchers resorted to using terms like 'school climate' or 'instructional leadership', language which is 'fuzzy' and of limited value to teachers and administrators (Cuban, 1983). Usually constructs such as 'school climate' were operationalized with only one or two 'proxy' variables (see Bridge, Judd, and Moock, 1979). Perhaps the most serious limitation of input-output research was that the models used did not include all of the relevant pupil-background factors — factors that affect schooling outcomes and are confounded with the school attended. Failure to include all of the relevant pupil-background factors can lead to inaccurate and biased estimates of the effects of schools or the effects of school policies and practices.

An understanding of how monitoring systems are related to the input-output model is important because the weaknesses of input-output research underlie many of the criticisms of performance monitoring. Knowledge of the weaknesses can help one assess the validity of inferences made from monitoring data. It also provides a basis for developing stronger models for monitoring school performance. The next section classifies monitoring systems into three types according to their purposes. Each type emphasizes a different aspect of the input-output model. The section that follows suggests ways that monitoring systems can be strengthened. These stress the importance of incorporating school 'processes' as part of the input-output model, and the advantages of using longitudinal data.

Purposes of Monitoring Systems

Richards (1988) classifies educational monitoring systems according to their underlying assumptions about what motivates educational improvement:

> those that monitor for regulatory compliance, those that monitor for instructional diagnosis and remediation, and those that monitor for school improvement or outputs. (p. 496)

The three types of monitoring systems are described below.

Compliance Monitoring
Compliance monitoring systems emphasize schooling inputs, particularly teacher and fiscal resources. These systems attempt to ensure that certain standards of educational provision are being met. A compliance monitoring system might include, for example, measures of average class size, pupil-

teacher ratios, expenditures on instructional materials, size of the library, teacher qualifications, number of support staff, or the proportion of pupils receiving special education. Typically some sanction is applied to schools not meeting specified standards. For example, a school may be required to submit a plan for correction, or in an extreme case, be subject to closure. The assumption underlying the use of compliance monitoring is that if schools meet specified standards on various input measures, then adequate levels of performance will necessarily follow.

Diagnostic Monitoring
Diagnostic monitoring systems emphasize the output side of the input-output model, particularly academic outcomes. Their goal is to determine whether specific aspects of the curriculum are being mastered by the majority of pupils. In the same manner that teachers use classroom tests to identify areas where certain pupils need further instruction and remedial activities, diagnostic monitoring systems seek to identify particular skills and concepts that require greater emphasis in certain schools.

The outcome measures of diagnostic monitoring systems are typically criterion-referenced tests (CRTs). CRTs focus on a delimited domain of learning outcomes tied closely to the content of the curriculum. Scores are interpreted in terms of the particular skills that pupils have mastered (Gronlund, 1985). Results of a CRT in mathematics, for example, might suggest that 80 per cent of pupils in a particular school had mastered a set of algebraic algorithms, but only 40 per cent were able to apply them to solve related word problems. Diagnostic systems require frequent testing and immediate feedback, so that teachers can shift the emphasis of their instruction or provide remedial activities.

Diagnostic monitoring systems place little emphasis on schooling inputs, because their main purpose is to identify specific strengths and weaknesses in academic skills, irrespective of pupils' characteristics. Consequently, they are not as useful for making comparisons between schools or school districts. School districts in Minnesota operate a diagnostic monitoring system with support from the state. The state develops the assessment instruments with input from teachers concerning content and standards. Districts are required to administer annually a test in one curricular area at three grade levels. Although districts must publicize summaries of the results, the emphasis of analysis and interpretation is not on comparisons of schools or districts, but on achieving local criteria, making better use of resources, and improving instruction (Richards, 1988).

Performance Monitoring
The third type of monitoring system, which Richards (1988) calls performance monitoring, includes measures of both schooling inputs and outputs. Typically the outcome measures are standardized achievement tests, which are less curriculum-specific but cover a broader domain of skills. Performance monitoring systems strive to make comparisons between schools and school districts in their outcomes. In some cases the comparisons include adjustment for schooling inputs. The explicit intention of these systems is to make schools publicly accountable through market forces. The belief is that inter-school or

inter-district comparisons will stimulate competition and motivate educators to provide a better education.

The standardized achievement tests used in performance monitoring have been standardized on nationally representative samples. Thus, the scores of individuals or the average scores of schools or districts can be compared with national norms. Norm-referenced achievement tests (NRTs) cover a large domain of academic skills, but have few items covering any specific set of skills. Test items tend to be of average difficulty; this increases the likelihood that total test scores will discriminate amongst individuals (Gronlund, 1985). Wide-range achievement testing with NRTs is less expensive and requires less testing time than criterion-referenced testing. There are trade-offs, however, which are discussed in Chapter 7.

In the past, administrators and government policy-makers have used data on examination results as general indicators of the health of the educational system, somewhat in the same way that economists have used economic indicators (Murnane and Pauly, 1988). Analyses were limited to examinations of long-term trends, or to comparisons between ethnic, racial, and social-class groups, and between males and females. Recently, however, with a renewed emphasis on accountability, administrators have used performance indicators to compare schools. Typically they compute a mean score for each school, and rank-order the schools according to their mean scores. In some cases, an adjustment is made to take account of the differences between schools in the composition of their pupil intake.

In California, for example, schools are rank-ordered on a composite index of socioeconomic status (SES) and then banded into particular SES categories. The SES index is based on pupils' and teachers' reports of the educational and occupational attainment of the pupils' parents. Comparisons between schools in their achievement test scores are made amongst schools in each SES band (see Haertle, 1986; Richards, 1988). Florida's state assessment system employs a different strategy based on multiple regression. With this approach, a 'predicted' or 'expected' achievement score is estimated for each school, based on the relationship between achievement scores and indicators of SES for all schools in the state. The discrepancy, positive or negative, between a school's actual mean achievement score and its expected achievement score is its index of school performance.

These techniques are simple, and therefore appealing. However, data describing pupils' SES are insufficient to control for all of the out-of-school factors relevant to a child's progress in school (Willms, 1986), and estimates based on data that are aggregated to the school level, such as school mean achievement or SES, are biased (Aitkin and Longford, 1986; Bryk and Raudenbush, 1987).

Stronger Models for Monitoring Schools

Incorporating Data on School Process

Research based on the 'input-output' model of schooling was criticized because it did not offer much to educators about how to improve school practice (Levin, 1980). Schools were viewed simply as 'black boxes' which begged to be 'illuminated' (Parlett and Hamilton, 1976). During the past decade, a new literature has emerged that emphasizes school processes instead of resource inputs (Good and Brophy, 1986; Purkey and Smith, 1983; Ralph and Fennessey, 1983). Researchers have attempted to define 'school climate' (Anderson, 1982), and to examine the effects of factors such as parental involvement, pupil-teacher interactions, and norms and expectations for high achievement (see Brookover, Schweitzer, Schneider, Beady, Flood, and Wisen-baker, 1978; Moos, 1979).

This literature led to the so-called 'five-factor model' for effective schools, which was held up by many educational reformers as a blueprint for educational improvement (see Cohen, 1981; Odden, 1982). The model postulated that effective schools had some combination of the following characteristics:

1 strong administrative leadership;
2 a safe and orderly climate;
3 an emphasis on basic academic skills;
4 higher teacher expectations; and
5 a system for monitoring pupil performance

(see Ralph and Fennessey, 1983)

However, much of the literature on school process has been based on small comparative case studies, or ethnographies of exceptional schools. Critics claimed that the methods employed in these studies did not meet the standards of social science research: most studies did not control adequately for the background characteristics of pupils entering the schools, and a number of them may have suffered from observer bias (Purkey and Smith, 1983; Ralph and Fennessey, 1983). Although the five-factor model has considerable face validity, the empirical evidence that these five factors are more important than some other set of factors is not compelling.

Some performance monitoring systems have included measures of school process in addition to input and output measures. Data on school process are important because they can be used to determine why some schools are performing better than others. In most cases, however, analysts have not combined input, process, and output variables in a single model. Typically, they present average scores for the process measures for each school alongside average scores on a number of outcome measures. By showing the relationships between process measures and outcomes in this way, they suggest that if schools improved their schooling processes in the prescribed measurable ways, better scores on the outcome measures would follow.

This may not be the case. The problem is that many of the processes that make for an effective school are correlated not only with schooling outcomes, but also with the intake composition of schools. Taking the five-factor model as an example, head teachers of high social-class schools probably can display strong administrative leadership and establish a safe and orderly climate more easily than head teachers of schools in deprived areas. Similarly, teachers in high social-class schools probably find it easier to maintain high expectations for academic success, and are more likely to monitor their pupils' performance. Therefore, although school-level averages on process and outcome

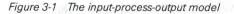
Figure 3-1 The input-process-output model

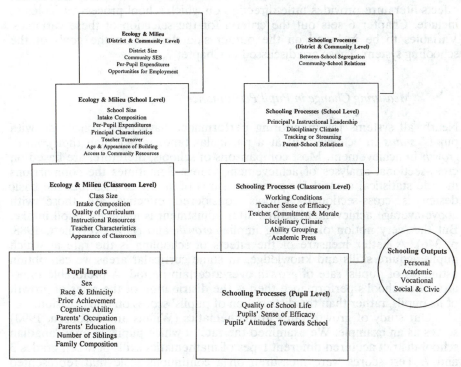

measures may help schools identify strengths and weaknesses, they are insufficient for purposes of accountability.

Figure 3-1 depicts an input-process-output model similar to others in the literature.[1] The foremeost box on the left shows the main factors that comprise pupil inputs. The boxes behind the pupil-input box list factors describing the ecology and milieu of the school. Ecological factors describe the physical and material aspects of the environment; milieu factors describe characteristics of the school staff. The boxes in the middle of the diagram list schooling processes for each level of the schooling system. The circle lists four general domains of schooling outcomes.

The model is an improvement over the basic input-output model because it recognizes the multilevel structure of the schooling system, and separates school processes from factors that lie outside the control of teachers and administrators. This separation is important for the statistical modelling of school effects (see Chapters 4 and 10). The model is not fully comprehensive. The set of pupil inputs is reasonably complete. The rationale for the selection of these variables is presented in Chapter 5. Any additional variables would probably be highly correlated with this set and therefore redundant (e.g.,

---

[1] For other examples, see Barr and Dreeben, 1983; Shavelson, McDonnell, Oakes, Carey, and Picus, 1987).

Alexander, Pallas, and Cook, 1981; Willms, 1985a). However, the school effects literature provides little direction on which school process variables to include. Chapter 6 sets out the criteria for the selection of these variables. Variables to be included on the output side depend on the goals of the schooling system. These are discussed in Chapter 7.

Measuring Change in Pupil Performance

Nearly all systems for monitoring performance have been concerned with pupils' *status* in achievement at a particular time, rather than their *rate of growth* in achievement. Most comparisons of schools, therefore, are based on cross-sectional analyses of achievement scores. Sometimes the comparisons include statistical control for prior measures of ability or SES, but the basic design is cross-sectional. Schools considered effective are those with above-average achievement scores after adjustment is made for pupil intake. But the 'very notion of learning implies *growth* and *change*' (Willett, 1988, p. 346). A better measure of the effects of schooling is the rate at which pupils acquire skills and knowledge. In some curricular areas we can obtain estimates of pupils' rate of growth over a certain period. A preferable indicator of a school's performance then is the distribution of the rates of growth of its pupils, rather than the distribution of pupils' scores on one occasion.

Our study of growth rates in mathematics (Willms and Jacobsen, 1990) serves as an example. We examined the rate at which pupils in one Canadian school district acquired different types of mathematics skills between grades 3 and 7. Test scores were measured on a continuous scale that represented achievement in terms of months of schooling completed. One of our findings was that there were large differences between the thirty-two schools in the district in their average rates of growth in mathematics. The differences were sizable, even after controlling for pupils' initial cognitive ability: there were four schools in the district where a pupil with average initial ability grew at a rate of only nine months of schooling per ten-month school year, whereas there were four schools where a pupil with comparable initial ability grew at a rate of more than eleven months per ten-month school year. After five years of schooling, therefore, the gap between comparable pupils attending one of the top-performing schools in the district and those attending one of the lowest-performing schools, was equivalent to one full year of schooling.

Bryk and Raudenbush (1988) showed how growth analyses can be used to study patterns of children's growth, even with a small number of subjects. They examined the growth trajectories of vocabulary development from twelve to twenty-six months for eleven children, using data collected by Huttenlocher, Haight, Bryk, and Seltzer (1988). Their analysis showed that the rate at which children acquired new words accelerated over the period. The amount of maternal speech observed during typical daily activities was related to the rate at which the children acquired new words, and this association increased over the period. In another analysis they used data from the Sustaining Effects Study (Carter, 1984), which described the progress of 600 pupils in their reading and mathematics from grades 1 to 3. The analysis included measures at both the pupil and school levels. The most important finding stemming from their analysis was that the variance between schools in pupils' growth rates was considerably larger than in pupils' status at a particular grade level. Their work suggests that researchers' attempts to understand the effects of important school policy or process variables will likely have greater success if they use longitudinal data which describe pupils' growth over three or four years.

Recent developments in statistics, computing, and test design have made these types of analyses possible. Test developers have constructed batteries of achievement tests that include separate tests targeted for pupils at different grade levels. A test for any particular grade includes items that overlap in their content and difficulty with some of the items in the tests for previous and subsequent grades. This makes it possible to map scores onto one long continuous scale that covers several years of schooling. The developers try to build the scale such that it has equal intervals over the entire scale. Under the assumption of equal intervals, one can then measure children's growth in achievement in the same way that one measures growth in height or weight.[2]

The simplest measure of growth is the change in a pupil's score between two time points. For several years researchers have eschewed 'change scores', believing they lacked reliability. Rogosa and Willett (1983, 1985) pointed out that they are not necessarily unreliable; if researchers can obtain data on at least three occasions, then more reliable estimates of growth are possible. Bryk and Raudenbush (1987); Raudenbush and Bryk (1986); Raudenbush (1989) and Goldstein (1987) developed multilevel statistical models appropriate for describing pupil growth, and for assessing school performance. Several computer programs have been developed that can be used to estimate school effects based on their models. The multilevel model is discussed further in Chapters 4 and 10.

Growth rates are better than scores measured at one time point for comparing schools because they are less sensitive to the intake composition of schools. Growth rates describe improvements in performance over a specified period, and so the controls for prior ability and family background are to a large extent built into the measure. Therefore, schools that serve predominantly low-ability or low-social-class pupils are more likely to fare better on an indicator of pupil growth during a particular period of schooling, than on an indicator of pupil achievement taken at the end of that period (Shim, 1991).

Measuring Change in School Performance

If monitoring systems are to be used for purposes of accountability, then estimates of school performance need to be accurate and capable of distinguishing between aspects of performance attributable to good school practice and those due to wider social factors, or due to random fluctuation. The performance of a school might vary from year to year for several reasons. Variation could be due to changes in school organization and practice, or due

---

[2] Objections to this conception of learning are discussed in Chapters 7 and 11.

to changes in the involvement and efforts of teachers. But variation can be due also to social and economic changes in the community, such as the availability of local employment or the migration of certain sub-populations. Schools can have 'good years' and 'bad years', seemingly random fluctuations associated with the interests and abilities of each cohort of pupils. Some of the fluctuation is truly random, contributing to what statisticians call measurement and sampling error. For example, performance indicators based on test scores contain some random error due to idiosyncrasies in the way pupils answer certain questions and the way tests are administered. On average this error is greater for small schools, the same schools that are often most vulnerable when administrators consider school closures.

To separate the effects on schooling outcomes attributable to schooling *per se* from those attributable to other factors or to random fluctuation, one requires data describing schooling inputs, processes, and outputs for successive cohorts on at least two occasions; three or more are preferable. The section above on measures of growth suggested that stronger models for assessing school effects were possible with repeated measures of performance on individual pupils. This section calls for repeated measures on schools. After a monitoring system has been in place for a few years, this data will naturally become available. The point to be made, though, is that data for successive cohorts can be used in a longitudinal design that provides richer and more accurate information about the effects of schools.

Willms and Raudenbush (1989) showed how longitudinal data on schools can be incorporated into the multilevel model, with time as one level of the model. The estimated 'effect' of each school in a system is partitioned into two components: a long-term average effect, or a trend, plus an effect specific to each time point. The model provides more accurate estimates of each school's performance as well as a means for assessing whether variation in its performance is attributable to changes in school policies and practice. Longitudinal data on schools also provide a means for assessing the effects of specific interventions implemented by particular schools in an authority. Details of the approach and an example are provided in Chapter 10.

Guidelines for Developing a Monitoring System

1 **A monitoring system should include schooling inputs, processes, and outcomes** (see Figure 3-1).
2 **Performance indicators should describe aspects of schooling at various levels of the system, such as the pupil, family, neighbourhood, classroom, school, school district, and community.**
3 **Attempts should be made to relate school performance to specific schooling processes associated with school organization and teaching practices.** It is incorrect to simply measure schooling outcomes and presume that the quality of instruction is inferior in low-performing schools.
4 **Measures of growth are preferable to measures of status at one time point.** Growth measures are more reliable if they are based on measurements taken on at least three occasions.

5 **A monitoring system should permit a longitudinal assessment of schools.** Evaluations based on cross-sectional assessments are often inadequate. A longitudinal assessment requires data on successive cohorts of pupils. In the analysis, each school serves as its own control. This allows for a more powerful evaluation whereby changes in school performance are related to changes in school policies and practices. A longitudinal assessment also provides more accurate estimates of school effects.

Chapter 4

The Estimation of School Effects

A Definition of School Effects

Educators, administrators, and researchers use the term 'school effects' in a number of ways. Many use it to refer to the effects of particular school policies or practices, or the effects of some intervention. For example, what is the effect on academic achievement of increasing per-pupil expenditures? What is the effect of increasing instructional time in mathematics? What have been the effects of comprehensive reorganization? Most of the literature describing the large-scale cross-sectional studies of the late sixties and early seventies used the term in this way.

The 1966 study *Equality of Educational Opportunity*, popularly known as the Coleman study (Coleman, Campbell, Hobson, McPartland, Mood, Weinfeld, and York, 1966), estimated the relationship of over 400 input variables to measures of academic achievement. The 'school effects' of variables that could be manipulated by school policies, such as per-pupil expenditures or the type of curriculum, were relatively small compared with the effects of family background. These findings, and Jencks *et al.*,'s conclusion that equalizing the quality of American high schools would not substantially reduce inequality (Jencks, Smith, Acland, Bane, Cohen, Gintis, Heyns, and Michelson, 1972), led to the popular but pessimistic conclusion that 'schools don't make a difference' (see also Averch, Carroll, Donaldson, Kiesling, and Pincas, 1974).

The work of Coleman, Jencks, and their colleagues provoked a widespread search for 'school effects' using the input-output approach. Researchers developed more sophisticated models (e.g., Alexander, Pallas, and Cook, 1981; Burstein, 1980; Lau, 1979). They also used more sensitive outcome measures (e.g., Brimer, Madaus, Chapman, Kellaghan, and Wood, 1978; Madaus, Kellaghan, Rakow, and King, 1979) and input variables that were closely related to the teaching process (Brookover, Beady, Flood, Schweitzer, and Wisenbaker, 1979). The literature following the Coleman study suggested that school effects, conceptualized in this way, arise mainly from teacher practices — pupils learn more from teachers who have high expectations, and from those who carefully structure their lessons so that 'time on task' is maximized (Murnane, 1981). The literature suggested also that the intake composition of the school affects achievement: pupils from disadvantaged backgrounds perform better in schools with a significant number of children from advantaged backgrounds (Brookover *et al.*, 1979; Willms, 1985b, 1986). Other variables, such as school size, class size, or school expenditures do not appear to have strong direct effects; however, they may have indirect effects by facilitating better teaching, and contributing to staff motivation and commitment. Bridge, Judd, and Moock (1979) present a detailed summary of the effects of various schooling inputs and processes based on that literature.

Others use the term 'school effects' to mean the difference between a school's average level of performance and some standard, after adjusting statistically for the intake characteristics of the school (e.g., Aitkin and Longford, 1986; Willms and Raudenbush, 1989). When the term is used in this way, each school in the system is considered to have its own unique effect on pupils' outcomes. Thus, there is an 'effect' associated with attendance at a particular school. The standard to which schools are compared can be the average for a set of schools with comparable intakes, the average for the district, or the national average (e.g., Gray, Jesson, and Jones, 1984; Willms, 1986). Sometimes the standard is a pre-defined criterion, such as a goal based on the performance of the previous year. The term 'school effects' is used in the same sense when researchers compare sets of schools to some standard, or make comparisons between school sectors such as denominational and nondenominational schools (e.g., McPherson and Willms, 1986; Willms, 1985a).

Researchers sometimes use the term 'school effects' to refer to the extent of variation between schools in their outcomes; for example, a study might report that approximately 12 per cent of the total variation in pupils' test scores was between schools (e.g., Gray, 1988). Occasionally the term is used to describe the overall effects of attending school *versus* not attending school (e.g., Alexander, Natriello and Pallas, 1985).

Throughout this book I use the term 'school effect' in a sense similar to the second one described above: the 'effect' of a particular school will refer to the difference between the (estimated) average outcome score for a child with certain background characteristics attending that school, and the (estimated) average outcome score for the same child in the entire schooling system. A school's level of performance on an outcome measure depends on several factors. It depends not only on the policies and practices of the school, but also on the background characteristics of pupils entering the school, and on wider social and economic factors that lie outside the control of teachers or administrators. The overall ability and SES composition of a school also affects performance. In the next section I distinguish between two types of school effects: one refers to the overall effect of attendance at a particular school, and therefore includes the effects of school composition and wider social and economic factors; the other refers to the effects that are due specifically to school policies and practices. Both types of effects, which are called Type A and Type B effects, respectively (Willms and Raudenbush, 1989), include an adjustment for pupils' family background.

Two Types of School Effects

The estimation of Type A and Type B effects is based on a model that describes the influences affecting an individual pupil's outcome score. The statistical notation for this model and a description of the methods for the estimation of Type A and B effects are described in Chapter 10 and in the Technical Appendix. (See also Willms and Raudenbush, 1989.) Using broad terms, the model can be described as follows:

Pupil's outcome score =
  the average score for all pupils in the schooling system (e.g., school district, region, country)
  + the effects of pupil background (e.g., pre-entry ability, SES, sex)
  + the effects of school policies and practices (e.g., school resources, organizational structures)
  + the effects of school characteristics (e.g., class size, per-pupil expenditures)
  + the effects of school composition (e.g., average SES of the school)
  + the effects of social and economic factors (e.g., local unemployment rate)
  + any unmeasured effects unique to the child's school
  + random error (e.g., error in measurement due to unreliability of the test).

Type A Effects

The first type of 'school effect', referred to as a Type A effect, addresses the question: 'How well would we expect a pupil with average background characteristics to perform in school X, compared with the average performance of the entire schooling system?' Thus if we said that a school's Type A effect on grade 7 mathematics scores was 0.8 grade equivalents (GEs), and the district average GE was 7.1, we would mean that the expected score for a pupil with average background characteristics was 7.9 in that school. Type A effects can be either positive or negative.

A Type A effect includes the effects of school policies and practices, the effects of school composition, the effects of exogenous social and economic factors, and any unmeasured effects associated with school X. It does not include the effects of the pupils' background characteristics or measurement error. One might prefer to think of Type A effects as 'adjusted school differences' instead of 'school effects', because they include the effects of factors that lie outside the control of teachers and administrators.

Parents are especially interested in the Type A effects of a school. They want to predict the summative effects of schooling — from whatever source — on the schooling outcomes of their child. They are less interested in knowing whether a school is doing well compared with other schools that have similar social and economic constraints, or similar pupil compositions.

Type B Effects

The second type of effect, the Type B effect, includes only the effects of school policies and practices, and unmeasured effects associated with school

X. Type B effects address the question: 'How well does school X perform relative to other schools with similar composition and similar social and economic contexts?' Estimates of Type B effects therefore include statistical adjustment for the contextual influences arising from the social-class composition of the school, and for effects arising from social and economic factors that lie outside the control of the schooling system.

Teachers and administrators are more interested in Type B estimates because they include the effects of policy and practice, and exclude factors outside their control. If government agencies or school districts want to use performance indicators for purposes of accountability, decisions should be based on Type B effects, not Type A effects.

A precise definition of Type B effects is difficult, because it depends on the purpose of the analysis, and requires subjective judgements about which factors lie outside the control of teachers and administrators. For example, should the effects of per-pupil expenditures be included as part of the Type B effect? Per-pupil expenditures are largely determined by teachers' salaries and pupil-teacher ratios. One could argue for the inclusion of per-pupil expenditures in the Type B effect because by removing their effects one would be removing any effects of teacher competence and experience that was associated with teachers' salaries. But for some purposes one could argue for the exclusion of per-pupil expenditures, because the goal may be to compare schools in their performance, given comparable levels of expenditures. By excluding the effects of per-pupil expenditures, then, one could better isolate the effects of particular policies and practices. The definition of Type B effects therefore is variable, depending on the purpose of the analysis. This is not a problem in practice if the data comprise a fairly complete list of relevant policy variables, because the analyst can estimate the separate effects of specific policies, practices, or school characteristics.

Contextual Effects
The distinction between Type A and Type B effects is important because the composition of a school's intake can have a substantial effect on pupils' outcomes over and above the effects associated with pupils' individual ability and social class (Brookover *et al.*, 1978; Henderson, Mieszkowski, and Sauvageau, 1978; Rumberger and Willms, 1991; Shavit and Williams, 1985; Summers and Wolfe, 1977; Willms 1985b, 1986). Schools with high social-class or high ability intakes have some advantages associated with their context: on average they are more likely to have greater support from parents, fewer disciplinary problems, and an atmosphere conducive to learning. They are more likely to attract and retain talented and motivated teachers. Also, there are peer effects that occur when bright and motivated pupils work together (Heath, 1984). Contextual effects can occur also at a classroom level when schools allocate pupils into different classes on the basis of their ability (Willms and Chen, 1989). The size of contextual effects can vary also across school districts (Willms, 1987), and can change over time (Willms and Raudenbush, 1989).

Figure 4-1. Estimates of Type A and Type B effects

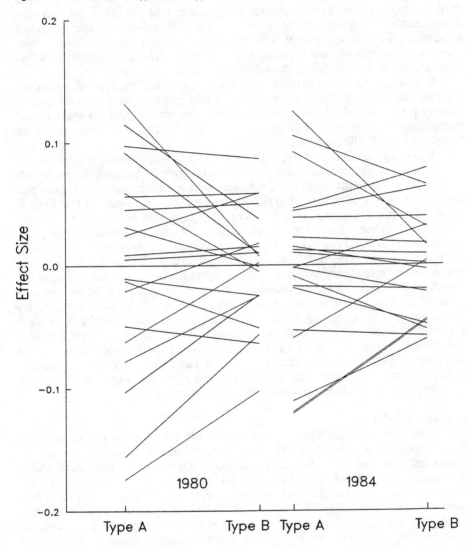

An Example of Type A and Type B Effects

Figure 4-1 shows estimates of Type A and Type B effects on overall examination attainment for twenty schools in the Fife Education Authority for 1980 and 1984. The attainment measure is a nationally standardized measure describing the number and level of O-grade and Highers awards attained on the Scottish Certificate of Education examinations. The model used to estimate the Type A effects included statistical controls for the sex of the pupils, their verbal reasoning ability, the number of children in their families, their fathers' occupations, and their mothers' levels of education. The estimation of

Type B effects employed these measures plus the mean socioeconomic status of the school. (For details, see Willms, 1986). The effects were estimated using hierarchical linear modelling techniques, which are described in Chapter 10 and the Technical Appendix.

The magnitude of the school effects are expressed as 'effect sizes'. These are estimates of the effects of each school measured as a fraction of a standard deviation of the outcome measure. For example, an effect size of 0.1 means that the estimated attainment score of a pupil with average background characteristics was 10 per cent of a standard deviation higher in that school than the national average attainment score. In terms of percentiles, an effect size of 0.1 places a child at the 54th percentile, instead of the 50th percentile. On the attainment scale in Figure 4-1, an effect size of 0.1 is approximately equivalent to one additional O-grade.

Estimates of school effects can be reported in a number of different metrics, or units. Percentage points, percentiles, grade equivalents, and effect sizes are metrics that can be explained and interpreted fairly easily. For example, one might state that the intake-adjusted reading score for a particular school was 2.3 percentage points, 13 percentiles, .19 grade equivalents, or .15 of a standard deviation above the national average. Effect sizes are a useful metric because they permit comparisons across different types of outcome measures, and to some extent across schooling systems. Also, the substantive significance of effect sizes can be judged to some extent by relating them to the average effect sizes reported for particular educational interventions. Many review articles, particularly meta-analyses, summarize findings in terms of effect sizes. For example, Levin, Glass and Meister (1984) estimated that peer-tutoring programs bolstered achievement by approximately .75 of a standard deviation, daily 10–minute computer-assisted-instruction sessions were associated with an effect size of .17, and a reduction in class size from thirty-five to twenty pupils was associated with an effect size of .16.

The Type A effects of Fife's secondary schools ranged from about –.15 to .15 in 1980. This suggests that a hypothetical pupil with average background characteristics, whose verbal reasoning quotient at the end of Primary 7 was 100, attained roughly three additional O-grade passes if he or she attended the top-performing secondary school instead of the lowest-performing secondary school. For this pupil, attending the better school would make the difference between finishing at the 56th percentile instead of the 44th. The range in Type A effects was slightly smaller in 1984.

The Type B effects were smaller, ranging from about –.10 to .10. These effects can be thought of Type A effects with the effects of school composition removed. These effects are more likely to be due to specific school policies.

Analysts often present the rank order of schools based on their estimates of school effects. The results shown in Figure 4-1 demonstrate that rank orders can be misleading. The majority of schools in the figure are tightly clustered around the EA average, with effects ranging from –.07 to .07. Any small fluctuation in a school's estimated effect, including a difference due to measurement or sampling error, would dramatically change its rank in the distribution. Generally, rank orders of schools should be avoided because they accentuate differences between schools that have effect sizes at or near the middle of the distribution.

Data Requirements for Accurate Estimation of School Effects

'School effects', as defined above, refer to the effects of schools on individual pupils, not their effects on some aggregate of pupils. The estimation of school effects therefore requires data collected at the individual level. Aggregate data, such as school mean attainment or school mean SES, are insufficient. Researchers have criticized the use of aggregate data for the estimation of school effects for some time (Aitkin and Longford, 1986; Burstein, 1980; Cronbach, Deken, and Webb, 1976; Hannan, Freeman, and Meyer, 1976). Their principal objection is that estimates based on aggregate data can be biased because they do not take account of the hierarchical structure of educational data. If one could assume that the relationship between pupils' outcomes and the relevant background variables were identical across schools in a system, then estimates based on aggregate data would be similar to what I refer to as Type B effects. However, this assumption does not hold in most schooling systems, and generally estimates based on aggregate data are inaccurate and misleading. Also, with aggregate data one cannot estimate Type A effects, or determine whether schools have differential effects for pupils with differing sex, ability, or family backgrounds.

Even with individual-level data, school effects cannot be measured with perfect accuracy. The accuracy of estimation depends on several factors: the size of the samples from each school; the reliability and validity of the input, process, and outcome measures; and the extent to which all of the relevant control variables are included in the model. If estimates are based on a model that does not include the necessary controls for pupils' intake characteristics, the estimates will be systematically biased. A systematic bias is introduced also if the controls are not measured reliably. The bias stemming from poor model specification is commonly called 'selection bias'. If the outcome variable is not measured reliably, the estimates of school effects include a non-systematic or random error. Estimates based on small sample sizes have the same problem. The requirements for adequate model specification are discussed in the next section, followed by a section describing the effects of measurement and sampling error.

Controls for Pupil Intake

The critical requirement when attempting to estimate school effects is to separate the effects on schooling outcomes associated with pupil intake from those that are associated with the schools pupils attend. Pupils are not randomly assigned to schools; they are selected by formal and informal selection mechanisms. Apparent differences between schools in their outcomes are attributable, in part, to differences in the characteristics of pupils before they enter school. These include, *inter alia*, gender, race, ethnicity, general ability, specific academic competencies, and the influences of family background. Most approaches for making comparisons between schools in their examination results consider schools to be 'treatments' in a quasi-experimental design; differences between pupils allocated to treatments are controlled for by some method of statistical adjustment. However, unless the researcher adjusts for the relevant factors associated with intake, the estimates will be biased (Boardman and Murnane, 1979). The controls for pupil intake are inadequate in many monitoring systems. The result is that schools with more advantaged intakes appear to be performing better than they are; schools with dis-advantaged intakes appear worse.

The set of relevant intake factors required for statistical control includes those that are associated with schooling outcomes and confounded with school membership. The set is 'incomplete' in a statistical sense if there are other variables that are related to school membership and correlated with the outcome measure, given the variables already included in the set. In practice, many of the important differences between schools in their intake that are relevant to subsequent academic performance can be captured with one or two measures of pupils' entry-level academic achievement (e.g., see Willms, 1985a, 1986), or with measures of general verbal and quantitative ability. When attempting to estimate school effects for secondary schools, measures of family SES are useful also, but are less important than premeasures of academic ability. Measures of SES may be more important for the estimation of school effects on achievement at the elementary level, but they are not a substitute for good measures of cognitive ability (e.g., see Jacobsen, 1990). The measurement of SES and the adequacy of various models are discussed in detail in Chapter 5.

One way to reduce selection bias and thereby make fairer assessments is to test pupils on several occasions, estimate their rates of growth on the outcome measure, and then compare schools on the basis of average rates of growth. Generally, assessments based on measures of growth will be less susceptible to selection bias than those based on testing on a single occasion, because growth measures indirectly take account of pupils' initial status (Shim, 1991). The use of growth measures does not eliminate selection bias, however, and does not preclude the need for control measures describing pupils' background characteristics.

Measures of School Process

Unbiased estimates of Type A effects can be obtained with pupil-level data describing outcomes, prior achievement, and family background. To estimate Type B effects, however, one also requires data describing the relevant school policies and practices that potentially explain variation between schools in their outcomes (Raudenbush and Willms, 1988). Type A effects can be estimated essentially by starting with the overall differences between schools and removing the effects of pupils' prior achievement and their background characteristics. This approach is simpler and less expensive than collecting data on school policy and practice, compositional effects, and other factors, and estimating Type A effects by summing the effects of these factors.

The accurate estimation of Type B effects, however, has more stringent data requirements. Type B effects are estimated by collecting direct measures of educational policies and practices, and determining their differential effects for each school. Rough estimates of Type B effects can be obtained by start-ing with the overall differences between schools and removing the effects of pupils' background characteristics and school composition. The estimates shown in Figure 4-1 were obtained in this way. However, because some aspects of school practice and policy are correlated with school composition, there is the danger of removing some of the effects of policy and practice when removing the effects of composition. The resultant estimates therefore underestimate the true Type B effects.

Measurement and Sampling Error

The accuracy with which Type A and Type B effects can be estimated depends on the extent of measurement error in the outcome variable and the number of pupils sampled from each school. One can estimate both types of school effects with data describing samples of pupils from each school; however, even with 50 per cent samples, the sampling errors for smaller schools may be too large for most policy purposes. It is preferable, therefore, to obtain data on entire cohorts of pupils. The costs of collecting data on entire cohorts are to some extent compensated for by saving the administrative costs of taking random samples within each school.

Even with complete sample coverage, however, estimates of school effects include measurement error. These errors will also be greater for smaller schools. Estimates based on the Hierarchical Linear Model (HLM) make adjustments for this error by borrowing strength from the data set as a whole. The estimates of school effects are differentially 'shrunk' towards the mean outcome score for the entire sample. The amount of shrinkage depends on the sample size for a particular school and the reliability with which school effects are estimated (Raudenbush and Bryk, 1986). The shrinkage of estimates for small schools is greater than the shrinkage for large schools. All schools are shrunk somewhat towards the grand mean, depending on the reliability of the outcome measure.

Figure 4-2 shows an example of an adjustment of Type A effects for three separate samples. The first two diagrams show estimates of Type A effects on attainment for the twenty secondary schools in Fife in 1980 and 1984. The third diagram shows estimates of Type A effects on reading scores for seventy-five of the primary schools in 1984. The Type A effects were estimated in two ways: the first used a separate Ordinary Least Squares (OLS) regression equation for each school; the second used an HLM. OLS estimates are unbiased; that is, they do not include any systematic error in a particular direction. However, they include error due to sampling and measurement. The HLM estimates include an adjustment for sampling and measurement error, and although they are biased, they present a more accurate picture of the variation between schools. The controls used in the model to estimate these effects for the seconday schools were the same as those used in the previous example. The controls for primary schools included the pupils' sex, socioeconomic status, and measures of their reading and verbal reasoning ability in Primary 3. The 1980 estimates were based on approximately 50 per cent sample coverage (see Willms, 1986). The 1984 estimates, for both secondary and primary, were based on 100 per cent sample coverage.

Figure 4-2. Adjustment of Type A effects for measurement and sampling error

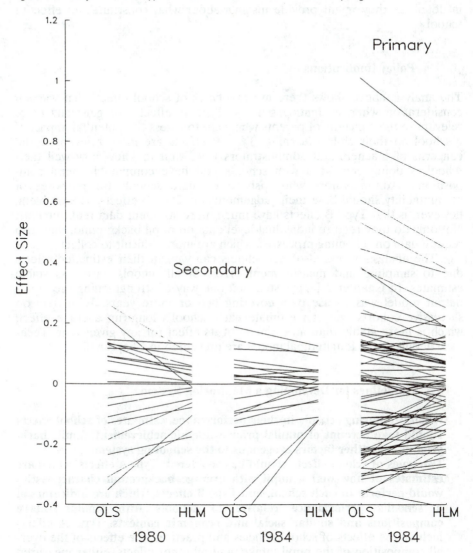

Before using HLM to adjust for measurement and sampling error, the range in the secondary school effects was over 0.60 of a standard deviation. With HLM the range was reduced by nearly one-half. The most dramatic changes were for schools with large effect sizes, either positive or negative. There appears to be little difference between the 1980 and 1984 estimates in the amount of shrinkage; thus, 50 per cent samples appear to be sufficient.

The range in primary school performance was very large, even after adjusting for measurement and sampling error. However, most of the schools had Type A effects that were within .20 of a standard deviation from the EA average. A few schools had particularly large effect sizes — greater than .25

or less than –.25. These 'outliers' would be particularly interesting to study in detail, as they might provide insights about what constitutes an effective school.

Policy Implications

The analysis above shows there are two types of school effects that warrant consideration when evaluating schools. Type A effects are generally more relevant to the concerns of parents who want to assess the potential impact of a school on their child's learning. Type B effects are more relevant to the concerns of teachers and administrators who want to know how well their school is doing compared with schools that have comparable pupil compositions. Administrators who wish to evaluate schools for purposes of accountability should base their judgements on Type B effects. The problem, however, is that Type B effects have much more stringent data requirements. Not only do they require individual-level data on pupil background, they also require data on schooling processes, which are more difficult to collect.

The analysis shows also that schools can vary in their estimated effects due to sampling and measurement error. Small schools have less stable estimates. In Chapter 3 I suggested that one way of strengthening the input-output model was to use data covering two or more years. With data on successive cohorts one can estimate each school's long-run average effect, which is more stable than an estimate of its effect for any given year. Technical details of the longitudinal model are presented in Chapter 10.

Guidelines for Developing a Monitoring System

1   **When comparing schools in their performance, estimates of school effects should take account of pupils' prior academic achievement, family background, and other factors exogenous to the schooling system.**
2   **Two types of school effects should be considered: Type A effects, which are estimates of how well a pupil with average background characteristics would perform in each school, and Type B effects, which are indicators of a school's performance relative to schools with similar intake compositions and similar social and economic contexts.** Type A effects include the effects of school policies and practices, the effects of the overall composition of the pupil intake, and all other effects, either measured or unmeasured, such as those stemming from wider social and economic factors. Only the effects of pupils' background characteristics are held constant. Type B effects include the effects of school policies and practices, and other unmeasured school-related factors, but exclude the individual-level effects associated with pupils' backgrounds, and the school- and community-level 'contextual effects' attributable to the composition of a school's intake, and to wider social and economic factors.
3   **The distinction between Type A and Type B effects is important because a school's examination results are related not only to the individual characteristics of pupils that attend it, but also to its overall social-class**

and ability composition. Schools with a high proportion of disadvantaged pupils, on average, have poorer examination results than schools with a low proportion of disadvantaged pupils, even after controlling for pupils' ability and background at the individual level.

4   **Data on pupils' background characteristics must be collected at the individual level and include measures of prior academic achievement or cognitive ability.** These are the most important control measures, and without them estimates will be biased. Measures of SES are also important, but fairly accurate estimates of school effects can be obtained without them. Estimates of school effects based on aggregate data are usually biased and should not be used.

5   **Unbiased estimates of Type A effects can be obtained with pupil-level data describing outcomes, prior achievement or ability, and SES. Estimates of Type B effects, however, require data describing the relevant school policies and practices that potentially explain variation between schools in their outcomes.**

6   **Estimates of school effects should include an adjustment for measurement and sampling error.** Estimates of school effects based on 100 per cent samples are preferred.

7   **The estimation of school effects can be accomplished more accurately when measures on successive cohorts are available.** In a longitudinal design, each school serves as its own control, and effects for each school at each time point are measured relative to the school's long-run average effect.

8   **Reports of the differences between schools in their effects should specify the size of observed differences in a metric that can be interpreted easily. Reports should not rank-order schools in their effects.** Effect sizes are particularly useful because they provide a convenient metric for making comparisons across schools and across different outcome measures. Also, the substantive significance of effect sizes can be judged to some extent by relating them to the average effect sizes reported for various educational interventions. Rank-orders can be misleading because they accentuate small differences between schools that have effect sizes at or near the middle of the distribution.

Chapter 5

Measuring Pupil Inputs

Socioeconomic Status and its Relationship with Academic Achievement

The relationship between pupils' family background characteristics and schooling outcomes is well established. However, researchers disagree about the magnitude of the relationship, and therefore debate the role that measures of family background should play in studies of schooling. Sociologists have devoted considerable effort to constructing measures of socioeconomic status (SES), but the measures have not been used consistently in the study of schooling (Mueller and Parcel, 1981). Researchers sometimes avoid using measures of SES because of social and political issues concerning the collection of information on pupils' family backgrounds, but often they avoid using them because they are unclear about their role in analysis. In some applications SES may have a limited role if measures of pupil ability or pretests of academic achievement are available.

In this chapter I assert that schools vary substantially in their intakes, and that the relationship between pupils' background characteristics and schooling outcomes warrants consideration. If analysts wish to estimate the effects of particular school practices or policies, or to compare schools in their achievement, they must include valid and reliable measures of schooling inputs. This chapter discusses the role of SES and background characteristics in analysis, and makes recommendations for their measurement. To do this I strive to establish a 'best set' of input measures for the study of school effects. This is an impossible task, of course, but the attempt serves to clarify many of the problems associated with the measurement of SES and pupil characteristics.

Researchers use the term 'socioeconomic status' (SES) to refer to the relative position of a family or individual on an hierarchical social structure, based on their access to, or control over, wealth, prestige, and power (see Mueller and Parcel, 1981). Operationally, the SES of pupils is ascribed to a wide range of background measures describing the occupational prestige, educational levels, and economic positions of pupils' parents. White (1982) conducted a meta-analysis of over 200 studies that reported the relationship between composite measures of SES and academic achievement. The average of the 489 individual-level correlations reported in his meta-analysis was .25, but what was particularly interesting was the variability in the correlations across studies. Estimates ranged from small negative values to positive values of about .80; the standard deviation was .16. Some of the variation could be explained by how SES was measured, the heterogeneity of the sample, and the number of measures comprising the SES composite.

White concluded that when pupils were the unit of analysis, there was little utility in using measures of SES as control or predictor variables. However, his estimate is lower than those typically found in studies based on large, nationally representative samples. Estimates of pupil-level correlations between a composite measure of SES and achievement test scores for the 1982 US. *High School and Beyond* study were .33 for reading, .34 for general mathematics, and .30 for science (Willms, 1983, Table 4-2). Estimates for Scotland for a similar SES composite and the 1980 national O-grade examination results were .41 for arithmetic, .39 for English, and .47 for overall attainment (Willms, 1986). Madaus, Kellaghan, Rakow, and King (1979) reported multiple correlations for Ireland that ranged from .33 to .43 for standardized tests of Irish, English, and mathematics, and from .19 to .48 for national certificate examinations.

The large-scale national studies have shown also that schools vary substantially in their SES intakes. Schools vary in their inputs in part because of residential segregation (Massey and Denton, 1988) and parental choice of schools (Echols *et al.*, 1990), but also because of certain organizational and structural features of schooling systems. These include the way school catchment boundaries are drawn, the location of magnet programs and special services, school admission and expulsion policies, and the 'creaming' of more able pupils into private schools. A useful index of the extent to which pupils are segregated along lines associated with their backgrounds is the proportion of total variation in SES that is between schools. A score of zero on this index means that all schools in a system are identical in their intakes and thus there is no variation in SES between schools; a score of 1.0 means that within schools pupils have the same SES, and thus all variation in SES is between schools. (In practice, these extremes do not occur.) For the US this index was .25 in 1980, based on the *High School and Beyond* data; however, much of the school segregation in the US is inter-racial: in that year the segregation indices for measures of race and ethnicity were .45 for Blacks and .36 for Hispanics (Willms, 1983, Table 4-3). Other research shows that urban areas tend to have larger segregation indices than rural areas (e.g., Zoloth, 1976).

The estimate of between-school segregation for Scotland in 1980 was remarkably similar: .22. An index of .22 represents a substantial degree of between-school segregation: more than 10 per cent of the Scottish schools served populations where about 90 per cent of the families lived in government-owned 'council' houses, about 20 per cent of the parents were available for work but unemployed, and 15 per cent of the families had only one parent. These school catchments are a stark contrast to those served by schools in the top 10 per cent of the distribution, where only 5 per cent of the families lived in council houses, 2 per cent were unemployed, and 2 per cent were single-parent families (Willms, 1986). Moreover, the index was higher for Scotland's four major cities: Glasgow, .35; Edinburgh, .32; Aberdeen, .25; Dundee, .29.

The macro-level analyses demonstrate the importance of using measures of pupils' family background in analyses of school effects. They show that schools vary substantially in their intakes, even within local communities. Also, the relationship between measures of family background and schooling outcomes is large enough to affect estimates of school effects and estimates of the effects of school policy and practice. The next section discusses generally the roles that measures of SES can play in analyses of schooling.

Purposes of Measures of SES and other Pupil Characteristics

Measures of SES and other pupil characteristics can be used in analysis in one or more of the following roles:

Statistical Control

A *confounding factor* in an experiment is one that is distributed differently across 'treatment' groups and correlated with the outcome measure. In the assessment of school effects, each school can be thought of as a 'treatment' in a quasi-experiment. SES would be a confounding factor if its distribution differed across schools, and if it was correlated with the outcome measure. In most schooling systems this is the case. The same can be said of prior ability and measures of race and ethnicity. If confounding factors are ignored in an experiment the results will be biased, because part of the effect of the confounding factor on the outcome appear as an effect of the treatment. If SES is ignored in the estimation of school effects, what appear to be the effects of schooling may be the effects of SES. Researchers refer to this type of bias as selection bias.

Similarly, SES or pupil characteristics can be a confounding factor in the estimation of the effects of some organizational feature or school policy. SES would be a confounding factor if it were correlated with both the policy variable and the outcome measure. For example, if a researcher is attempting to estimate the effects of computer-assisted instruction (CAI) on pupil achievement, SES would be a confounding factor if high-SES pupils received more CAI than low-SES pupils, or *vice-versa*, and if SES were correlated with the measure of achievement. SES is not the only potentially confounding factor. In many studies, race, ethnicity, prior ability, and gender can be confounding factors. If the effects of these factors are not controlled, the findings can be biased.

Confounding factors can bias results at higher levels of aggregation also. For example, a researcher may be interested in the effects of some policy that was implemented in some schools in a district, but not in others. If the schools that received the 'treatment' differed from others in their mean SES, the researcher must control for both individual- and school-level SES.

Several methods are available for controlling for confounding factors. The best way is by random assignment of pupils to treatments. Random assignment ensures, within the limits of probability, that the distributions of all potentially confounding variables are identical across groups. But in most educational settings random assignment is not feasible for political reasons. A notable exception is the Tennessee study on class size, in which kindergarten pupils and teachers were randomly assigned to large and small classes within each school (Finn and Achilles, 1990). Without random assignment, the researcher must use some method of statistical control. Analysis of covariance (ANCOVA) is the most common approach, but there are other approaches which are more appropriate in some applications. These involve matching pupils on relevant variables, using information describing the population to standardize the findings, or stratifying the sample into groups based on values of the confounding variables (Anderson, Auquier, Hauck, Oakes, Vandaele, and Weisberg, 1980).

Increased Precision and Statistical Power
One of the difficulties in conducting research in classrooms or schools is that pupils usually differ in their outcomes to the extent that the effects of particular classroom or school interventions are difficult to discern. Even if one is comparing the achievement scores of a treatment group with those of a control group, and the two groups are comparable in their family backgrounds, the effects of the intervention may be quite small compared with the range of achievement scores within each of the two groups. The problem is one of statistical power; that is, the researcher is not able to reliably determine whether an observed difference between groups is due to the effects of the schooling intervention, or due to chance factors associated with measurement and sampling error. To the extent that researchers can identify pupil characteristics correlated with the outcome measure, and can control for them, the likelihood that they can detect statistically significant effects stemming from the intervention increases. Thus, one of the major purposes of including SES and pupil characteristics in the design of an experiment is to control for variance and thereby increase the precision of an experiment.

Assessment of Interactions
Occasionally educational 'treatments' or interventions affect certain kinds of pupils more than others. For example, Stahl and Miller (1989) reported that whole language and language experience approaches to beginning reading instruction were equal in their effects on reading achievement to traditional basal reading approaches. However, basal reading approaches tended to produce stronger effects with populations specifically labelled as disadvantaged. The inclusion of measures of SES and pupil characteristics in the design of a study allows one to investigate whether there are interactions between the treatment and pupils' background characteristics. In other words, one can make generalizations about the effects of a treatment across different subpopulations (see Cook and Campbell, 1979, Chapter 2).

An Aggregate Descriptive Variable
SES and other pupil-level measures can be aggregated to the class or school level, and used as a descriptive indicator of the social-class intake of a set of classes or schools. For example, in the discussion of segregation above, individual-level data on SES were used to estimate segregation indices, and the indices proved to be a useful summary of the extent of SES segregation. Even more can be learned by examining how school means on SES are distributed within each school district and within each community. In our Scottish research we found that the examination of simple scatterplots of

mean SES and mean attainment furthered our understanding of the system considerably, and allowed us to generate hypotheses about school effects that could be tested with more detailed individual-level data (see McPherson and Willms, 1986, 1987). Aggregate measures of SES and pupil characteristics are useful also in the study of contextual effects, and in the assessment of school effects (see Chapter 4).

Generalization of Findings
Measures of SES and other pupil characteristics can be useful for assessing the extent to which the findings of an investigation are generalizable to some larger population. Most educational studies are conducted within schools or school districts with no formal random sampling for representativeness. By collecting descriptive information on SES and pupil characteristics, researchers can strengthen their case for the generalizability of their findings to other schools or districts.

Identifying a 'Best Set' of Pupil Background Measures

The above set of purposes helps delimit the range of variables that one might include in a set of input variables. As control measures for the estimation of school effects, one wants to include only those variables that are clearly exogenous to the schooling system. For example, the extent to which parents participate in schooling activities may be a confounding factor, but it can be affected by school policies and the efforts of school staff. Thus it is not clearly exogenous. By removing its effect through statistical control, one might remove also some of the effects of schooling. The amount of time spent on homework is also a factor that is influenced by both the school and the family.

White (1982) makes the point also that there may be reciprocal effects between academic achievement and variables associated with the learning atmosphere at home; for example, do parents take an interest in their child's education because the child is enthused and doing well at school, or does the child become enthused and do well because of the parents' interest? Variables associated with parents' expectations and aspirations fall into this category. In this chapter I limit the discussion to variables that describe family and pupil characteristics, but are not affected by the schooling system. Variables associated with home atmosphere that can be affected by the schooling system are classified as school process variables and discussed in the next chapter.

I also distinguish between family-related factors that might comprise a composite measure of SES, and other pupil characteristics, such as ability, race, and ethnicity. Measures of SES are almost always correlated with these pupil characteristics, and studies often lack sufficient power to determine their separate effects (e.g., Willms and Chen, 1989). Also, measures of pupil ability or prior performance can attenuate the effects of family SES on achievement, because the prior measure to some extent includes the earlier effects of SES. This is especially a problem in studies of short duration, or studies that measure pupil ability at the same time as the outcome measure (Alexander, Pallas, and Cook, 1981). For purposes of statistical control and precision, the distinction between SES measures and pupil characteristics is less important because the researcher does not usually need to combine variables into a single composite. But if the purpose is mainly to examine interactions, or to describe a sample, a composite measure of SES can be useful. In these cases, we want to distinguish between variables that represent the construct SES and variables representing other constructs, such as ability, or race and ethnicity. To determine which variables represent SES, we should consider how well variables represent the theoretical construct of SES rather than how well they predict achievement.

Two other problems come immediately to mind when one attempts to identify a 'best set' of background measures for the study of school effects. 'Best', in the context of the first two purposes set out above, implies that we want a set of variables that explains a high proportion of the variance in schooling outcomes. The 'best set' therefore depends on the outcome measure. Madaus *et al.*, (1979) found that the proportion of variance accounted for uniquely by sets of individual and family variables differed dramatically across outcome measures. The choice of background measures depends also on the social, political, and economic context of the schooling system. For example, one might expect variables associated with race and ethnicity to play a bigger role in a study of schooling in Los Angeles than one in Edinburgh.

Another consideration is the cost of data collection. The measurement of any construct is improved if one collects multiple measures of the same construct (Cook and Campbell, 1979). Thus, a composite measure of mothers' and fathers' education, occupation, and income would produce a more reliable and valid indicator of SES than a single measure of either mothers' or fathers' occupation. But the collection and analysis of multiple measures means greater costs for administration, testing time, data entry, and analysis. The means used to collect data are also related to costs. For example, interview data are more likely to furnish a better measure of SES than questionnaire data, but for purposes of monitoring the costs of interviewing are usually prohibitive. Census data can be obtained easily, but in most cases are less valid than questionnaire data.

An Analysis for One Education Authority

The analysis in this section is a search for the best set of input variables for predicting schooling outcomes. It is based on data describing Fife Educational Authority. The inquiry is limited in that the outcome measures describe only academic outcomes, and the input measures are based solely on questionnaire data. Also, Fife Education Authority comprises only a few small cities and townships; much of the Authority is rural. Compared with urban authorities, between-school segregation is small. Nevertheless, the analyses are useful in that the data are typical of the kind that school districts or EAs can collect easily with questionnaires administered to classes of pupils.

A common method for assessing the importance of a predictor variable is to estimate the percentage of variance in the outcome variable it explains. Predictor variables are usually correlated with each other, and the collective contribution of a set of variables is not simply the sum of their individual contributions. Thus the analysis must consider the *unique* proportion of explained variance associated with each variable, and the proportion *common* to other variables in the model. The same applies to sets of variables entered as 'blocks' into a regression analysis. A problem with this approach is that the proportion of variance explained, denoted R^2, can be a misleading indicator of the substantive significance of a variable. A variable might have large effects in substantive terms, but because of its distribution in the sample, contribute little to explained variance. Thus the analysis must consider R^2 and the substantive significance of the effect of a variable.

Table 5-1 shows, for a number of primary and secondary outcome measures, the proportions of variance explained (R^2) by measures of prior performance, sex, and family background. The outcome measures for primary schooling include pupils' reading and verbal reasoning scores taken at the end of Primary 7. The secondary school outcomes include measures of pupils' fourth year O-grade examination results in arithmetic, English, and science; an overall measure of examination attainment describing both O-grade and Highers results; and a dichotomous measure indicating whether pupils remained in school beyond the fourth year (see Willms, 1986, for a description of the scaling of these variables). The Primary 7 reading and verbal reasoning scores were used as measures of prior performance for the secondary analysis, while similar measures taken at the end of Primary 3 were used for the primary school analysis. The family background measures were derived from questionnaire data collected at the end of the fourth year of secondary school. They include mothers' and fathers' occupational prestige scores, based on the Hope Goldthorpe scale, mothers' and fathers' education, number of siblings, and whether the family was a single- or two-parent family.

The complete set of predictor variables explained approximately 52 per cent of the variance in pupils' primary 7 reading scores. The measures of prior performance and sex, by themselves, explained over 50 per cent of the variance.[1] The family background measures, by themselves, explained about 15 per cent of the variance; however, 13 per cent of the variance was common to the measures of prior performance. Thus the family background measures made a unique contribution of only about 2 per cent.

The decrease in R^2 associated with each variable provides an indication of its unique contribution. Primary 3 reading was the strongest predictor of Primary 7 reading; removal of this variable from the model resulted in a loss of over 10 per cent of the explained variance. Verbal reasoning was next in importance, with a unique contribution of about 6 per cent. Fathers' occupation was the most important measure of family background, followed by mothers' education and fathers' education. The remaining family background variables contributed uniquely less than one-tenth of 1 per cent to the explained variance.

---

[1] Nearly all of the explanatory power of this block was attributable to the measures of prior performance. Sex had a negligible contribution; it was included in this block for convenience of computation and explanation.

Table 5-1 Percentage of Variance Explained and Decreases in R² Associated with the Removal of Predictor Variables

	Primary		Secondary				
	P7 Reading	P7 VRQ	Overall SCE Attainment	S4 Arithmetic	S4 English	S4 Science	Staying On at School
Total R²	52.01	58.94	54.91	58.81	63.57	44.22	22.40
Percentage of Variance Explained by							
Prior Performance and Sex	50.07	57.84	51.30	57.18	61.74	39.88	19.87
Family Background	15.28	14.10	22.27	18.39	20.12	20.22	10.67
Commonality	13.34	13.00	18.66	16.76	18.29	15.88	8.14
Decrease in R² Associated with Removal of:							
Prior Performance	36.73	44.58	32.41	40.40	40.69	23.32	11.19
Verbal Reasoning	5.96	9.14	3.40	8.14	2.49	2.49	.90
Reading	10.89	11.02	4.21	2.16	7.67	2.98	1.79
Sex	.48	.03	.06	.22	2.09	1.03	.37
Family Background	1.94	1.10	3.61	1.63	1.83	4.34	2.53
Father's Occupation	.45	.31	.80	.37	.41	.86	.35
Mother's Occupation	.07	.09	.10	.11	.10	.14	.00
Father's Education	.10	.04	.22	.04	.09	.53	.46
Mother's Education	.14	.07	.22	.12	.11	.23	.09
Number of Parents	.02	.00	.24	.12	.08	.08	.01
Number of Siblings	.09	.01	.18	.04	.07	.04	.08

The same general pattern was found for the prediction of Primary 7 verbal reasoning scores: about 58 per cent of the variance was explained by the complete set of predictors, but most of the explanation could be accomplished with the measures of prior performance. Prior reading scores was the most important predictor, followed by verbal reasoning ability, then fathers' occupation. Sex and the remaining family background variables could be removed from the model with little loss in explanatory power.

Measures of prior performance outweighed family background variables in the analyses of secondary outcomes also. The unique contribution of family background measures ranged from 1.63 to 4.34 per cent of the variance. Of the two measures of prior performance, reading was a better predictor than verbal reasoning for all outcome measures except arithmetic. Fathers' occupation was the best predictor amongst the family background measures across all outcomes except staying on at school, where fathers' education was marginally a better predictor. Mothers' education was either the second or third most important predictor amongst the family background measures. Mothers' occupation, number of parents, and number of siblings tended to contribute little to the explained variance, given the other variables in the models.

These findings suggest that if the goal of analysis is to estimate school effects or the effects of some intervention, then measures of prior performance are essential for statistical control. If the analysis does not include measures of prior performance, the estimates of effects will probably be biased. Measures of family background add marginally to the degree of statistical control.

Figures 5-1 and 5-2 show the extent of bias in estimates of school effects on primary reading scores, and on secondary SCE attainment scores, for various models. In both figures, the last set of estimates is based on an HLM analysis which employed the complete set of control variables. I refer to these estimates as *unbiased* estimates of Type A effects, but accept that there may be other relevant input variables with effects not captured by the input variables in this model.

The first set of estimates in Figures 5-1 and 5-2 shows the unadjusted differences between schools; that is, the simple mean scores of the outcome measures. As estimates of school effects, these are obviously biased. A measure of the extent of bias is the difference between the unbiased estimate and the unadjusted estimate. The average bias (absolute value) is about .30 of a standard deviation for the primary schools, and .19 for the secondary schools. The ratio of the variance in the estimates of bias to the size of the unbiased estimates, which I call the *bias-to-effect-size ratio*, is about 4.47 for the primary schools and 11.03 for the secondary schools. Moreover, the figures show that some schools had large unadjusted mean scores (either positive or negative), but had Type A effects that were close to the average for this set of schools.

The second set of estimates show the HLM means, without statistical control for prior performance, sex, or family background. These means have been adjusted for sampling and measurement error, based on the size of each school sample, and the variability in outcome scores within and between schools. This adjustment reduces the bias-to-effect-size ratio to .88 for

Figure 5-1. *Bias in estimates of school effects on primary reading scores*

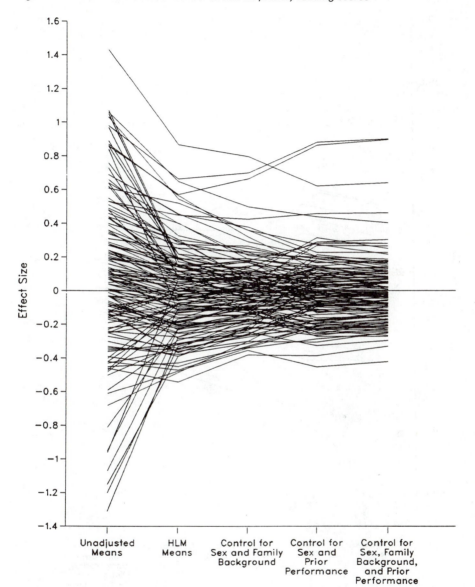

primary schools and to 8.24 for secondary schools. The extent of 'shrinkage' of the primary school estimates is much greater than that of the secondary schools. This is because the average sample size was 30.2 for the primary sample, compared with 292.4 for the secondary sample. There were sixty primary schools with sample sizes less than twenty and their estimates were not very stable.

Figure 5-2.   Bias in estimates of school effects on secondary attainment scores

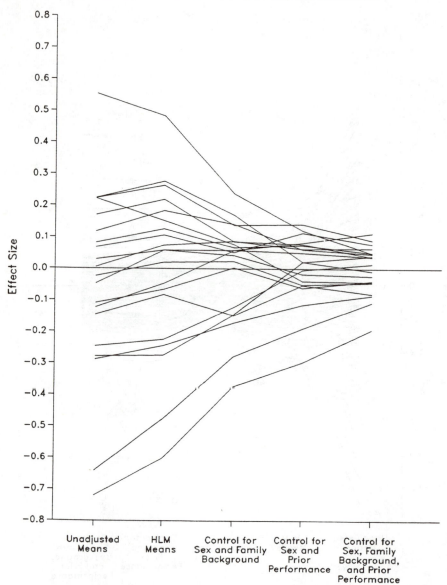

The third set of estimates includes adjustment for measures of family background and sex, but does not include adjustment for prior performance. The average bias for these estimates is .09 of a standard deviation for both sets of schools, and the bias-to-effect-size ratios are .37 and 2.14, for the primary and secondary schools respectively. The fourth set of estimates shows the extent of bias when the model includes only prior performance and sex. The averages of the estimates of bias are .03 of a standard deviation for both primary and secondary schools, and the bias-to-effect-size ratios are .03 and .32 for the primary and secondary schools respectively. Together these two sets of results show dramatically the need for estimates of prior performance in the estimation of school effects.

A comparison of Figures 5-1 and 5-2 suggests that the adjustment for measurement and sampling error is particularly important for primary schools, and less important for secondary schools. Because the number of pupils at each grade level in a typical primary school is relatively small, estimates of the average performance on the outcome measures are not very stable. This means that estimates of school effects may vary considerably from year to year, not because of changes in school policy or practice, but simply because of the particular 'sample' of pupils attending the school each year. Estimates for the secondary schools are more stable because of the larger sample sizes at each level. Willms and Raudenbush (1989) examined the question of stability in greater detail for this set of secondary schools.

The two figures show, as did Table 5-1, that measures of prior performance are essential for the estimation of school effects. Without them the average bias was .09 of a standard deviation. Fifteen of the primary schools had estimates that were biased more than 20 per cent of a standard deviation, and four of the secondary schools had estimates that were biased more than 15 per cent of a standard deviation. Some of these were biased positively, others negatively; thus comparisons between two schools in their effects could be substantially biased if there were no controls for prior performance. Measures of SES were less important. If the model excluded SES, the estimates were biased, on average, by about .03 of a standard deviation. This is not large in substantive terms; however, in both samples there were schools that were biased as much as .10 of a standard deviation, both positively and negatively. Thus comparisons between two particular schools could be biased by as much as .20 of a standard deviation if the set of controls did not include measures of SES. Generally, the bias stemming from inadequate control is to the advantage of high SES schools, and to the disadvantage of low SES schools.

Methods for Handling Missing Data

One of the problems encountered when attempting to conduct regression analyses with survey data is that usually not all pupils provide answers to all questions. This is especially true of questions pertaining to family SES. Although the percentage of respondents with data missing on any particular question may be small, there is usually a large percentage who have not answered every question.

Most statistical software packages offer two options for handling missing data in regression analyses: listwise and pairwise deletion. The listwise method employs data for those respondents with complete data for every variable in the analysis. Those with missing data on any variable are deleted. The pairwise method constructs a correlation matrix using all available data for each pair of variables considered separately; regression coefficients are then based on this correlation matrix. When the sample size is large, and the proportion of respondents with missing data is small, both methods will provide accurate estimates. They are usually preferred because of their simplicity and availability.

Listwise deletion is the simplest and most straightforward method, and can be used with any multivariate analysis. Also, with listwise deletion one can easily construct a composite index derived from two or more variables. However, when an analysis involves several variables, and the pattern of missing information is random or close to random, then the number of cases with complete information can be relatively small. For the set of variables employed above, only 58.5 per cent of the cases had complete data on all measures of SES and prior performance. For this reason, I chose pairwise deletion. Kim and Curry (1977) suggest that when sample sizes are large, and the correlations between variables are moderate, the pairwise method may produce slightly better estimates of regression coefficients. These two conditions are usually met for data sets constructed to monitor school performance. However, there can be situations when the matrix generated by the pairwise technique is inconsistent (mathematicians use the term 'not positive definite') and produces bizarre regression results. This is most likely when sample sizes are small and data are not missing at random.

When listwise deletion is used for a data set with a large number of explanatory variables, the researcher usually has to employ some strategy to reduce the number of variables. Lockheed and Longford (1991) used a listwise approach when examining the effects of a number of pupil- and group-level variables on mathematics achievement in Thailand. Their initial regression model included thirty-two variables. They estimated coefficients for the model using listwise deletion across all thirty-two variables, and employed a conservative criterion (*t*-values less than 0.9) to exclude variables from the model. They then estimated coefficients for the reduced model using listwise deletion across variables in the new set, thereby obtaining a larger sample than was employed in the initial model. They proceeded in this fashion until arriving at their final regression model. This technique of backwards deletion, although a bit tedious, allowed them to achieve a much larger sample than if they had employed listwise deletion across the full set of variables.

Another way to reduce the number of variables is to construct a composite measure of variables describing a specific construct such as SES. The National Opinion Research Center, in constructing the *High School and Beyond* data set, used a straightforward method for constructing an SES composite. They standardized each of five indicators of SES: father's occupation, mother's and father's education, family income, and a scale of household possessions. The composite SES score was simply the average of all non-missing indicators. If a case had valid data for only one indicator, or none, it was assigned a missing value. This technique yielded valid data on the SES composite for 96.8 per cent of their respondents.

When a data set is small (say fewer than 1000 cases) and the correlations amongst variables are large, both listwise and pairwise deletion of missing data are inappropriate. In these cases the researcher can consider some method of imputing missing values. Some software programs provide the option of 'mean substitution'; that is, replacing the missing values with the mean score on that variable. I do not recommend this technique because if data are not missing at random, mean substitution will bias regression estimates. Beale and Little (1975) provide an iterative method as follows: impute missing values on the basis of regression relationships estimated with non-missing data; replace the missing values with the imputed values; reestimate the regression relationships; impute new values for the missing data; repeat the process until the estimates of the missing values converge. Paterson (1989) provides an example of this approach in a study of the relationship between SES and educational attainment. In general this approach will provide superior estimates to other methods. However, the process is tedious and time-consuming without software designed for the purpose. The BMDP statistical package has a routine that utilizes an iterative method for imputing missing values, and Kim and Curry (1977) offer some non-iterative methods which are less computing-intensive. Convenience and feasibility will to some extent dictate the choice of technique, and if the data set is large, the choice may make little difference (Beale and Little, 1975; Kim and Curry, 1977).

Guidelines for Developing a Monitoring System

1 **Measures of SES and other pupil characteristics are important indicators in a monitoring system.** They can be used in the following roles:

   - statistical control of confounding factors,
   - increased precision and statistical power,
   - the assessment of interactions,
   - an aggregate descriptive variable,
   - improving the generalizability of findings.

2 **Measures of prior academic achievement and cognitive ability are more important control variables than measures of SES or other pupil characteristics.** If data on prior achievement or ability are available, measures of SES and other pupil characteristics do not contribute substantially to analyses of school effects or the effects of policies and practice. Measures of SES and other pupil characteristics are valuable anyway, however, because they can be used to assess interactions, to describe a sample, and to generalize findings. The measures of SES and other characteristics should include sex, race and ethnicity, parental occupation and education, and family composition.

3 **Usually only a small percentage of pupils who are surveyed answer every question pertaining to SES and other characteristics. The analyst must adopt some strategy for handling missing data, such as listwise or pairwise deletion of data, or some iterative method.** When sample sizes are large, and correlations amongst variables are moderate, the pairwise method produces slightly better estimates than the listwise method. Iterative methods are necessary when sample sizes are small and the correlations amongst variables are large.

Chapter 6

Schooling Processes

The task of this chapter is to identify some of the key components of schooling processes that might be useful to teachers and administrators, and provide some strategies for their measurement. The first section lists some of the general problems entailed in collecting process data, and asks whether it is a worthy enterprise. The second section provides a map of the territory, and, like a world map, offers only one of many possible projections, and is necessarily on a large scale. The section that follows presents a list of key components of schooling processes and makes some suggestions for their measurement. The penultimate section discusses some of the issues concerning the measurement and interpretation of data on schooling processes. The chapter concludes with a list of guidelines for the development of indicators of schooling processes. In Chapter 10 I elaborate the idea of using process data as part of a school or district research program.

Should We Collect Data on Schooling Processes?

Researchers have demonstrated that there are statistically significant differences between schools in their outcomes (e.g., Gray, 1989; Lockheed and Longford, 1991; Murnane, 1975; Raudenbush and Bryk, 1986; Willms, 1986), but after two decades of serious effort, they have made little progress in determining *why* some schools are more successful than others. Reviews of the school effects literature provide long lists of variables found related to instructional outcomes, but most reviews consider only the statistical significance of observed effects, not their magnitude. Those that consider magnitude suggest that the effect of any particular school policy or organizational variable is weak (for example see Chapter 8, Section 5 of Bridge, Judd, and Moock, 1979). At best the literature points to general factors, such as those comprising the five-factor model: strong administrative leadership, a safe and orderly climate, an emphasis on basic academic skills, high teacher expectations, and a system for monitoring pupil performance (see Chapter 3).

Part of the problem is that there are so many factors that affect schooling outcomes, and most of them are complex and difficult to describe and measure. Factors like 'principal leadership' are multifaceted (Bossert, Rowan,

Dwyer, and Lee, 1982), and there is low intersubjective agreement amongst teachers in their ratings of principals' leadership skills (Rowan, Raudenbush, and Kang, 1991). Some factors are interactive; for example, Summers and Wolfe (1977) found that teacher experience had a positive effect on the achievement of high-ability pupils, but a negative effect on the achievement of low-ability pupils. Some factors have important indirect effects, even though their direct effects are weak. Teacher morale is a good example: although it does not have a high correlation with schooling outcomes (Brookover *et al.*, 1978; McDill and Rigsby, 1973), it may be a prerequisite for a school climate that is conducive to learning (Rosenholtz, 1989b). The identification of important schooling processes is complicated also because factors at each level of the system can affect schooling outcomes, and these factors can interact across levels, and have indirect effects through factors at higher or lower levels (Meyer, 1980; Raudenbush and Willms, 1988). The level of aggregation at which factors are measured is important too because factors can have different meanings at different levels of aggregation (Burstein, 1980). Finally, the task is difficult because the relationships may be unstable over time (Murnane, 1987).

Because of the scope and complexity of schooling processes, and because the research on school effectiveness has not identified strong links between processes and outcomes, some researchers question whether indicators of schooling processes are useful. Murnane (1987) cautioned against collecting data describing schooling processes because reliable and valid information on what teachers and pupils actually do is difficult to collect, given the diversity of activities in US schools, and the extent to which school policies and practices are ever-changing. He suggested also that the collection of indicators on schooling processes might lead to misguided efforts if educators try to improve their scores on process indicators that are only weakly related to schooling outcomes. Porter (1991) recommended the collection of indicators describing schooling processes, but emphasized indicators of curriculum content and teaching quality, because school quality 'is particularly difficult to assess' (p. 27).

I accept Murnane's misgivings about process data if administrators try to use them in a rational decision-making model (Sproull and Zubrow, 1981); that is, if they look at outcome data to determine which schools are performing below standard, turn to the list of process variables to diagnose the causes of low performance, and then prescribe a corresponding remedy. Our knowledge about how schools have their effects on instructional outcomes is inadequate to support this kind of management strategy. I believe also that the solution to shortcomings of input-process-output research does not lie in more sophisticated or more comprehensive research; I largely take Cohen and Weiss's (1977) view that 'the improvement of research on social policy does not lead to greater clarity about what to think or what to do; instead, it usually tends to produce a greater sense of complexity' (p. 68). I doubt whether another two decades of research will yield better theories about how schools have their effects on pupils' outcomes; nor will it help us specify a *model for all seasons* — a model that would apply to all schools in all communities at all times. Even if we could come close to an ideal model, its complexity would be overwhelming and the data requirements immense.

However, administrators make decisions based on their beliefs about how schools operate, and on information about the schooling system. Although much of their information comes from personal observations and comments from school personnel (Sproull and Zubrow, 1981), information derived from tests and questionnaires contributes to their working knowledge. Despite the problems associated with identifying, defining, and measuring schooling processes, certain indicators can be useful as part of the information used by teachers and administrators. The literature has provided some direction as to which general areas have the strongest links to schooling outcomes (Anderson, 1982, 1985). A few well-measured indicators covering these areas could be used alongside other information to help teachers and administrators understand how the system operates. Some general indicators of schooling processes might also provide direction for asking more specific questions that call for detailed comprehensive data. For example, indicators of pupil-teacher or pupil-pupil relations might direct attention to issues of race relations, calling for more intensive study in particular schools. Also, data on schooling processes can help strengthen the input-output 'shell', such that one can determine more accurately the effects of certain interventions. In other words, one could use information describing schooling processes in conjunction with input and output data to help evaluate individual schools' action plans, district-wide initiatives, or national and state policies.

What are Schooling Processes?

The word 'process' in the input-process-output model suggests that schools in some way *process* pupil inputs into schooling outcomes. For the moment I will use this conception of schooling processes because it is useful for delineating the territory covered by the term. Processes then are the many factors associated with schooling that affect outcomes, either directly or indirectly. They include factors describing the context and setting of schools, such as 'school enrolment', 'teachers' mean salary', and 'racial balance'; and evaluative factors associated with the 'climate' or 'culture' of schools (see Howe, 1977). The evaluative factors attempt to portray the internal workings of school life: how pupils and staff are organized for instruction, the formal and informal rules governing operation, the nature of interactions between participants in various roles, and participants' attitudes, values, and expectations.

One of the problems with delimiting a set of variables describing schooling processes is that the boundaries between input and process variables, and between process and output variables, are not clear. In the previous chapter I limited the set of input variables to those that were clearly exogenous to schooling, leaving endogenous variables to be included in the set of process variables. This means that variables like 'parental support of school activities', 'parent-teacher rapport', or 'parental press for academic achievement' are classified here as process variables, because they can be affected by school policies and practices. Conceptually this is a problem, because a variable like 'parental press for academic achievement' may be affected only minimally by school staff, and one may be inclined to classify it as an input variable. Other variables lie on the boundary between process and outcome variables. For example, one could argue that 'pupils' academic aspirations' or 'satisfaction with school' are process variables — they are part of what we call 'school culture' and they affect schooling outcomes. But equally one could argue they are outcome variables in their own right, every bit as important as academic achievement (see Epstein and McPartland, 1976; Sirotnik, 1984). I will classify variables depicting attitudes and values as process variables, but the distinction is relevant more for the statistical modelling of school effects than it is for administrative uses of indicator data.

Another problem with delimiting a set of process variables is that we are interested mainly in factors that can be influenced through school policy and practice (Williams and Bank, 1984). But immediately we must ask 'influenced by whom?'. Teachers may have relatively little control over factors like 'class size', 'length of the school day', or 'resources available for teaching materials'; conversely, district-level administrators have relatively little control over teachers' instructional strategies or their methods of motivating pupils. The characterization of schooling processes thus requires a multilevel formulation, and to be useful to teachers, principals, and district-level administrators, the 'input-process-output' model requires variables describing the system from different perspectives.

Figure 6-1 presents a list of constructs describing schooling process, classified according to a taxonomy of organizational climate specified by Tagiuri (1968). The list also classifies constructs according to level of measurement. I use the term 'constructs' rather than 'variables' because many items on the list are multidimensional and require several variables to describe them well. Some are not easily operationalized with quantitative methods. I relied heavily on Anderson's (1982, 1985) reviews to build the list, but have included also constructs from more recent work on school climate and school effects (e.g., Clark, Lotto, and Astuto, 1984; Oakes, 1989; Pallas, 1988; Porter, 1991; Rosenholtz, 1989b; Rowan *et al.*, 1991). The list attempts to be comprehensive in that it includes most of the major constructs that appear in the literature. Anderson (1982, 1985) discusses the research findings pertaining to many of the constructs. Not all of the constructs included have shown consistent and strong relationships with academic achievement or other schooling outcomes; some of them have weak or indirect effects, most have not been studied adequately.

Tagiuri's taxonomy of organizational climate comprises four categories: ecology, milieu, social system, and culture. The ecological constructs include those that describe the physical and material environment of the classroom, school, and district. The second category, milieu, includes variables describing characteristics of individuals at each level. Pupil characteristics measured at the individual level are not included here because they are exogenous to the schooling process. They were discussed in Chapter 5. The figure includes pupil composition, which is typically measured with aggregate measures of pupil characteristics (e.g., mean SES), because it is often used as a proxy for other schooling processes. I have enclosed it in brackets because it is largely exogenous to the schooling system. However, one could argue that pupil composition at each level is affected by schooling processes; for example,

Level of Measurement	Ecology (physical and material variables)	Milieu (student composition and characteristics of staff)	Social System (patterns and rules of operating and interacting)	Culture (norms, beliefs, values, and attitudes)
Student			type of instructional program participation in decision-making chose school program moved schools participation in school activities relationships with other students	peer norms for academic success parent norms for academic success sense of efficacy *vs.* futility attitudes towards school quality of school life work and study habits teacher attitudes sense of efficacy *vs.* futility commitment morale clear goals consistency cooperative emphasis flexibility (open to change)
Class	class size appearance of classroom instructional resources curriculum materials	(student composition) teacher characteristics years experience salary level of education	within-class segregation ability grouping disciplinary climate access to knowledge academic press time on academic instruction amount of homework high expectations success is rewarded emphasis on academics student-student relationships student-teacher relationships parent-teacher relationships	
School	school size appearance of building age of building per-student expenditures access to community resources	(student composition) teacher turnover principal characteristics teaching experience administrative experience salary duration of current position	within-school segregation tracking, streaming disciplinary climate instructional leadership extra support children with special needs counselling services staff participation in decisions retention and acceleration policy principal-teacher relationships teacher-teacher relationships community-school relationships parent involvement in school between-school segregation community-district relationships mechanisms for accountability	principal expectations of teachers of students coherence clear goals consensus curricular goals disciplinary standards
District	district size per-pupil expenditures	(student composition)		

schools with high academic expectations may attract certain types of pupils. Earlier I discussed the role of measures of pupil composition in the estimation of school effects (see Chapter 4). In Chapter 10, I discuss their role in helping to explain why some schools are more effective than others. Tagiuri's third category, social system, includes constructs associated with the patterns and rules governing how schools operate, as well as variables depicting the nature of relationships amongst and between pupils and staff. The fourth category, culture, includes those constructs depicting the norms and values of the school. These variables depict what many researchers refer to as the 'climate' or 'ethos' of the school.

Identifying a Set of Key Indicators

Researchers who have thought about which process indicators to include in a monitoring system agree that it is better to measure a few indicators well than attempt to cover the entire domain (Murnane, 1987; Oakes, 1989; Sirotnik and Burstein, 1987). Murnane (1987), who was writing mainly about state and national indicator systems, suggested four criteria:

- Is there evidence that this activity is related to critical performance measures?
- Will the collection and reporting of information on the activity lead to desirable responses?
- Can valid and reliable information about the activity be collected at reasonable cost?
- Are the categories used in collecting the information likely to be meaningful in 15 years? (p. 111)

Oakes (1989) also called for indicators that had clear empirical links with valued schooling outcomes. She based her choice also on whether an indicator would press schools towards emphasizing a broader range of schooling outcomes than those covered by standardized achievement tests. She believes that when schools try to 'look good' on indicators of organizational arrangements, teaching strategies, or classroom processes, they inadvertently put in place the conditions necessary for learning higher-level skills.

The literature on school effects provides only a rough guide for choosing process indicators. Nearly all of the constructs listed in Figure 6-1 could be said to have an empirical link with educational outcomes, but few of the findings have been tested in formal, 'true' experiments. Most of the work has been correlational and only a few studies have attempted to construct causal models that examine direct and indirect relationships between constructs, or interactions across levels of the system. Also, reviews of the literature have not attempted to quantify the strength of the relationships between constructs; they have simply reported their statistical significance. Finally, most of the research evidence pertains to links between ecology and milieu variables with achievement test scores. The important process-outcome links may be between social system or culture variables and affective outcomes. For these reasons, my selection of process indicators does not emphasize empirical links with schooling outcomes.

I propose the following criteria:

- **Which indicators provide a *balanced picture* of schooling across levels of the system, and across types of (Tagiuri) constructs?** A path diagram connecting the constructs in Figure 6-1 would be very complicated (e.g., see Figure 1 of Glasman and Biniaminov, 1981). But to a large extent the relationships would flow from left to right; that is, those on the left would have their effects on schooling outcomes indirectly through constructs on the right. For example, class size and instructional resources affect working conditions in the school, which in turn affect teachers' morale and commitment, which finally affect pupils' outcomes (e.g., see Rosenholtz, 1989b). These paths also cross levels of the system, both up and down. Thus, to get an accurate picture of the schooling system, it is necessary to have indicators across the four types of constructs, and across levels of the system.

- **Which indicators facilitate self-examination and the process of school renewal?** Sirotnik (1987) views evaluation as a process of *critical inquiry* — a dialectic around questions and activities pertaining to school renewal. Indicators are one form of information that can stimulate discussion about how certain aspects of schooling operate, why things are the way they are, whose interests are being served, whether change is called for, and if so, how to accomplish it (see Sirotnik, 1987, p. 42).

- **Which indicators are seen as tractable variables by school staff and administrators?** The early school effects literature emphasized the search for 'tractable' variables — those that could be manipulated through educational policies and practices (Bridge *et al.*, 1979). The problem is that the tractability of a variable is itself context-bound. Tractability depends on the level of the system at which one is working. It depends also on the availability of resources, which may or may not be seen as tractable. It can depend on wider social and political influences, such as the conditions set by a teachers' union or expectations voiced by active parents. Furthermore, what is tractable today may not be tractable in a few years' time. Thus, a set of 'key indicators' of schooling processes may be ever-changing, and must take account of a staff's needs and goals for the educational system. Murnane's criteria of long-term durability is applicable more to state or national indicators; district indicator systems need to provide the kind of information that teachers and principals find useful in their work.

- **Which indicators are easy and inexpensive to measure?** Most districts collect and maintain financial and demographic data describing salaries, expenditures on materials and equipment, the condition of physical plant, pupil and teacher characteristics, curricular materials, and program participation (Burstein, 1984). Information pertaining to virtually all of the ecology and milieu constructs, and many of the social system constructs, can be routinely collected at little expense, and thus should be included as part of a monitoring system. However, the costs associated with obtaining reliable and valid data on some social system and culture constructs is pertinent. For some it can be prohibitive.

Based on these criteria, an indicator system might collect information describing the following aspects of schooling:

I   Ecology and Milieu Constructs
II   Segregation
III   Disciplinary Climate
IV   Academic Press
V   Intended *versus* Enacted Curriculum
VI   Pupil Attitudes
          Sense of efficacy *versus* futility
          Attitudes towards school
          Quality of school life
VII   Teacher Attitudes
          Sense of efficacy *versus* futility
          Commitment and morale
          Working conditions
VIII   Instructional Leadership of Principals

To this list I would add two or three constructs relevant to the particular interests of pupils, teachers, and principals in the district. For example, a district in the throes of implementing a new program on multiculturalism may wish to develop a separate instrument pertaining to pupils' understanding and acceptance of differing cultural values. A district with strained labour relations may want to collect indicators pertaining to specific aspects of relationships between teachers and administrators.

To adequately measure all of these aspects of schooling processes on an annual basis may prove too costly, but I contend that it is better to measure a few aspects well than many cursorily. Some constructs require lengthy, detailed questionnaires to measure them well. Constructs such as disciplinary climate or principal leadership are best measured through a variety of methods, including observations and interviews. One strategy to reduce costs would be to measure particular constructs every other year, or in the case of pupil questionnaires, to tailor particular versions for each grade level. I do not recommend separate versions of questionnaires for subsamples of teachers in a school, or for subsamples of pupils at one grade level, because it unduly complicates administration and data analysis, and substantially reduces the reliability of school- and class-level estimates of the mean scores on the constructs of interest. Suggestions specific to the measurement of each aspect of schooling processes are specified below.

Ecology and Milieu Constructs

Data describing nearly all of these constructs can be obtained through a school-level questionnaire completed by the principal or a designated school administrator. The School Questionnaire used in the 1988 National Educational Longitudinal Study (NELS88) (US Department of Education, 1989), which is a forty-minute, self-administered questionnaire, is a good example. It includes items pertaining to teacher and pupil characteristics, school programs, and grading and testing policies. It also includes items on school policies and practices that are relevant to some of the social system variables. It does not include items describing the physical appearance or age of the school, or per-pupil expenditures. These could be obtained easily through school or district records.

Segregation

Segregation refers to the extent to which pupils from different groups are separated by the schools they attend, or the classrooms and instructional groups in which they are placed. Indicators of segregation should include measures of the extent to which pupils are separated according to social class, ability, academic achievement, gender, race, and ethnicity. They should include also information about the selection mechanisms that affect segregation. Segregation can occur between instructional groups within classes, between classes within schools, and between schools within communities or school districts. Thus the set of segregation indicators need to describe segregation at several levels.

Some simple measures of segregation can be constructed easily using measures of pupil inputs aggregated to the class, school, or district level (see Chapter 9). Massey and Denton (1988) provide a comprehensive review of the literature on segregation indices. Two of the indices are particularly useful at the school and district level. The Dissimilarity Index, D, pertains to the extent that minority group members are evenly distributed across schools within a district, or across classrooms within a school. The Isolation Index,[1] I, is a measure of the extent to which minority group members are isolated from members of the majority culture. It differs from the Dissimilarity Index in that it depends on the relative size of the groups considered; if a minority group comprises a relatively small proportion of the district's population, minority members will tend not to experience isolation from majority members, even though their enrolment is uneven across schools. Indicators of segregation for continuous variables, such as measures of SES or ability, can be constructed by estimating the proportion of variance that lies between groups within organizational units (for example, see Willms and Chen, 1989). This ratio is called η^2 (eta-squared), or the correlation ratio. The formulae for calculating the segregation indices are presented in Chapter 9.

---

[1] The converse of the Isolation Index is the Exposure Index, which measures the extent to which minority group members are exposed to majority group members (Massey and Denton, 1988). I prefer the Isolation Index because its direction is the same as the Dissimilarity Index (0 represents no segregation, 1 represents high segregation).

Figure 6-2 School-Related Behaviors covered in Questionnaires Measuring Disciplinary Climate

Class attendance	Violates School Rules
truancy	fighting
cutting classes	rough-housing, rowdy behavior
tardiness	profanity
leaving without permisson	smoking
Classroom behavior	inappropriate dress or appearance
disruptive behavior	inappropriate intimacy
inattentiveness	eating or drinking in the wrong place
incomplete homework	littering
cheating on tests, plagiarism	locker misuse
disobedience of teacher directives	gum-chewing
Relationships	Illegal Behaviors
disrespect to teachers	use of drugs or alcohol
disrespect to peers	rape or other acts of assault or violence
racial friction	vandalism
bullying	gang activity
	theft

The indicators describing the selection mechanisms can be derived from questions asking about policies and practices associated with ability grouping, tracking and streaming, and admission criteria to programs and schools. For example, the NELS88 School Questionnaire includes items that ask whether a school has formal admission or application procedures, and if so, how many pupils applied, how many were selected, and whether consideration was given to particular selection criteria. Gamoran (1990) constructed a number of indicators associated with high school tracking, based on the work of Sorensen (1970) and Rosenbaum (1976). These would be useful in a detailed analysis of the effects of a system's tracking policies.

Disciplinary Climate

The disciplinary climate of a school is often measured through teachers' and pupils' reports of the extent to which pupils comply with certain rules of conduct. A typical question is: 'To what extent are each of the following matters a problem in your school?' This is followed with a list of behaviors that are rated on a Likert scale (e.g., serious, moderate, minor, not a problem). Figure 6-2 provides a list of the behaviors that could be included (see DiPrete, 1981; Duke and Perry, 1978; Wynne, 1980). This type of question does not fully characterize the 'disciplinary climate' of a school because the subjective evaluation of what constitutes 'a problem' may vary considerably amongst pupils and teachers, and the question does not distinguish clearly aspects of misbehavior from rule enforcement and disciplinary standards.

Social control theories of discipline and delinquent behavior maintain there are institutional links between the school and pupils, and that pupils need to be taught the norms and values of the school. Disciplinary climate refers to the extent to which pupils internalize these norms and values, and conform to them. Schools which have positive disciplinary climates have organizational structures which reinforce beliefs and commitments to these norms and values. Parents and the wider community can also contribute to this socialization (see DiPrete, 1981; Kornhauser, 1978).

From this perspective, an important aspect of disciplinary climate is whether there is a clear set of school rules, and if so, how rules are perceived and enforced. Are rules set by school policy or do teachers set their own rules? Do pupils participate in setting rules? How are rules enforced? Do teachers feel they have the backing of parents and administration in enforcing rules? Do pupils understand the rules and have clear expectations about the consequences for non-compliance? Do pupils feel the rules are acceptable? Do they consider disciplinary measures fair and consistent? Answers to these questions provide a more complete picture of the disciplinary climate of a school than tallies of particular behaviors. To address these questions well requires interviews and detailed observations (see Duke and Perry, 1978; Wynne, 1980).

Academic Press

The term 'environmental press' or 'academic press' is used to describe the extent to which school staff value academic achievement and hold high expectations for their pupils (Anderson, 1982; Mitchell, 1968). Schools with high academic press place a greater emphasis on academic skills, which is manifest in a number of school routines and processes. The belief that all pupils can master the curriculum is projected by the principal and teachers, such that pupils are more likely to engage in challenging activities (Oakes, 1989) and to establish high norms of their own for academic success.

A set of indicators measuring academic press should include a number of evaluative items covering teachers' expectations of pupils, especially in academic areas. It should include also items concerning how time and resources are used; for example, what proportion of time is spent on academic instruction? Do non-academic activities or routines interfere with instruction? Do teachers start classes on time and place high demands on their pupils throughout their lessons? Do teachers make special efforts to challenge the most able pupils, and do they provide extra help to pupils struggling with the material? What is the type and amount of homework assigned? Finally, the items should assess pupil norms for academic success. To what extent do pupils value academic success for themselves and their peers? Are pupils confident they can master the curriculum? Do they spend adequate time doing homework? Is there cooperation amongst pupils in the completion of assignments?

Intended versus Enacted Curriculum

One of the important factors arising out of recent research attempting to explain differences between schools in their academic outcomes is whether pupils have covered the relevant topics. Lee and Bryk (1989) found, for example, that schools where pupils take a high number of academic courses, and where there is less latitude in the choice of courses, are more likely to have higher levels of achievement and a more equitable distribution of achievement. The Second International Mathematics Study (McKnight, Crosswhite, Dossey, Kifer, Swafford, Travers, and Cooney, 1987) obtained information on the intended and enacted curricula. The study found that within the US there were marked differences between classes in the mathematics curriculum and the way mathematics was taught. Coverage of topics on the international test was at or below the international average in most content areas, and instruction tended to be less intense than in other participating countries. The study suggested that fewer 'opportunities to learn' relevant topics may have accounted for the mediocre results of US pupils. Important questions for administrators, therefore, are whether the intended curriculum is well specified, and whether there is a tight connection between the intended and enacted curriculum.

Porter (1991) suggested collecting indicators of the strength and intent of curriculum policy instruments (also see Porter, Floden, Freeman, Schmidt, and Schwille, 1988). He lists six relevant characteristics of the documents: *prescriptiveness* (how well does a document specify desired practice?), *consistency* (are documents at different levels of the system mutually reinforcing?), *nature of the content specified* (what content does the document actually prescribe?), *accuracy* (is the content of the specified curriculum correct?), *authority* (is the document persuasive?), and *power* (are there rewards and sanctions tied to compliance?). Indicators of these characteristics need to be based on an assessment of a wide range of curricular instruments including district and school policy documents, course outlines, textbooks, pupil assessments, and requirements for graduation and for college and university entrance. The amount of time allocated to particular subject areas also defines the intended curriculum.

Defining the enacted curriculum and constructing valid indicators of its content are more difficult. The enacted curriculum depends on the content of each lesson, the method of instruction, and the relative emphasis placed on each topic. The task is complicated too because increasingly teachers are integrating the curriculum across subject areas. One strategy to measure the enacted curriculum is to ask pupils whether they have covered particular topics, but pupils may tend to recall being taught only the material they learned well. If this strategy is used, the analyst must construct class-level indicators based on aggregates of pupil responses. Another strategy is to ask teachers directly what topics they have covered, but this too has problems in that their responses do not necessarily capture the depth of coverage and the method of instruction.

Pupil Attitudes

One of the major factors differentiating high- and low-achieving schools in the Brookover *et al.*, (1979) study was pupils' sense of efficacy *versus* academic futility. The term referred to the extent to which pupils felt that they had control over their school successes and failures, whether teachers cared about their progress, and whether other pupils punished them if they did succeed. For example, three of their items were as follows:

> *'People like me will never do well in school even though we try hard'.*
> (Strongly agree, Agree, Disagree, Strongly disagree)

> *'Of the teachers you know in this school, how many don't care if the
> students get bad grades?'* (Almost all of the teachers, Most ...., Half ...,
> Some ..., Almost none ...)

> *'How many students in this school make fun of or tease students who get
> real good grades?'* (Almost all of the students, Most ..., Half ...,
> Some ..., Almost none ...). (p. 201)

The items measuring this construct are similar to items measuring the psychological construct *locus of control* (Lefcourt, 1982), which refers to the
extent that pupils attribute their successes or failures to their own efforts
(*internal* locus of control) or to chance or fate (*external* locus of control). The
Brookover *et al.* items, however, were directed more specifically to schooling.

Other questionnaires of pupils' attitudes have emphasized pupils' satisfaction with school or their assessment of the quality of school life. Epstein
and McPartland (1976) developed a twenty-seven-item scale that was used to
assess quality of school life for pupils in grades 4 through 12. They defined the
construct 'quality of school life' in terms of three dimensions: pupils' general
sense of well-being, pupils' academic behavior and life plans, and pupils'
relationships with teachers.

Teacher Attitudes

Considerable research has attempted to relate teacher commitment and
morale to pupils' academic achievement (Hoy and Ferguson, 1985; Kushman,
1990; Rosenholtz, 1989a). Underlying this research is the notion that schools
with committed, satisfied teachers have less teacher absenteeism, lower turn-
over, less burnout, and less dysfunctional classroom behavior (Rosenholtz,
1989b). The most important aspect of morale and commitment is that
teachers have a sense of efficacy about their work: 'The primary psychic rewards for most teachers come from students' academic accomplishments
— from feeling certain about their own capacities to affect student growth
and development' (Rosenholtz, 1985, p. 355). The Brookover *et al.* questionnaire included items pertaining to teachers' sense of academic futility
which tap this dimension. Teachers scoring high on academic futility were less
likely to push their pupils to do well and felt there was little they could do to
ensure that all pupils achieved at a high level. For them, the custodial function of schooling outweighed the educative function. An important aspect of
teacher efficacy, not covered directly by the Brookover *et al.* questionnaire, is
teachers' confidence in managing pupil behavior. Particularly for beginning
teachers, efficacy has more to do with managing behavior than affecting pupil
learning (Blase, 1986; Denscombe, 1985).

Commitment and satisfaction with work also entail the belief that work is
meaningful. Teachers who believe they are making an important contribution

to the well-being of their pupils and to society in general, will show greater commitment and job satisfaction. The meaningfulness of teaching is an important part of their value system.

Finally, commitment and morale require an acceptance of organizational goals and values (Mowday, Steers, and Porter, 1979). Teachers are more likely to be committed to their work if the school staff sets specific goals for pupil learning, if teachers are given opportunities to participate in decision-making and the setting of goals, and if teachers are given a high degree of autonomy in accomplishing school goals (Lortie, 1975; Rosenholtz, 1989b).

A set of indicators measuring commitment and morale therefore should include direct measures of these three aspects of morale and commitment: efficacy, meaningfulness, and acceptance of school goals and values. The set should include also indicators of a number of factors associated with working conditions that indirectly contribute to commitment and morale. These include, but are not limited to, the following: opportunities for professional growth and development (conferences, professional days, curriculum workshops, collaborative activities), type and frequency of evaluation, salaries, class size, time available for non-instructional activities, and the extent of collegial decision-making.

Instructional Leadership of Principals

Attempts to define and measure the leadership qualities of principals have been fraught with problems (Murphy, 1988). Many research studies have defined instructional leadership through a set of tasks considered to be the most important functions of administrators (e.g., Boyd, 1983; Duke, 1982; Hallinger and Murphy, 1985; Murphy, Hallinger, and Mesa, 1985). These lists have been used to construct scales that produce a single indicator of principal leadership; for example, the Administrator and Teacher Survey included a 14-item scale covering a number of activities, such as the setting of plans and priorities and ensuring they are carried out, the acquisition of resources for the school, ensuring staff involvement in decision-making, and the recognition and support of school staff (see Stern and Williams, 1986). Murphy (1988) raises several objections to this task-based approach to the measurement of principal leadership. Two objections relevant to performance indicators are that behaviors are not necessarily additive and that they depend a great deal on the situation or context. Also, the checklists tend to miss or undervalue some of the less visible leadership activities, such as establishing routines or setting school policies. Sometimes the informal, 'behind-the-scenes' strategies that principals employ have more important effects on pupil outcomes than the observable behaviors captured by questionnaires. These shortcomings suggest that scores on individual items in a questionnaire covering principal leadership may be more interesting and relevant as separate indicators than a composite indicator of principal leadership.

The literature on school effectiveness provides some direction on the types of principal behaviors most relevant to schooling outcomes. Generally, it emphasizes the indirect effects of principals' actions through shaping the attitudes and behaviors of teachers and pupils, and by establishing policies and procedures that facilitate teaching and learning (Rosenholtz, 1985). The literature pertaining to shaping attitudes and behavior is consistent with the perspective on pupil and teacher attitudes presented above. Effective principals set high standards and create incentives for pupil learning, and transmit the belief that all pupils can achieve at a high level. They set clearly-defined goals and priorities for pupil learning, and prescribe means to achieve them. They enhance teacher commitment by involving teachers in making decisions, by providing opportunities for teachers to improve their skills, and through consistent and fair evaluation.

The policies and procedures set by effective principals have to do with what organizational theorists call 'buffering the technical core' (Rosenholtz, 1985; Thompson, 1967). This means that they minimize the extraneous and disruptive influences that keep teachers from teaching and pupils from learning. Protecting teachers from excessive paperwork or providing non-teaching personnel to assist teachers with classroom and school managerial tasks can help to maximize teaching time. Principals can also ensure that disruptions for announcements or school assemblies are kept to a minimum. Clear policies about discipline and school behavior, and support from the principal in dealing with behavioral problems, can help teachers focus their energies on teaching activities.

Issues Concerning Measurement and Interpretation

Figure 6-1 includes several broad constructs, such as 'disciplinary climate', 'instructional leadership', 'academic press', and 'quality of school life'. There are nearly as many definitions of these constructs, and ways of operationalizing them, as there are research studies that use the terms. This section discusses some of the problems associated with definition, method of measurement, and level of analysis that are relevant to the construction of indicators of schooling processes.

Problems of Definition

If you asked a number of administrators what the term 'disciplinary climate' meant, you would likely get several different answers. Some might define it in terms of teachers' styles of discipline, ranging from permissive to authoritative. Others might consider whether there are rules of order in place, and the extent to which these are enforced. Others might say it referred to the orderliness of the classroom, and the extent to which pupils are noisy or disruptive. Some definitions might emphasize work and study habits. If you then asked teachers or pupils, they would probably offer yet another set of definitions. Lightfoot (1983) found that in attempting to portray the character and culture of secondary schools, the meaning of constructs varied also with the contextual circumstances of the school setting.

Two of the problems of definition, therefore, are that the constructs have different meanings for constituencies at different levels of the system, and many of them are multidimensional. Also, there are few models or theories to inform the definition of constructs. One could produce a list of 'disciplinary climate' variables that have been associated with schooling outcomes, and base the definition of 'disciplinary climate' on the domain covered by the variables. But without an underlying model or theory, the indicators derived from the definition probably would not be useful to teachers or administrators.

A useful starting point, therefore, is to specify the theoretical framework associated with the construct and to identify the dimensions of the construct relevant to different actors. Oakes (1989) does this nicely for the construct 'press for achievement', which enables her to distil a list of indicators that might be used to assess a school's program.

Objective versus Subjective Methods

One of the debates concerning the measurement of schooling processes, particularly school 'culture' or 'climate', is whether to admit variables derived from the perceptions of observers or participants (Anderson, 1982). Of the constructs listed in Figure 6-1, the ecology and milieu constructs, and some of the social system constructs, tend to represent *factual* circumstances which could be operationalized with a few objective measures. Some of the social system constructs, and nearly all of the culture constructs, tend to represent activities and attitudes derived from participants' personal *values* and *interpretations* of events. These require subjective measures of the perceptions of observers or participants. The debate concerns whether subjective data are valid and reliable indicators of social system and culture constructs.

Howe (1977) set out two criteria for construct validity: a consensus amongst group members and significant differences between groups within the same organization. Consider a measure of teachers' perceptions of principals' 'instructional leadership'. Howe's criteria would require that teachers within a school give similar ratings to their principal, but the average scores for principals must vary across the district. Consensus amongst teachers bespeaks validity because it suggests teachers have a common view of 'instructional leadership' and their reported perceptions accurately represent the leadership behaviors exhibited by the principal. Variance amongst the mean scores of principals indicates that the instrument can reliably distinguish between different levels of leadership ability. The problem is there may be a lack of consensus amongst teachers even though they share a common view of instructional leadership and report it accurately. Ratings might depend on teachers' own experience and needs, or their status within the school. Some teachers may have greater opportunity to observe principals' behaviors, and some may witness critical but isolated incidents of leadership behaviors (see Anderson, 1982; Moos, 1979; Murphy, 1988). There may be 'subclimates' within schools, stemming from departmental divisions or informal subgroups, which would also contribute to within-school variance. Therefore, although within-school agreement increases validity and reliability, the essential criteria is that of significant between-school variation.

Rowan *et al.* (1991) found that teachers within the same high schools varied considerably in their views of working conditions. Within-school variance on measures of principal leadership, staff cooperation, teacher control, and classroom order was on average about four times greater than between-school variance. Their scales included between seven and fourteen items, with internal consistencies (reliability) ranging from .77 to .92. (The ratio of within- to between-school variance was even greater on their measure of teacher morale, which had only four items and an internal consistency of .66.) However, because the scales were sufficiently reliable, and because they had a sufficient number of teachers sampled per school (about twenty-five on aver- age), they could reliably distinguish between schools on these measures. Between-school reliabilities ranged from .74 to .83 across the four measures. These results suggest that with sufficiently reliable scales, and large enough within-school samples, subjective data can provide reliable indicators of some of the constructs listed in Figure 6-1.

Level of Analysis

The level-of-analysis problem is not simply a statistical consideration about the appropriate level at which to conduct analyses. It concerns also the substantive meaning that can be attached to scores on a set of items (Sirotnik, 1980). The referent group implied by particular items, the level at which a construct is measured, and the meaning of a construct at different levels of aggregation are relevant to the development of performance indicators. These considerations govern the choice of level of analysis.

When children are presented a statement about their attitude towards school and asked to rate it on a 7-point scale (e.g., 'strongly disagree' to 'strongly agree'), do they consider the item phenomenologically, thinking about how satisfied they are compared with how satisfied they might be, or do they ask themselves how satisfied they are compared with their peers? If the latter, then which peers — their classmates, other pupils in the school, or all pupils in the community? The wording of items is critical. Care must be taken to ensure that the reference group is explicit and consistent across items in the scale. Ambiguity about group referent can cause confusion about whether an item is measuring a property of the individual or the group. Howe (1977) distinguished between *evaluative* items, which were associated with personal values and the meaning people attach to certain organizational processes, and *descriptive* items, pertaining to people's observations about the processes. Sirotnik (1980, p. 261) suggested that items using the first person singular (e.g., 'I am generally a trusting type of person') tend to reflect individual attributes, whereas those stated in the third person plural (e.g., 'Staff mem- bers trust one another at this school') tend to describe group character- istics. Items using 'we' are inclined to include both an individual and group effect.

Some constructs, such as 'academic press' or 'pupil-teacher' relationships can be measured at several levels. The question is not whether pupils' perceptions are more valid than teachers' or principals' perceptions of these constructs; rather, it is what meaning can be attached to the construct at differing levels of measurement. Pupils' perceptions of 'academic press' may be more important in determining pupil achievement than teachers percep- tions, even though teachers may have a broader view because of their experi- ence and knowledge of other schools.

The level of aggregation at which a school process variable is analyzed and reported is also relevant. Pupils' 'attitudes towards school' measured at the individual level means something quite different from the school mean of 'attitudes towards school'. At the individual level it is more representative of personal beliefs and values, which are affected by family, school, and other influences. At the school level the variable distinguishes between attributes of schools, and is affected predominantly by factors such as how material is taught, the way teachers relate to pupils, and the reward structure. Similarly, correlations at the individual level have a different substantive meaning than correlations at the class or school level (Cronbach, *et al.*, 1976; Sirotnik, 1980).

Guidelines for Developing a Monitoring System

1   **Data on schooling processes can contribute to the working knowledge of teachers and administrators and can prompt discussion about how schools operate.** However, our knowledge about how schools have their effects on instructional outcomes is inadequate to support the use of process data for diagnosing the causes of low performance and prescribing attendant remedies.
2   **It is preferable to measure a few schooling processes well than many cursorily.** Schooling processes encompass the many factors associated with schooling that affect outcomes, either directly or indirectly. They include factors describing the context and setting of schools, and evaluative factors associated with the 'climate' or 'culture' of schools. It is not possible to specify a definitive set of process indicators that would apply to all schools in all communities at all times.
3   **Selection of indicators should be based on the following criteria:**

   • **Do they provide a balanced picture of schooling?**
   • **Do they facilitate self-examination and the process of school renewal?**
   • **Do they describe processes that can be altered through policy and practice?**
   • **Are they relatively easy and inexpensive to measure?**

4   **Those constructing indicators of schooling processes should begin by specifying the theoretical framework associated with the processes, and by identifying the dimensions of the process relevant to different actors.** The referent group implied by particular items, the level at which a construct is measured, and the meaning of a construct at different levels of aggregation are relevant to the development of indicators of schooling process.

Chapter 7

Schooling Outcomes

Most monitoring systems include only a small range of outcome measures, usually emphasizing academic achievement. In many instances, the outcomes are limited to achievement tests of basic skills in reading and arithmetic. These typically comprise a small number of multiple-choice items aimed at covering the skills taught in the majority of public schools. Many teachers and educational researchers are critical of the testing technology and have called for alternative forms of assessment (Wolf, Bixby, Glenn, and Gardner, 1991). This chapter discusses some of the issues relevant to identifying the goals of schooling and selecting tests to measure them. The first section argues for monitoring that encompasses a wider range of goals, and the second section calls for monitoring that stresses equity as well as excellence in goal attainment. The next three sections discuss the validity and reliability of outcome measures, and considerations relevant to selecting tests. These sections are followed with a section describing the new forms of 'authentic assessment' that have been proposed as an alternative to norm-referenced, multiple-choice tests. The chapter concludes with a list of guidelines for developing a monitoring system.

Identifying Goals

Monitoring systems are often limited to the measurement of academic achievement because it is easier to measure than personal, social, and vocational development. Considerable effort has been devoted to developing reliable, standardized tests of academic achievement. Tests measuring constructs such as self-concept, efficacy, or effective communication, however, are less well developed and tend to be unreliable. Also, some evaluators believe that success in academic achievement is one of the few goals that is common across schools. Although schools vary in their stated purposes, and in the emphasis of their curriculum and instruction, nearly all schools view the development of basic skills in literacy and numeracy as one of their main goals. Another reason is that some of the impetus for national testing and monitoring systems has stemmed from a belief that standards of achievement have fallen, and that parents want schools to place greater emphasis on basic academic skills.

Goodlad (1984) challenged the assumption that parents want schools predominantly to teach the basics. He and his colleagues at UCLA surveyed over 8,000 parents to find out whether they were generally satisfied with their children's education, and to determine the expectations they held for schools. Their study was conducted in the late 1970s, when American schools were widely criticized in the press because of declining test scores.

Their data suggested that parents were not as dissatisfied with their schools as the press suggested; however, parents did feel that schools were not all that they could be. Goodlad's sample included parents of children in thirty-nine elementary, thirty-six junior, and thirty-nine secondary schools. The parents were asked to grade their child's school on a five-point scale (A, B, C, D, Fail). With the exception of two elementary schools, which received an average grade of A, all schools received an average grade of B or C. About 10 per cent of the parents were clearly dissatisfied with their schools — they gave a D or Fail grade — but no schools received an average grade below C.

The same type of question has been asked for several years in the Annual Gallop Poll of the Public's Attitudes towards the Public Schools (Elam and Gallop, 1989). Responses to the items suggest that parents may be more satisfied with the public schools in their community now than ten years ago. Of those responding to the question in 1979, about 8.5 per cent gave the schools a failing grade, compared with only about 4.5 per cent in 1989. The percentage of respondents giving the schools an A or B grade increased from about 41.5 to 47.5 per cent over the ten-year period. We need to be cautious, however, in concluding there is widespread satisfaction with the public schools. The 1989 Gallup Poll found that respondents who were nonwhite, less well educated, or had lower than average incomes gave the schools significantly lower grades. Also, respondents who were from large cities (over one-half million) gave the schools a lower grade.

Goodlad's (1984) study also asked questions about parents' expectations of schools. They covered four broad areas of goals:

1   academic, embracing all intellectual skills and domains of knowledge;
2   vocational, geared to developing readiness for productive work and economic responsibility;
3   social and civic, related to preparing for socialization into a complex society; and
4   personal, emphasizing the development of individual responsibility, talent, and free expression. (p. 37)

On average, parents considered all of these goals 'very important'. When asked to make a single most preferred choice, about half of the parents rated academic goals as the most important, while nearly one-third preferred personal and social goals. They also asked teachers and pupils in the sampled schools to state their preferences. Teachers placed greater emphasis on personal and social goals than did parents, with about 45 per cent choosing one of these two areas as their preference. Pupils spread their preferences more evenly across the four goal areas. Overall, Goodlad concluded that 'most parents want their children to have it all' (p. 39). The same could be said of teachers and pupils.

Although schools share many goals, they vary in the relative emphasis placed on academic, personal, social, and vocational goals. On average, schools serving pupils who are predominantly from disadvantaged backgrounds place less emphasis on academic goals, and greater emphasis on goals in the other three areas. Even within the academic domain, schools vary in the relative emphasis placed on instruction in certain subject areas. Research on the relative performance of Catholic and non-denominational schools, for example, suggests that Catholic schools place greater emphasis on instruction in English than in mathematics or science (see, for example, Haertle, James, and Levin, 1987, and McPherson and Willms, 1986).

There is also the issue of breadth *versus* depth: some schools may encourage pupils to take a wide array of different courses, while others might prefer pupils to study a few subjects in greater depth. The large comprehensive public high schools in the US have been portrayed as 'shopping malls' (Powell, Farrar, and Cohen, 1985) because of the wide array of elective courses and because of the differentiation of core courses into levels for pupils of varying ability. It is important, therefore, that those developing monitoring systems take account of the variation between schools in their goals, and include a wide range of outcome measures in all four goal areas. Any single measure of overall school performance is likely to misrepresent the performance of some schools.

Excellence or Equity

Schools vary also in their allocation of resources to pupils with differing ability and social backgrounds. Some schools devote considerable energy towards bringing their least able pupils up to some minimum level of academic competency, while others strive for excellence for a small number of talented pupils. There is some evidence that specific school policies affect the distribution of outcomes within a school (Burstein and Miller, 1979; Lee and Bryk, 1988). The streaming of pupils according to their prior performance is one example. Syntheses of the research suggest that in schools where children are differentiated into classes according to their ability, the more able pupils tend to do better, while the least able pupils fare no better, or perhaps do worse (Kulik and Kulik, 1982, 1984). Slavin (1987) suggests the results may stem from the effects of specialized programs. Schools with heterogeneous classrooms tend to have more uniform distributions of achievement (Dreeben and Gamoran, 1986; Kerckhoff, 1986; Rowan and Miracle, 1983; Willms and Chen, 1989).

How does one compare, then, the mathematics achievement of a Scottish secondary school where nearly all of its pupils obtained a C or B award in O-grade arithmetic, but few pupils received an A, with a school where only about half of its pupils were presented for the examination, but amongst those who were presented, a high proportion received As and decided to study mathematics at the Highers level? A simple approach would be to assign weights to each grade (e.g., Fail = 0, C = 1, B = 2, A = 3), and compare the average performance of each school. But this approach might suggest the two schools were comparable in their performance, and thus would mask some of the important differences between them. When describing a school's performance, it is important to show the entire distribution of scores.

A related problem is determining the appropriate weights when scaling an outcome measure. The relative performance of the two schools described above would depend on the weighting assigned to various levels of O-grade awards (e.g., see Spencer, 1983). The scaling of the test requires judgements about the relative worth of A, B, and C awards. Educationists, however, would undoubtedly differ in their judgements depending on the goals of their school and their views about education. The scaling problem becomes even more difficult when one attempts to construct a single scale from two or more different criteria, such as overall attainment on the O-grade and Highers examinations (e.g., see Robertson, 1988).

Validity of Outcome Measures

Validity refers to whether a test measures what it is supposed to measure. If a test is supposed to measure primary school arithmetic ability, it should reflect the domain of content and skills considered to be a part of the primary curriculum in arithmetic. Performance on the test should not depend heavily on pupils' reading or science ability. It should assess arithmetic skills that have been taught and learned at school.

Validity is tied to the purposes for which test scores are to be used; a test can be valid for some purposes but not for others. A test of reading proficiency, for example, might be valid in the sense that it is predictive of later academic success, but not valid as an indicator of pupil mastery in the many skills involved in reading. Gronlund (1985) states that 'validity refers to the appropriateness of the interpretations made from test scores and other evaluation results, with regard to a particular use' (p. 55).

If performance indicators are to be useful they must reflect the qualities that administrators and teachers want to influence, and be susceptible to improvement through changes in policies and practice. Haertle (1986) calls these properties *intrinsic validity*. A problem with indicators of school performance is that once numbers have been assigned to various qualities, people tend to emphasize the size of the numbers and forget what they really represent. The number of days that pupils are truant is not the same as pupils' satisfaction with school. Verbal reasoning quotients are not the same as aptitude for success in high school. The acquisition of three O-grade awards is not the same as mastery of the content in three academic subjects.

The intrinsic validity of an indicator is related also to the kinds of actions that might improve scores on the indicator (Haertle, 1986). Some indicators have low intrinsic validity because teachers or administrators can boost a school's scores on the indicators without actually changing the qualities they represent. For example, if a school's performance in English were based on the average O-grade scores for pupils who presented for the examination, then a school could boost its apparent performance by adopting more restrictive presentation policies. Similarly, if the scores on a particular achievement test were susceptible to manipulation by 'teaching to the test' or coaching, they would be considered to have low intrinsic validity. A desirable test produces scores that are sensitive to conscionable actions by administrators and teachers, such as the provision of a more enriched curriculum, or the improvement of classroom instruction.

Reliability of Outcome Measures

Reliability refers to the consistency of scores on an evaluation instrument. One desires outcome measures that would yield the same or similar scores if they were repeatedly administered under identical conditions. There are particular types of consistency, and thus different types of reliability (Gronlund, 1985). A set of scores can be reliable, for example, over different periods of time, over different forms of a test, or across different raters.

We can think of a pupil's *observed* score for a particular setting and time as the sum of two components: his or her *true score* and *measurement error*. The measurement error can be either positive or negative. A set of observed scores is reliable if they accurately discriminate between high- and low-scoring pupils. If the spread of scores is large, then errors due to measurement will have less influence on the relative position of any individual in the group. Generally, a set of scores is more reliable if the test is not too easy or too difficult for the targeted group, and if there are few items that require subjective scoring. Reliability is also affected by the length of a test: the longer a test, the more reliable are its scores. Scores on short tests are more easily distorted by chance factors. Reliability can be enhanced by standardizing the timing and method of administration of a test, and the scoring procedures.

Considerations in Selecting Tests

When selecting a test to be used as a performance indicator, the evaluator must consider both its validity and reliability. One of the arguments against the use of standardized, norm-referenced tests. (NRTs, see Chapter 3) is that they are not valid indicators of what is taught and learned in school. These tests can produce reliable sets of scores; however, if they are not measuring the trait of interest, reliability is of secondary importance. Conversely, teacher-made criterion-referenced tests (CRTs) can be valid in the sense that they cover the curricular material on a particular topic well, but because CRTs are designed so that nearly all pupils achieve mastery, reliability tends to be low. Ideally, we would like to select tests that are both valid and reliable, and this should be possible given that psychometricians have developed sophisticated techniques for measuring very complex learning outcomes. However, tests can be valid and reliable for some purposes and not for others, and their validity and reliability depend on the level at which test scores are to be used. The choice of tests also must take account of the costs associated with test development, administration, scoring, and displaced teaching time. These considerations are discussed below.

Purpose of Testing

For a typical classroom at the grade 3 level, the range of grade-equivalent scores on most norm-referenced achievement tests spans about four grade levels. This means that the teacher will likely have a few pupils who score at the same level as the average grade 1 pupil, and a few who achieve scores at the grade 5 level. By grade 7, the range is about one-and-a-half to two times that size (e.g., Martin and Hoover, 1987; Willms and Jacobsen, 1990). One cannot infer, however, that pupils with low grade-equivalent scores have not acquired some of the skills taught at their current grade level, or that pupils with high grade-equivalent scores have mastered all of the skills taught at their grade level. What it does mean is that the range of skills for which pupils have achieved mastery spreads beyond those taught in any given year.

If the purpose of testing in a monitoring system is to examine long-term trends in achievement or to assess inequalities between racial and ethnic groups, the achievement tests must include items that span a considerable range. At the primary level, considering pupils' attention span and the length of scheduled class periods, a test of about forty multiple-choice items in a particular subject area might be appropriate. But with forty items, a test can include only about ten items covering the curriculum at each of four grade levels. For the classroom teacher, however, ten items are not sufficient for diagnostic purposes. Also, the test scores will probably not be sensitive to changes in teaching practice. For a teacher's purposes, the test would be better if it included items that covered forty curricular objectives at that grade level. But a test that included items covering skills only at one grade level would not discriminate as well between pupils at high and low levels of overall achievement. The choice of test, therefore, depends on its intended purpose. One must ask what kinds of decisions will be based on the test scores.

Low reliability is tolerable when the data are to be used more for formative than summative evaluation. In formative evaluation, data are used to inform decisions that are usually temporary, reversible, and of relatively minor importance. For example, a teacher may wish to identify which pupils need extra help with a particular topic, or whether more time should be devoted to a certain lesson. District personnel might use a wide-range audiometric screening test to identify pupils that may have a hearing loss and therefore require a more thorough, reliable assessment. Summative evaluation usually entails decisions that are permanent, and relatively more important. Data to inform such decisions require high reliability. The decision to place a child in a special class, for example, should be made only after thorough assessment based on data from a number of sources, including test scores with high reliability. Similarly, data used to inform decisions at the district level that are final and irreversible, such as closing a school, demand high reliability.

Level of Use

The reliability of a set of aggregate scores, such as school mean test scores, depends on the reliability of the scores at the individual level, the size of the samples comprising the aggregates, and the variability of the aggregate scores. An individual's observed score on a test includes a certain amount of measurement error, unless the test is perfectly reliable. The observed score is the sum of a person's *true score* and *measurement error*. Measurement error can be either positive or negative. When we average scores across individuals in a group, measurement errors to some extent cancel each other out, depending on the size of the group. If the group is large, the estimate of the mean score can be reasonably accurate, even when individual scores have low reliability.

But the reliability of a set of aggregate scores depends also on the extent to which the groups differ in their 'true' value of the aggregate score. Reliability at this level refers to the extent that we can distinguish between groups. Error at this level includes two components: measurement error, stemming from the unreliability of the test, and sampling error, which depends on the size of the samples used to estimate the aggregate scores. If the groups do not differ substantially in the trait being measured, the aggregate scores can have low reliability even if the individual scores are highly reliable. Conversely, if groups are relatively heterogeneous, the aggregate scores can be quite reliable, even when individual scores have low reliability, provided the within-group sample sizes are sufficiently large.

The implication of these statistical properties is that tests which produce scores with unacceptable levels of reliability at the individual level may be adequate for administrative purposes. For example, if sample sizes are large, then short, easy-to-administer achievement tests may have sufficient reliability for examining trends in achievement, estimating the performance of different types of pupils, or comparing schools in their performance. Reliable tests are always preferable, but usually there are some trade-offs between the degree of reliability and costs.

Costs

Several factors are related to the costs associated with testing. If the tests are to be prepared by district or school personnel, then account must be taken of the costs of test development. Attention must be paid also to the degree of expertise required to administer and score tests. Finally, there is an opportunity cost for pupils related to the time devoted to testing instead of instruction. These issues are discussed below.

Test Development   The development of reliable and valid achievement tests can be an expensive enterprise for an individual school or district. The advantage of using published tests is that people with expertise in writing and evaluating items have assembled reliable tests that have been normed on a large representative sample. The items have appropriate levels of difficulty and discriminate well between pupils with varying levels of achievement. The tests include standardized procedures for administration, scoring, and interpretation. Usually there are alternate forms of the tests, and tests targeted for pupils with varying levels of achievement. The disadvantage of published tests is that often they do not cover all of the topics taught in a particular subject area, or do not give the desired emphasis on particular topics. Thus there can be trade-offs between reliability and validity, which to some extent are determined by costs.

Ease of Administration   Some tests have simple, clear instructions, and can be administered by school personnel with little training. Administration becomes more complex if tests require timing for specific parts of the test, or if they include items that are completed by only a subset of the respondents (e.g., branching items). Group-administered tests tend to be easier to administer than individually administered tests.

Objective *versus* Subjective Scoring   Outcome measures that predominantly include objectively-scored items, such as multiple-choice items, tend to produce more reliable scores than tests based on essay questions. The problem is that it is difficult to write objective items that measure complex learning outcomes such as the ability to explain cause-and-effect relationships, to organize and synthesize ideas, or to make inferences from a set of facts. Subjective items also are considerably more expensive to score. But the more complex learning outcomes are often the most important part of any curriculum. Thus there are trade-offs that need to be considered with regard to validity and reliability, costs, and the purpose of the monitoring system.

Displaced Learning Time   One of the main concerns about the implementation of a monitoring system is the costs in learning time required for testing. It is important that the tests be long enough to be sufficiently reliable, but not so long that they displace a significant amount of teaching time. Usually reliable results for a general measure in some area, such as mathematics achievement, can be obtained in thirty or forty minutes (Gronlund, 1985), but to obtain detailed results describing scores in particular subtopics requires more testing time.

Authentic Assessment

Much of the criticism levelled against the monitoring of school performance has been directed at the use of multiple-choice tests. The chief concern is that they emphasize lower-order thinking skills isolated from a wider context, and that they equate learning with the pursuit of a single correct answer (Collins, 1988; Shepard, in an interview by Kirst, 1991). Another concern is that they emphasize the relative ranking of pupils, instead of describing their degree of learning in terms of external criteria (Wolf *et al.*, 1991). Multiple-choice tests do a relatively poor job of measuring pupils' ability to think, collect data, make inferences, plan, or synthesize information from a variety of sources. They also emphasize individual knowledge over collective knowledge (Resnick, 1987).

The call is for assessment based on longer term accomplishments that can be demonstrated through performances, oral presentations, debates, pupil-led conferences, in-depth projects, journals, portfolios, and exhibitions. These assessment tasks are 'authentic' in that they are 'real instances of extended criterion performances' (Shepard, in an interview by Kirst, 1991, p. 21). Outside of school, pupils have been judged with performance-based assessments for years in areas such as swimming, music, or driver training. In most cases, professionals in these areas have identified and described developmental sequences of skills that represent growth in learning. Learning at each stage is assessed by judges who are deemed competent in assessment of those skills. Pupils seldom object to this kind of assessment; in fact, many of them find it challenging and motivating. Many of the performance-based tests might not withstand the rigors of psychometrics; however, they have high face validity. Also, the stakes are not usually high; failure generally implies that a pupil must repeat a series of lessons and take the test again. The essential element in authentic or performance-based assessment is the tight connection between learning and assessment.

Unlike some proponents of authentic assessment who call for the abandonment of multiple-choice tests, I do not view the two forms of assessment as inherently incompatible. They simply serve different purposes and could be viewed as complementary. However, many monitoring systems overemphasize the use of norm-referenced, multiple-choice tests. A shift towards monitoring that incorporates criterion-referenced testing and alternative forms of assessment would be welcome.

Guidelines for Developing a Monitoring System

1 **A monitoring system should include performance indicators that reflect the goals of the school, and particularly qualities that administrators and teachers want to influence.** A set of indicators should include a wide range of outcomes, covering not only academic outcomes, but also personal, social, and vocational outcomes. Monitoring is more likely to be beneficial if the scores on indicators are susceptible to improvement through changes in school policies and practices.

2 **Analyses of school performance should examine the distribution of scores on each outcome measure, and not be based only on school averages.** Some schools are especially effective for pupils with high ability, but not for those with low ability, and *vice versa*. Similarly, differences between the sexes and between racial and ethnic groups in their schooling outcomes can be large in some schools and small in others.

3 **Analyses should include an assessment of equity issues, such as how large the achievement gap is between social-class groups, and between the sexes.**

4 **The choice of outcome measures cannot be separated from the purposes of monitoring.** Tests can be valid for some purposes, yet invalid for others. A test can produce reliable scores for one set of pupils, but not for another. Reliability can depend also on the level of aggregation at which the scores are to be used.

5 **Monitoring systems need to be cost-effective.** Schools and districts do not have unlimited resources to test pupils, score tests, and analyze data. In designing a monitoring system and selecting measures one must weigh likely benefits of certain information against the costs of administration and displaced teaching time.

Chapter 8

Design of a Monitoring System

The purpose of this chapter is to present a design for a monitoring system for assessing elementary and secondary school performance in a school district or education authority (EA). Between 1988 and 1990 I assisted in the design of two monitoring systems, one for the assessment of secondary schools in the Fife Regional Authority in Scotland, the other for the assessment of elementary and secondary schools in a medium-sized school district in Canada. Recently, I have been involved in the analysis of data from the California Assessment Program (see Rumberger and Willms, 1991). The design presented here is largely based on these experiences. There are several important differences between schooling systems in North America and the UK and the purposes of monitoring differ substantially between countries and across districts and EAs (see Chapter 2). However, there were enough similarities in the designs of the monitoring systems that I felt a separate presentation for each type of system would entail too much redundant material. Thus the chapter offers a single design, but includes discussion pertaining to both types of systems.

The design is not fully comprehensive. My intention is to provide some starting points for a district or EA that is in the early stages of developing a monitoring system. The proposed design emphasizes the collection of indicators that would be used mainly for diagnostic and performance monitoring by district and school administrators, rather than classroom teachers, or state and national administrators. The design presumes that data suitable for general assessment and for diagnosing learning problems at the individual level would be collected at the school level. Part of the district's role in monitoring would be to support school-level monitoring activities. Also, the proposed design does not entail the collection of qualitative data through classroom and school observations, interviews, or teacher logs and diaries (see Porter, 1991). As such, the design only constitutes a shell for a more comprehensive system. Because the collection of qualitative data is usually more expensive, I recommend that it be collected to examine issues relevant to the needs of individual schools and districts.

The chapter includes three sections. The first specifies the kind of data that might be collected routinely by a district or EA, and the indicators that could be derived from the data. The second section describes issues pertaining to confidentiality. The third section discusses how indicators for a

Figure 8-1   Proposed Tests and Questionnaires

	K	Primary/Intermediate							Seconday				
		P1	P2	P3	P4	P5	P6	P7	S1	S2	S3	S4	S5
School Records (SR)	●	●	●	●	●	●	●	●	●	●	●	●	●
Entry Screening Battery (ESB)	●												
Student Questionnaires (SQ)					●			●		●			
School-Leaver Questionnaires (SLQ)												●	●
Parent Questionnaires (PQ)	●				●			●		●			●
Vertically-Equated Achievement Tests (AT)		●	●	●	●	●	●	●	●	●	●	●	●
Affective Measures (AM)					●			●		●		●	
Fitness Tests (FT)		●	●	●	●	●	●	●	●	●	●	●	●
Teacher Questionnaires (TQ)	●	●	●	●	●	●	●	●	●	●	●	●	●

district or EA can be contextualized and informed by data collected at the classroom, school, state and national levels. The last section provides an approximate time line.

Data to be Collected

The proposed design entails intensive data collection from pupils and their parents at five critical 'transition points': the end of kindergarten and the beginning of grade 1; the end of primary schooling (end of grade 4); the end of intermediate schooling (end of grade 7); the end of the second year of secondary school; the end of secondary school. I have assumed the system includes seven years of primary and intermediate schooling, and five to six years of secondary schooling. [I use the alpha-numeric labels K for kindergarten, P1 through P4 for the primary grades, P5 through P7 for the intermediate grades, and S1 through S5 (or S6) for the secondary grades.] The design entails annual achievement testing in a number of areas, pupil surveys at critical transition points, regular tests of physical fitness, and an annual survey of all teachers. Figure 8-1 outlines the various tests and surveys that would be administered at each grade level. Figure 8-2 specifies the indicators of schooling inputs, processes, and outcomes that would be derived from the tests and questionnaires. The kinds of data to be collected from school records and the tests and questionnaires are discussed below.

School Records
School records are the primary source of demographic information and information on attendance and truancy. School records are useful also for keeping accurate track of pupils as they move from school to school, or leave the district.

Entry Screening Battery
Several school districts in Canada and the US routinely administer batteries of screening instruments in an attempt to identify pupils who require special

Figure 8-2   Indicators Derived from Tests and Questionnaires

Schooling Inputs
  Age at Entry (SR)
  Sex (SR)
  Indicators of Socioeconomic Status (PQ4, PQ7, PQ10)
    Mother's and Father's Occupation
    Mother's and Father's Education
    Number of Siblings
    Family Composition
  Race and Ethnicity (PQ4, SQ7)
  English as a First Language (PQ4)

School Process
  Ecology and Milieu (SR)
    Class, School, and District Size
    Per-pupil Expenditures
    Age and Appearance of Building
  Segregation (SR, TQ)
  Disciplinary Climate (SQ, TQ)
  Academic Press (SQ, TQ)
  Student Attitudes (SQ, SR)
    Sense of Academic Futility
    Satisfaction with School
    Attendance and Truancy
  Teacher Commitment and Morale (TQ)
    Efficacy
    Meaningfulness
    Acceptance of School Goals and Values
    Working Conditions
  Instructional Leadership of Principals (TQ)
    Shaping Attitudes and Behaviors
    Establishing Policies and Procedures

Schooling Outcomes
  Academic Achievement (AT)
    Mathematics
    Reading
    Language Arts
    Science
  Personal and Social (SQ, FT)
    Self-Concept
    Locus of Control
    Participation in Sports
    Physical Fitness
    Participation in Extra-Curricular Activities
  Vocational (SQ, SLQ)
    Work Experience
    Skills in Vocational Subjects
    Attitudes towards Work
    Post-School Destinations

educational services. The practice of screening is based on the assumption that school-related problems can be alleviated if treatment is begun early (Mercer, Algozzine, and Trifiletti, 1988). However, poor screening systems can be costly: if children are mistakenly classified as being 'at risk', district resources are wasted, and children and their families may suffer the negative consequences of labelling (Salvia, Clarke, and Ysseldyke, 1973). Also, poor screening techniques can result in some children being denied early remediation when they may be candidates who would benefit. Not surprisingly, many policy-makers and legislators are calling for better documentation of the costs and benefits of early screening and intervention (White, 1986).

Evidence pertaining to the efficacy of screening measures for predicting later achievement is contradictory, and it is difficult to compare studies because of the variety of screening instruments and outcome measures used. Jacobsen's (1990) study of the validity of kindergarten screening found that considerable improvement in identifying children 'at risk' could be attained by administering several measures at different times during the kindergarten year. I recommend using a battery of measures covering skills in the following domains: language, motor skills, social-emotional development, and pre-academic skills.

Pupil Questionnaires

The pupil questionnaires would include a number of items covering schooling inputs, processes, and non-cognitive schooling outcomes. The design includes the administration of pupil questionnaires to all pupils in P4, P7, and S2. These grade levels were chosen for at least three reasons. First, they coincide with the years that state or national examinations are given in many systems, and thus allow for more detailed reporting of pupils' progress at these levels. Second, these levels to some extent represent transition points in the pupils' schooling careers. Therefore data derived from the questionnaires can be used as 'posttest' data for one stage, and 'pretest' data for the next stage. Third, after three years the P4 and P7 cohorts will be administered the questionnaire again, when the majority of the pupils are in P7 and S2. This design therefore provides longitudinal data on individual pupils, which are useful for some types of analyses.

School-Leaver Questionnaires

This questionnaire would be administered as a postal survey to pupils approximately eight months after leaving school. It would ask a number of questions about their reasons for leaving school, and their post-secondary school or employment experiences. It could also ask pupils to reflect on some of their high school experiences. The questionnaire could be modelled after the school-leaving questionnaires used in England, Scotland, and Ireland, and the Follow-up Student Questionnaire used in the *High School and Beyond* study.

Parent Questionnaires

The parent questionnaires would be administered at roughly the same time as the pupil questionnaires. They would emphasize parents' satisfaction with their children's schools and their support for school activities. Information on family socioeconomic status too could be gathered with these questionnaires. The questionnaires could include also a number of items about home processes relevant to schooling outcomes, such as norms for academic achievement, and time spent on homework and watching television. They might incorporate questions pertaining to styles of parenting, similar to those asked of adolescents by Dornbusch, Ritter, Leiderman, Roberts, and Fraleigh (1987).

Vertically-Equated Achievement Tests

There are several types of achievement tests which are commercially available in North America and the UK, such as the Stanford Achievement Test and the Iowa Test of Basic Skills. Many Canadian school districts use either the Canadian Test of Basic Skills (CTBS) or the Canadian Achievement Test (CAT), which cover a number of academic skills for pupils in grades 1 through 12. Both tests are well suited to monitoring because their items were based on objectives stated in a number of curriculum guides and textbooks used in Canadian schools.[1] Also, scores from these tests can be placed on a vertically-equated scale. This means that the tests at each level include items that overlap in their content and difficulty with some of the items in the tests set for previous and subsequent grades. This makes it possible to map scores onto one long continuous scale that covers the twelve years of schooling. With scores on a vertically-equated scale, one can make more accurate estimates of pupils' rates of growth in academic achievement, rather than simply check their status at a particular point in time (see Willms and Jacobsen, 1990). As mentioned earlier, the use of growth scores is a more reliable and valid means for assessing school effects.

One of the advantages of the CAT over other achievement tests is that it includes eight overlapping levels. Each level of the test includes a larger number of items covering material at each grade level than is typical of most norm-referenced achievement tests. In other words, the tests attempt to strike a balance in the coverage *versus* test length dilemma discussed in Chapter 7. The tradeoff, however, is that a single level of the test will not cover the entire ability range of all pupils at a particular grade level. For example, suppose a teacher uses the Level 15 battery to test a class of grade 5 pupils. The Level 15 battery covers skills for grades 4.6 to 5.9. Recall that the range of achievement scores in a typical grade 5 classroom spans about four grade levels. Therefore, it is likely that several pupils would attain scores at or near the 'floor' of the Level 15 tests (e.g., at grade level 4.6), when their 'true' levels of achievement were actually lower. Similarly, several pupils would score at or near the 'ceiling' of the tests (e.g., at grade level 5.9), when their 'true' levels of achievement were considerably higher. This problem can be circumvented by using the 'locator' tests that accompany the battery. The locator tests are brief tests which aid in the selection of the best level of test. This two-stage process makes administration more difficult, but it affords advantages in terms of enhanced curriculum coverage.

Affective Measures

The literature includes a number of measures of various social-psychological constructs such as self-concept, locus of control, loneliness, academic motivation, and attitudes towards school. Some of these measures can be administered in a separate session or included as part of the pupil questionnaires. There are also a few commercially available tests that have separate subtests for a number of constructs.

---

[1] However, note the limitations of these tests, which are discussed briefly in Chapter 7, and in detail by Wolf *et al.* (1991)

The construct 'self concept' is described in the literature as an individual's perception of self in relationship to his or her environment (Shavelson, Hubner, and Stanton, 1976). People form their concept of self through an interpretation of hundreds of life experiences; the formation is influenced particularly by significant others in their environment, such as parents, teachers, and peers. Because a person's environment is complex and includes a multiplicity of interactions, the construct of self concept is considered to be multidimensional (Marsh and Shavelson, 1985). One of the best instruments for the measurement of self concept, and one which has been used widely in academic research, is the Self-Description Questionnaire (SDQ). There are three levels of the instrument designed for pupils at elementary, intermediate, and secondary levels. The SDQ measures thirteen separate components of self concept: academic, verbal, mathematics, problem-solving, physical ability, physical appearance, relations with same-sex peers, relations with opposite-sex peers, relations with parents, honesty, emotional stability, religion, and general self concept. The SDQ includes separate subscales for measuring each component; Marsh and O'Neill (1984) describe the reliability and validity of the subscales and the total test.

Fitness Tests
There are a number of short, easy-to-administer tests of physical fitness measuring various components of fitness such as strength, flexibility, speed, and cardio-vascular endurance. The Canada Fitness Award Test and the American Alliance Health, Physical Education, Recreation and Dance Test are two measures that provide good coverage. Many pupils enjoy doing these tests and charting their own progress. It would be preferable to administer them at least twice per year to all pupils. The analysis of the data from these tests would emphasize pupils' growth on various aspects of physical fitness.

Teacher Questionnaires
This questionnaire would be administered annually to all teachers in the district. It would address questions about between- and within-classroom segregation, disciplinary climate, academic press, and instructional leadership of the principal. It would include also several questions pertaining to the measurement of teacher morale and commitment. I recommend the development of separate versions of the questionnaire for primary, intermediate, and secondary teachers.

Confidentiality Issues

The identification of individual pupils is necessary for matching questionnaire data to data from other sources, such as parent questionnaire data, achievement test data, and data from school records. But it is essential that individuals cannot be identified on data that are made public. The thorny issue is whether pupils, parents, and teachers should have access to achievement test scores. On the one hand, they would likely see more value in the exercise if they were privy to the results. However, the argument against revealing test scores from tests like the CTBS or CAT is that *at the individual level* they do not provide as reliable and valid an indication of a child's progress as many other forms of assessment. There is the argument that some teachers may use the data to make judgements about the potential of some children, and these judgements may become self-fulfilling prophecies. On balance, I recommend not to reveal this type of data at the individual level. It would be preferable to direct energy towards other forms of assessment that are valid and reliable at the individual level. However, I would make class-level and school-level results available to teachers and principals. Also, the achievement test results could be used for screening purposes to identify children who require additional testing.

It is essential that the questionnaires be administered within the school during a class period. Preferably, they should be administered by someone other than the classroom teacher. If they are sent home with the pupils it is likely that the response rate will be low and the achieved sample will be biased. However, because some parents would not want their children disclosing information on their occupation or level of education, it may be necessary to send parents a copy of the questionnaire, a letter explaining its purpose, and a form for requesting exemption. The letter can state that if they do not want their child to answer the questionnaire they can return the exemption form to the principal. Also, the questionnaires should contain a statement at the beginning telling pupils what will be done to ensure confidentiality, and offering them the option to leave blank any questions they do not wish to answer.

The Center for Educational Sociology has taken the issue of confidentiality seriously. They have developed procedures for maintaining confidentiality of their school-leaver survey data that could serve as a model for school districts and EAs. Upon receipt of the questionnaires, the staff assign identification numbers and remove the pupils' names. The link between identification numbers and pupils' names and addresses is maintained on a secure identification file to which only the Head Programmer and the Directors have access.

The anonymity of schools is also potentially contentious. Generally, districts and EAs want data on individual schools, and would not want to implement a monitoring program if the identification of individual schools were not possible. The question becomes whether data describing schools' results are made available to principals, teachers, and parents. My position is that if monitoring data are to enhance the process of school renewal, principals and teachers need to have access to the information. However, the kind of information that will be available to parents and the wider public needs to be carefully negotiated, and clear to all parties at the outset.

Data Collection at Other Levels

Data collected at the state or national level can augment the district information system, and similarly district data can complement and extend the monitoring activities of individual schools.

State- and National-Level Data

Data collected routinely by the state or national education agencies, or by other government bodies at these levels, can add to the district's monitoring system. Some examples are discussed below.

National Census Data   Data from the National Census can be linked in some countries to pupil-level data via postal codes or enumeration districts. The census data include information relevant to the socioeconomic status and living conditions of families in each postal-code area. Data describing the proportion of single-parent families, the proportion of youth who are unemployed, or the extent of overcrowding or amenity deficiency can be used to construct variables that describe local neighbourhoods. For example, Garner and Raudenbush (1991) constructed an index of neighbourhood deprivation for Scottish Education Authorities based on analyses conducted by the Scottish Housing Association. They found that the level of neighbourhood deprivation had an effect on pupils' SCE examination attainment over and above the effects of their family background or the schools they attended.

Young Peoples Surveys   Large-scale surveys of pupils who are in their senior years of secondary school, or who have recently left school, are conducted in Scotland, England, and Wales. In the US there are the national surveys conducted by the National Center for Education Statistics. One of the chief strengths of the national surveys is that they have better coverage of course-taking patterns and post-secondary destinations than is usually obtained by education authorities or school districts. Education authorities in Scotland have made use of the Scottish Young Peoples Survey (SYPS) conducted by the Centre for Educational Sociology by paying for enhanced coverage of the survey in certain schools, contracting specific analyses of the SYPS data relevant to EA needs, and merging SYPS data with EA data to examine particular policy issues. Raffe's (1991) evaluation of the Technical and Vocational Education Initiative and Echols *et al.*'s (1990) examination of parental choice of schools are examples where data from the SYPS were used in conjunction with EA data. During the early 1980s the Centre for Educational Sociology conducted a successful program of collaborative research whereby teachers and administrators contributed items to the questionnaire, and participated in the analysis and writing of research monographs.

Another useful strategy is to include items in the district questionnaires that are identical to those used in national surveys. This allows the district to situate the results of their surveys in a national context. For example, the pupil, parent, and teacher questionnaires administered by the district could include some of the school process questions used in the 1988 National Education Longitudinal Study.

State or National School Census   Some state and national education agencies conduct an annual school census. For example, the Scottish Education Department collects school-level information on levels of staffing and resources, subjects taught, and enrolments. Their data also include information on each subject area, including the time allocated to that subject per week, the type of class organization, the number of teaching groups, and the size of each group. These data can easily be merged with district school-level data, and used in analyses to help explain some of the variation between schools in their performance in particular subject areas.

Classroom- and School-Level Data

Much of the data collected by teachers is obtained for the purpose of monitoring the performance of individual pupils, and diagnosing particular learning problems. Sometimes it is used for certification and accreditation. Teachers also use data to inform their teaching — to determine which areas require further instruction, the kinds of errors pupils are making, and how a topic can best be taught. Assessment at the classroom- or school-level might include the following:

- criterion-referenced tests in each subject area;
- diagnostic tests to assess particular learning problems;
- pupil dossiers of critical incidents and special events in the pupil's life, athletic awards, academic accomplishments, letters of recognition, and other noteworthy items;
- regular classroom tests, unit tests, marks on assignments;
- other informal assessment such as teachers' appraisals of reading logs, writing folders, and notebooks;
- pupil self-assessment.

The district-level monitoring system can inform school-level monitoring efforts by identifying general areas of academic strengths and weaknesses that might be assessed in greater detail. The assessment of school processes at the district level can enable the school to assess more accurately whether its local interventions and action plans are having an impact on the social and learning climate of the school. District monitoring can also contextualize the schools' criterion-referenced results by determining district norms for particular sets of items. This avoids the danger that the schools' local norms are unduly affected by factors such as the history of the school or its social-class and ability intake. Contextualizing school-level results can best be accomplished if there are items in the CRTs used by the schools that are common to the NRTs used by the district. Also, some of the district-level tests can serve as screening instruments to identify pupils who require further testing. The district instruments will likely be too blunt for adequate diagnosis of specific learning difficulties, but can serve as a first filter so that school-level testing efforts can be directed towards pupils who are at the greatest risk of school failure.

Stages in the Development of a Monitoring System

The specification of a schedule for the development of a monitoring system is difficult, because it depends largely on its priority amongst other projects, and the amount of district resources that can be allocated to monitoring. Outlined below are three of the main tasks required for the first stages of its development.

Pupil Identification System

The first requirement in the development of the monitoring system is to establish a means of tracking all elementary and secondary pupils. The task is not as easy as one would envisage, because some pupils change their name for various reasons, sometimes there are duplicate names, many pupils change schools, and pupils are continually entering and leaving the district. The point at which pupils drop out or complete school varies, and for many the time of leaving is not well defined.

I recommend that the identification system be defined in terms of 'age cohorts'. For example, the set of pupils with birthdates in 1985 would comprise the '1985 cohort', irrespective of their current grade placement or when they entered the first grade. I prefer age cohorts over grade or entry cohorts for two reasons. One is that the age and ability composition of grade cohorts can vary across schools because of differences between schools in their policies regarding grade retention and acceleration. If estimates of school effects are based on grade cohorts, then a school which tends to retain more pupils than average for the district, and accelerate fewer pupils than average, would have a better chance of showing above-average performance. Another reason is that a pupil's age relative to his or her classmates is related to achievement: after accounting for pupils who have repeated or accelerated a grade, pupils who are older than their average classmate tend to have above-average achievement scores (Willms and Jacobsen, 1990). These two reasons are particularly important in systems with dual or variable entry dates into primary school. For example, the British Columbia government instituted a dual-entry program in 1990–91, which allowed pupils to begin their primary schooling in either September or January. The time spent in primary school was to vary from three to four years, depending on the child's rate of development.

For each cohort, schools could collect basic demographic information: full name, birthdate, sex, address, postal code, and the date that the pupil began schooling in the district. All pupils would be assigned a pupil ID number that would be used for administration purposes throughout their schooling years in the district. The first two digits of the ID would designate the year of their cohort. The schools could then fill in an entry or exit form for any pupils that entered or left the system. In the first year of the development of the system, this information would need to be collected for all pupils, kindergarten through 12, but thereafter only for pupils entering the district.

Data Management System

The costs of data management and analysis are usually underestimated. After data from tests or questionnaires are entered into computer files, considerable work is required to 'clean' the data (check for incorrect entries, set codes for missing data) and to prepare the data for analysis (prepare labels for each value of each variable, examine frequency distributions of each variable, and merge the data with existing files). Analyses are seldom as straightforward as one expects; I have known even the most experienced researchers to underestimate the time required by a factor of two or three. For many purposes, graphics are useful, and these too are time-consuming.

Some of the costs of data preparation and analysis can be reduced by starting with a computer program that is capable of both data management and analysis, and by setting some standards for the construction of the data base. I have found that monitoring data for districts with about 10,000 pupils can be adequately handled with a 386 IBM-compatible PC (with 5K extended memory, a math co-processor, and an 80 MB hard drive). Data entry and cleaning can be done on less powerful machines, but one of this capacity is necessary for analyses.

Construction and Piloting of Questionnaires
One of the most costly and time-consuming aspects of getting started is the construction and development of questionnaires. Although many of the items can be based on those available in the literature, time is required to obtain permission for their use. Also, in most cases the district will want to construct several items relevant to its particular needs. A rough estimate is that it requires two person-months for the development and piloting of each questionnaire. However, not all of the questionnaires need to be constructed in the first year.

Time Line for the First Two Years

A time line for the first two years of the development of a monitoring system is described below:

First School Year (July to June)

July to September
    Establish pupil identification system
    Purchase of computing equipment and software
    Develop and pilot grade 7 questionnaire
October to December
    Develop grade 4 and grade 10 questionnaires
    Develop parent questionnaires
    Construct data management system
January to March
    Pilot grade 4 and grade 10 questionnaires
    Pilot parent questionnaire
April to June
    First administration of grade 7 questionnaire
    First administration of Self-Description Questionnaire
    First administration of CAT, all grades
    Develop data base for measuring CAT growth scores

Second Year (July to June)

July to December
    Develop school-leaver questionnaire
    First estimates of school effects, adjusted for SES
    Integrate data from other sources (e.g., provincial tests, school
        records)

January to June
First administration of parent questionnaire
Second administration of grade 7 questionnaire
First administration of grade 4 and 10 questionnaires
Pilot school-leaver questionnaire

A Unique Design

The proposed design was based on designs previously set out for two medium-sized districts, one in Scotland and one in Canada. These districts are in the process of developing their monitoring systems. There are several features of the design which distinguish it from other district-level monitoring systems. They are as follows:

- **The use of entire age cohorts rather than grade cohorts.** The use of age cohorts provides a more accurate means for assessing schools, and allows for the assessment of the effects of school, district, state, or national interventions.
- **Measurement of personal, vocational, social, and academic outcomes.** Most performance monitoring systems include information describing only pupils' academic performance. The inclusion of data describing non-cognitive outcomes provides a more comprehensive picture of the performance of schools.
- **Measurement of pupil growth.** Estimates of the effects of schools on academic achievement will be based, in part, on pupils' rates of growth, rather than on a cross-section of scores taken at one time point. Although educational researchers strongly advocate the use of growth scores, few monitoring systems use them.
- **Estimates of school effects adjusted for family background.** Most monitoring systems compare schools without controlling for pupils' family backgrounds. Some systems use crude techniques for adjustment based on data aggregated to the school level. The proposed system entails the collection of individual-level data, which allow the analyst to employ the recently-developed multilevel modelling techniques. These techniques take account of pupil background and adjust for measurement and sampling error.
- **Measurement and analysis of data on school policies and processes.** The system will be capable not only of assessing how much schools vary in their performance, but also of addressing questions about why they vary. The analytical approach assesses how much of the variation in school performance is attributable to differences between schools in their policies and practices.
- **Complements monitoring efforts at higher and lower levels.** The proposed monitoring system uses data collected at higher levels of the schooling system to provide a wider context for data collected at the district and school levels. The district monitoring system also enhances the information systems of individual schools.

Chapter 9

Analyses for an Annual Report

This chapter describes several types of analyses that are useful for summarizing and displaying indicator data. Its purpose is not to prescribe the specific content of an annual report, but rather to set out some of the types of analyses that may be useful in a report, and to show how they can be displayed. The presentation is not prescriptive because the kind of report a district might prepare for internal use by teachers and administrators would probably differ substantially from one prepared for the school board, or for parents and the wider community. Also, a district might prepare separate reports for each school, and schools might prepare their own reports for district administrators, parents, or the school board.

Table 9-1 lists eight types of analyses that could be included in an annual report. The table lists the statistical techniques required for each analysis, and gives an example of the type of plot that could be used to display the findings. The examples are drawn from the work discussed earlier pertaining to indicator programs in Canada, Scotland, and the US. The purpose of most analyses is to summarize and organize a large set of data and to communicate the results as precisely and richly as possible. In deciding which statistical analyses were appropriate, and which type of plot to use to display results, I strived to achieve four desirable properties:

- **Interpretable and Economical** Often more complicated statistical techniques and graphical presentations help researchers understand the complexity of schooling phenomena, but the findings cannot be communicated easily to a wide audience. The goal is to present findings in a way that can be understood easily be administrators, teachers, and parents. Economy of display is also desirable. Sometimes a graph can display results for all schools in a district without being unduly cluttered.
- **Displays Distributions** A display of the distribution of scores on an indicator is preferable to summary statistics such as means or medians (see the discussion in Chapter 3). Plots such as box plots, dot plots, and frequency distributions show how scores on an indicator are distributed for an entire district or for separate groups.
- **Contextualizes Results with District, State, or National Norms** A presentation of results is often more useful if it provides comparisons

Table 9-1   Analyses and Displays for an Annual Report

Type of Analysis	Statistical Technique	Type of Plot	Figure
Comparing School Scores to District Norms (or District Scores to State or National Norms)	Descriptive Frequencies	Bar Graph Cumulative Freq. Distribution	9–1 9–2
Describing Variation Between Schools	Descriptive Frequencies Descriptive	Box Plots Histograms Dot Plots	9–3 9–4 9–5
Describing Changes in Year-to-Year Performance (for the District or Individual Schools)	Frequencies Frequencies	Line Graphs Cumulative Freq. Distribution	9–6 9–7
Describing the Extent of Segregation	Calculate P, D	Pie Charts Dot Plots	9–8 9–9
Describing Adjusted Results (for the District or Individual Schools)	Running Regressions	Smoothed Scatterplots	9–10 9–11
Describing Differences in Scores between Ethnic, Racial, and Socioeconomic Groups, and between the Sexes	Running Regressions	Smoothed Scatterplots	9–12 9–13
Estimating Type A and B School Effects	Hierarchical Linear Regression	Dot Plots	See Chapter 10
Estimating Rates of Growth (for the District or for Individual Schools)	Hierarchical Linear Regression	Line Graph	See Chapter 10

with district, state, or national norms. Sometimes this can be made easier by scaling the data in a certain way and by presenting results using a common metric.

- **Easy to Compute and Display** Many of the most informative analyses require only simple statistical techniques, such as the computation of means, standard deviations, and frequencies. The first four types of statistical analyses listed in Table 9-1 are of this type; they can be accomplished easily with basic statistical packages such as MINITAB, SPSS/PC, or SYSTAT. The routines for 'smoothing' data are included in some basic packages, but not all of them. The hierarchical linear regressions are more difficult and require specialized software, such as HLM (Bryk, Raudenbush, Seltzer, and Congdon, 1986), ML3 (Rasbash, Prosser, and Goldstein, 1991), or VARCL (Longford, 1986). Most of the plots can be produced with commercially-available graphics packages, such as Harvard Graphics or Graph-in-a-Box.

This chapter discusses the first six types of analyses listed in Table 9-1. The analyses and figures pertaining to Type A and Type B effects, and to pupils' rates of growth are presented in Chapter 10 and the Technical Appendix. They are presented there because they require more statistical sophistication than the analyses in this chapter, and because they require a discussion of hierarchical linear modelling, which is relevant also to the research program set out in Chapter 10.

Figure 9-1   Bar chart: Grade 5 test results on the Canadian Test of Basic Skills

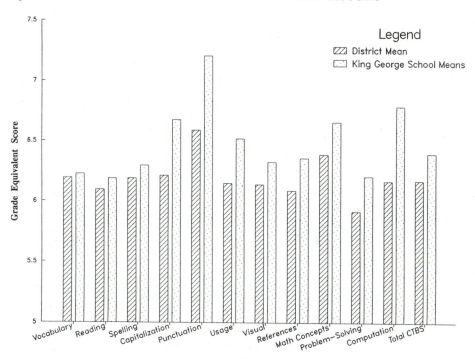

Comparing School Scores to District Norms
(or District Scores to National Norms)

Bar Chart

A bar chart is one of the simplest types of graphs for presenting scores on a set of indicators. It can be used to make comparisons of school scores with district and national (or state or provincial) norms. Figure 9-1 shows a graph of grade 5 test results on the Canadian Test of Basic Skills (CTBS) for one elementary school. (The school name 'King George' is fictitious.) The test was taken in May of 1989 by all grade 5 pupils in the district. The national norms, based on the norming sample of the test, is a grade-equivalent score of 5.9 for all subtests. The figure shows two bars for each subtest, one for the district means, the other for the school's means. Although this graph does not show the distribution of scores for each subtest, it provides an easily interpreted comparison of school scores to district and national norms.

Cumulative Frequency Distribution for a Continuous, Equal-Interval Indicator

The average score on an indicator often masks important variation between pupils in their scores. Therefore, analyses that display the distribution of scores on an indicator are also useful. The cumulative frequency distribution (CFD) is an effective device for showing the entire distribution of scores on an indicator. It allows also for comparisons of the distribution of scores for a

Figure 9-2   *Cumulative frequency distribution: Grade-equivalent scores in reading*

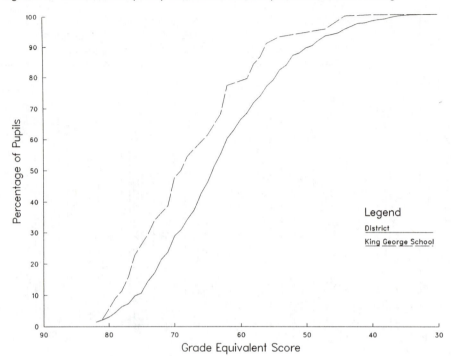

school to the distribution for the district, or to the national distribution. It can be used with scores that are on a continuous scale, such as grade-equivalent scores or percentages, or with scores that are on an ordinal scale, such as grades on a test. The CFD described in this section uses continuous data.

A CFD shows the percentages of pupils scoring at or *above*[1] each score on the X-axis. The construction of CFDs is described in several elementary statistics texts (e.g., Hopkins and Glass, 1978). Figure 9-2 shows the CFD of grade-equivalent scores in language arts (based on the 4 CTBS language arts subtests) for King George Elementary School and for the entire district. One can use the CFD to determine the percentage of grade 5 pupils that achieved at or above each grade level. For example, approximately 78 per cent of the grade 5 pupils in King George scored at or above a grade-equivalent score of 6.0, compared with 66 per cent for the district. These were determined by drawing a vertical line from 6.0 on the X-axis, and reading the percentages on the Y-axis where the line crossed the CFD for the school and district. Similarly, about 95 per cent of the King George grade 5 pupils were at or above a

---

[1] Many textbooks describe the CFD as showing the percentage of students at or *below* a particular score. Generally I prefer reversing the scale on the X-axis because the height of a cumulative frequency line then corresponds with a higher overall score on the X-axis (outcome) measure.

grade-equivalent of 5.0 (or 5 per cent of the pupils were below this level), compared with 88 per cent for the district.

The CFD can be used also to determine percentiles. One draws a horizontal line from the Y-axis at the desired percentile, and reads the grade-equivalent score on the X-axis at the point where the horizontal line crosses the CFD line. For example, the fiftieth percentile (e.g., the median) in language arts for King George was 6.8, and for the district was 6.4. The CFD line for King George is above the district CFD line, which shows that King George's scores for language arts were above the district average. In particular, the King George line rises more steeply from the origin, indicating that King George had more pupils at the top end of the distribution.

Sometimes CFD lines for a school cross the district line. This happens, for example, when a school has relatively more pupils scoring at the top and bottom end of the distribution, and relatively fewer pupils scoring in the middle. When the indicator is measured on an ordinal scale, such as grades or levels of attainment, interpretation of the CFD is improved by scaling the ordinal measure such that the cumulative frequency of the national (or state or district) results lie on the diagonal. This is demonstrated in Figure 9-7, which is discussed in the section pertaining to comparisons of year-to-year performance.

Describing Variation Between Schools

Box Plots

Box plots are a convenient way of displaying the distributions of scores for a large number of schools. CFD plots can be used to compare schools in their distributions of unadjusted scores on an indicator; however, when more than two or three CFD lines are on the same graph, they usually overlap and become difficult to read. Box plots do not display the entire distributions of scores, as do CFD plots. Box plots display only a five-number summary of each distribution. But for many purposes the five-number summary is adequate.

Figure 9-3 shows a set of box plots describing scores on the Edinburgh Reading Test for pupils entering the twenty secondary schools in Fife Education Authority in 1980. The tops and bottoms of the boxes represent the upper and lower quartiles (e.g., the 25th and 75th percentiles) of the distributions for each school; the line dividing the box is the median (50th percentile). The tails above and below each box show the range of data from the 10th to 25th percentile and 75th to 90th percentile for each school.[2] The widths of the boxes are drawn proportional to the square root of the school size.[3]

---

[2] Sometimes box plots show the outliers as dots above and below the upper and lower tails. Outliers could be defined as those with scores above the 90th percentile or below the 10th percentile. However, care must be taken to ensure that the scores of individual pupils cannot be identified.

[3] This is conventional because several measures of variability are proportional to the square root of the sample size.

Figure 9-3   Box plots: Scores on the Edinburgh reading test for primary 7 pupils

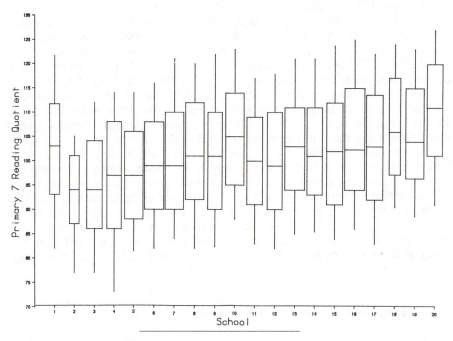

McGill, Tukey, and Larsen (1978) describe box plots in greater detail and offer some variations that are appropriate for other applications.

Each box plot provides a convenient summary of the distribution of reading scores for a school. The chief advantage of using box plots over simply listing means or medians is that box plots allow one to observe and compare distributions of scores across schools. For example, School 1 in Figure 9-3 has about the same median reading score as School 13, but the range of scores in School 1 is much larger. Teachers in School 1 therefore were likely to have had more heterogeneous classes than those in School 13. The upper tail for School 2 is very short — from 101 to 105. Only 10 per cent of the pupils entering that school had scores above 105. It is possible that the most able pupils in the catchment left the catchment to attend other schools.

Histograms
Box plots are useful for data describing variables that are on a continuous, equal-interval scale. When data are categorical, however, the summary measures provided by box plots are less useful. For categorical data, histograms are more useful. Figure 9-4 shows a set of histograms describing truancy rates for each of the twenty schools. The chart shows the percentages of pupils in each of four truancy categories: never truant, truant a lesson here and there, truant a day here and there, and truant several days or weeks at a time. The figure shows on a single page the distribution of the truancy indicator for all schools in the EA.

Figure 9-4   Histograms: Truancy rates for twenty secondary schools

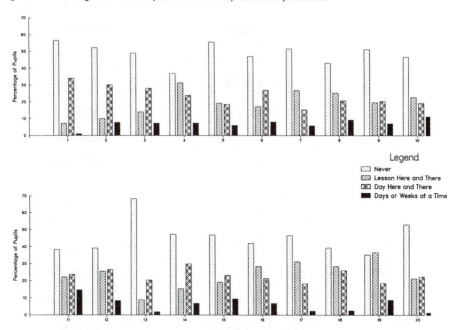

The figure allows one to identify immediately those schools where serious truancy is high. In School 11, for example, more than 10 per cent of the pupils were truant days or weeks at a time, and more than 20 per cent reported being truant a day here and there. The figure also shows that in some schools (e.g., Schools 1, 2, and 3) pupils were more likely to be truant for an entire day than they were to skip a lesson here and there.

Dot Plots
A dot plot simply describes a batch of data with a dot for each observation on a horizontal or vertical scale. Figure 9-5 shows the mean CTBS scores for each CTBS subtest for the thirty elementary schools in the Canadian data. The small circles show the mean scores for each school and for each subtest, and the short vertical lines show the district means for each subtest. The long vertical line at a grade-equivalent of 5.9 is the national norm. The advantage of this type of graph is that it allows the analyst to view the entire distribution of scores for several indicators, and to identify outliers. At the school or class-room level, dot plots can be used to display the scores of individual pupils across a number of indicators.

Describing Changes in Year-to-Year Performance

Line Graphs
The most common type of graph for displaying trends in a set of data is the line graph. It shows the average score on an indicator plotted against time.

Figure 9-5   Dot plots: School mean CTBS scores for each subtest

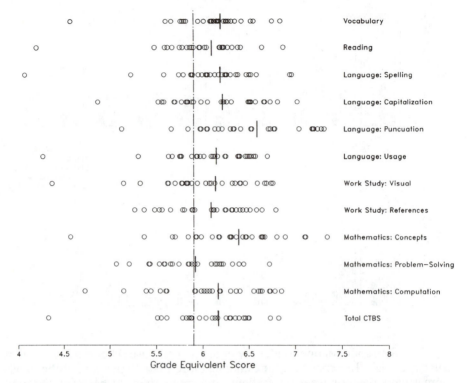

One can include several lines on a line graph, denoting the trends for different groups. Figure 9-6 shows the average arithmetic and English O-grade scores by sex and social class for all Scottish secondary pupils in 1976, 1980, and 1984. The O-grade scores were scaled on a logit distribution using a technique recommended by Mosteller and Tukey (1977), and then standardized to have a mean of zero and a standard deviation of one.[4] The graph shows several trends:

1   arithmetic scores were increasing for all social-class groups and for both sexes;

---

[4] The O-grade scores were scaled on a logit distribution using data for the entire country. Scaling a set of scores on a logit distribution is similar to scaling data on a normal distribution, except that scores at the upper and lower end of the scale are not as spread out. This type of scaling can be used for any set of scores on an ordinal scale. The scaled value for each grade is the value of:

$$Y = \frac{\psi(P) - \psi(p)}{P - p}, \text{ where } \psi(p) = p \log_e(p) + (1 - p) \log_e(1 - p),$$

where p is the fraction of pupils beyond the designated grade, and P is the fraction of pupils above and including the designated grade.

Figure 9-6   Line graphs: Social-class and sex differences in arithmetic and English O-Grade results

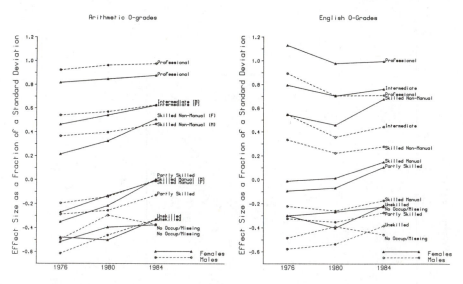

2   English scores were increasing for pupils from working-class families (unskilled, partly skilled, and skilled manual occupations), but were decreasing slightly or remaining about the same for pupils from middle-class backgrounds (skilled non-manual, intermediate, and professional occupations);

3   the gap between the average arithmetic and English scores of pupils from middle- and working-class backgrounds closed slightly, but remained large;

4   sex differences in arithmetic declined to virtually zero for all social-class groups except the professional group, whereas in English females maintained a strong advantage;

5   sex differences were very small compared with differences between social-class groups.

Again, a great deal of information is portrayed on a single page.

Cumulative Frequency Distributions for an Ordinal Indicator

Figure 9-7 shows how a CFD can be used to compare a school's scores on an ordinal measure with the results from a previous year, and with norms for the entire EA. The example is based on the Scottish data. The X-axis displays award categories that pupils can obtain on the SCE O-grade examination in English. The top five categories — 10 through 14 — are considered an *A* award (marks range from 70 to 100 per cent); 8 and 9 are a *B* (60–69 per cent); and 6 and 7 are a *C* (50–59 per cent). Categories 5 and below are not considered passing grades. The axis has been scaled such that the diagonal

Figure 9-7 Cumulative frequency distribution for an ordinal indicator: SCE O-grade English examination results

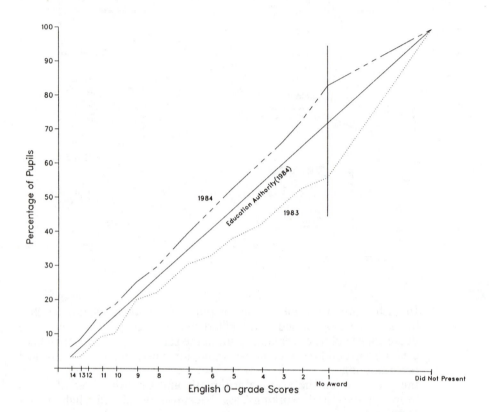

line describes the cumulative frequency of scores for Fife Education Authority in 1984. This was done by scaling the X-axis on an 100-unit scale and assigning the values between 0 and 100 that correspond to the authority's cumulative frequencies for each category. Thus the authority's norms determine the size of the gap between 14 and 13, between 13 and 12, and so on. The CFD lines for one (fictitious) school show its 1983 (dotted line) and 1984 (broken solid line) results. The CFD lines show that the school dramatically improved its results between 1983 and 1984.

The bottom category — 'did not present' — includes all pupils who did not present for the examination, either because they were not deemed capable by their teachers, or because they elected not to. The percentages at which the vertical line above the 'no award' category intersects the three CFD lines are the presentation rates for this examination. In 1984, 72.4 per cent of the pupils in the EA presented for the examination. In this particular school, only 56.3 per cent of the pupils presented for the examination in 1983. By 1984, the presentation rate had increased to 83.3 per cent.

Figure 9-8   Pie charts: Racial and ethnic distribution for San Francisco secondary schools

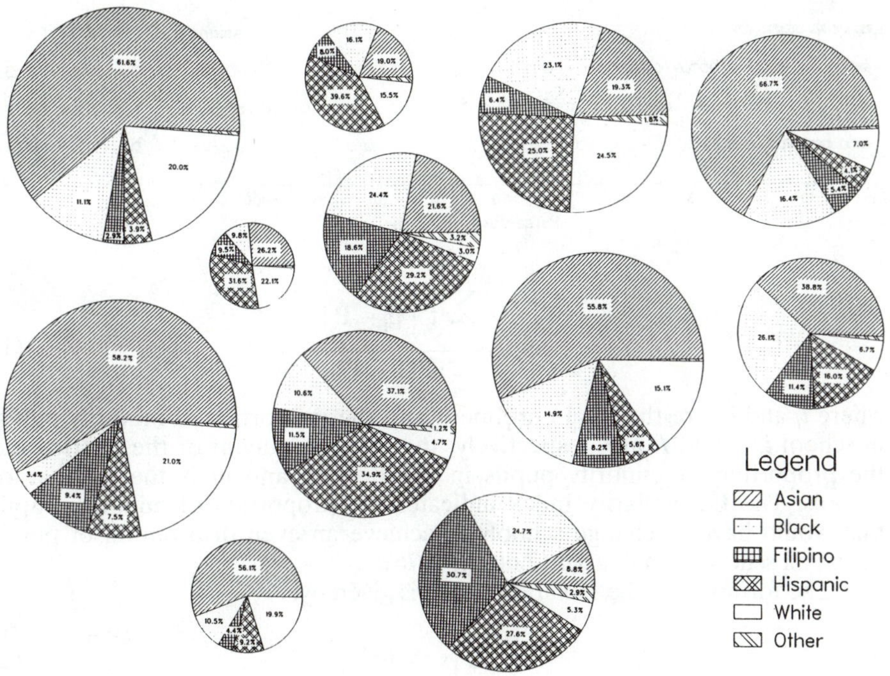

Legend

▨	Asian
⬚	Black
▦	Filipino
▩	Hispanic
☐	White
◪	Other

Describing the Extent of Segregation

Pie Charts

Pie charts can be used to examine the extent that racial, ethnic, or social-class groups are unevenly distributed across schools in a district. Figure 9-8 shows a pie chart of the racial and ethnic distribution for each of the secondary schools in San Francisco.[5] The area of each pie is proportional to the total enrolment of each school. The percentages were obtained from the 1988–89 California Basic Educational Data System (CBEDS). The 'Other' category includes American Indians, Alaskan Natives, and Pacific Islanders. These pie charts could be overlayed onto a map of the city to provide a useful description of the extent of segregation in the district.

Segregation Indices

Three segregation indices were discussed in Chapter 6: D, the Dissimilarity Index; E, the Exposure Index; and η^2 (eta-squared), the correlation ratio. All of these indices vary between 0 and 1, with 0 representing no segregation, and 1 representing total segregation. The formula for the Dissimilarity Index is:

---

[5] The percentages for most pies do not sum to 100 per cent. This is because of rounding error, and because the percentages for segments with less than 1 per cent are not printed on the graph.

Figure 9-9 Segregation indices: Los Angeles secondary schools

Asians	D = .393	I = .137
Whites	D = .542	I = .375
Hispanics	D = .460	I = .662
Blacks	D = .530	I = .423

$$D = \frac{\sum_{i=1}^{m} t_i \mid p_i - P \mid}{2TP(1 - P)} \tag{1}$$

where t_i and p_i are the total enrolment and the proportion of minority pupils in school i. T and P are, respectively, the total enrolment of the district and the proportion of minority pupils in the district, and m is the number of schools. The Dissimilarity Index indicates the proportion of minority pupils that would have to change schools to achieve an even distribution of pupils across all schools in a district (Zoloth, 1976).

The formula for the Isolation Index is given by:

$$I = \sum_{i=1}^{m} [x_i/X][y_i/t_i] \tag{2}$$

where x_i, and y_i are the school enrolments of minority and non-minority pupils respectively, and X is the district enrolment of minority pupils. As in Equation (1), t_i represents the total enrolment of school i, and m is the number of schools. The Isolation Index can be interpreted as the extent to which minority pupils are exposed only to one another, rather than to other non-minority pupils (Massey and Denton, 1988). The Isolation Index differs from the Dissimilarity Index in that it depends on the relative size of the minority group. For example, Filipinos may be unevenly distributed across schools in a district, but because they represent a small proportion of the total population in California school districts, they may not be isolated from pupils of other racial and ethnic backgrounds. The reverse is true for Hispanics, where in some districts they are the largest minority group.

The correlation ratio can be calculated using analysis of variance; it is the ratio of the between-group variance to the total variance.

Dot plots are useful for displaying how pupils from differing backgrounds are distributed across schools. Figure 9-9 shows the proportions of pupils from each racial and ethnic group in each of the secondary schools in Los Angeles. Each circle denotes the percentage of pupils in a school for the relevant group (e.g., p_i). The short vertical lines denote the percentages for the district (e.g., P). For example, the figure shows that the percentage of Asians in Los Angeles schools varied from 0 per cent to about 26 per cent in that year, and the district percentage was just below 10 per cent. The figure also shows the Dissimilarity Index and the Isolation Index for each group.

Figure 9-10 *Smoothed scatterplot: English versus P7 reading for Fife EA*

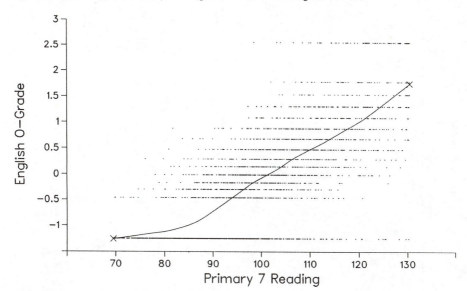

Asians were relatively less segregated than other ethnic and racial groups: D = 0.393 for Asians compared with .542 for whites, .460 for Hispanics, and .530 for blacks; I = 0.137 for Asians compared with .375 for whites, .662 for Hispanics, and .423 for blacks.

Describing Adjusted Results
(for the District or for Individual Schools)

Smoothed Scatterplots
Figures 9-3 through 9-5 (above) showed how box plots, histograms, and dot plots could be used to display variation between schools in their scores on some indicator. However, comparisons between schools based on these methods do not include an adjustment for the intake characteristics of pupils. Smoothed scatterplots provide a means to make a simple adjustment for pupil intake. Their advantage is that they show graphically how pupils at varying levels of initial ability, on average, score on some outcome measure. Generally smoothed scatterplots are used with data that are measured on a continuous scale. In the next four examples, the 14-category English O-grade results were transformed into a logit-scale and standardized[6] using the technique suggested by Mosteller and Tukey (1977) (see Note 4 above).

Figure 9-10 shows a smoothed scatterplot for O-grade English results against Primary 7 reading scores for Fife Education Authority in 1984. On this

---

[6] The scaled scores for the O-Grade English grades are as follows: 1 = 2.56, 2 = 1.79, 3 = 1.54, 4 = 1.31, 5 = 1.09, 6 = 0.88, 7 = 0.68, 8 = 0.47, 9 = 0.29, 10 = 0.14, 11 = –0.01, 12 = –0.17, 13 = –0.30, 14 = –0.46, Did Not Present = –1.25.

Figure 9-11   Smoothed scatterplot showing differences between schools

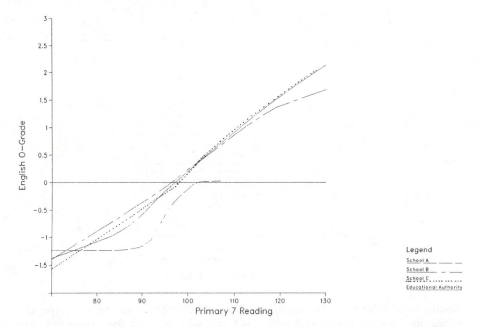

graph, each point represents the reading and English scores for one pupil. The 'smoothed' line is a summary of the relationship between English O-Grade scores and reading achievement for the authority. It can be thought of as the line that passes through the middle of the data. There are several different techniques for smoothing a set of data. This particular technique is called 'robust non-linear locally weighted regression' (Cleveland, 1979). In most cases, the various techniques produce similar results. Many commercially available statistical packages have the facility to draw smoothed lines through a set of data.

With the smoothed scatterplot one can estimate how well a typical pupil with a certain P7 reading score performed in the authority. For example, pupils who had a P7 reading score of 100, on average, had a scaled S4 O-grade English score of approximately −0.08. (A vertical line drawn from the X-axis at 100 intersects the smoothed line at −0.08.) This means that a pupil with an intake reading score of 100 scored approximately 8 per cent of a standard deviation below the EA average four years later. A pupil who had a P7 reading score of 85, on average, had an S4 English score of −1.00, and a pupil who had a P7 reading score of 115, on average, had an S4 English score of 0.75.

Figure 9-11 shows the smoothed lines for three schools and the education authority.[7] The lines for the individual schools were truncated at the 10th and 90th percentiles of their P7 reading scores. For School A (dashed line), which

---

[7] In this graph the O-grade scores are based on O-grades taken in S4, S5, and S6.

Figure 9-12   *Smoothed scatterplot showing differences between females and males*

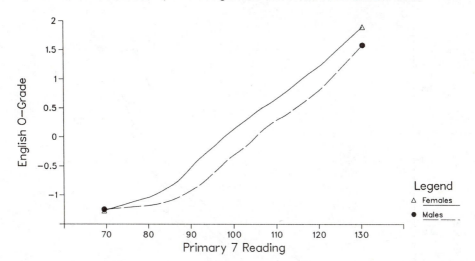

is a small school, the smoothed line runs parallel to the X-axis for pupils with P7 reading scores between 70 and 90. This means that very few pupils in this range presented for the exam. Pupils with P7 reading scores between 90 and 107 also fell below the authority standard (solid line). In School B (short-long dashed line), pupils at the low end of the range of P7 reading scores had O-grade scores that were slightly above the authority standard, but pupils at the high end of P7 reading had below-average scores. Pupils in School C (dotted line) were very close to the authority standard at all levels of P7 reading scores.

These estimates are similar to what were referred to as Type A effects in Chapter 4. They are estimates of how well a pupil with certain characteristics performed in each school. These estimates include statistical control for pupils' P7 reading scores, but do not include control for social class or other relevant background characteristics. Thus they are somewhat biased, although the bias is not extreme because P7 reading is a powerful predictor of O-grade English results. For purposes of comparing schools, smoothed scatterplots are not a good substitute for estimating Type A and B effects; however, they can be used easily by individual schools to gain a rough impression of their performance relative to the authority standard. They serve also to provide information about presentation rates and differences between different types of pupils in their performance.

Describing Differences in Scores between Groups

These types of plots are useful for examining differences between social-class groups, or between the sexes. Figure 9-12 shows the smoothed scatterplots of English O-grades against P7 reading scores separately for males and females. The figure shows that for pupils with P7 reading scores above 90, the sex

Figure 9-13   Smoothed scatterplot showing differences between social-class groups

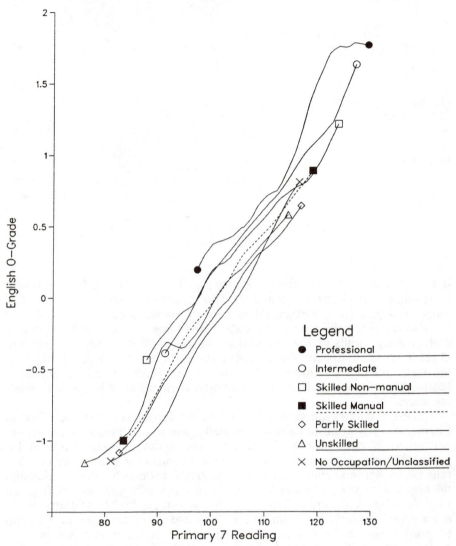

difference is about 40 per cent of a standard deviation, and is fairly constant across the range of P7 reading ability. Forty per cent of a standard deviation is a big gap: it is equivalent to at least two points on the 14-point scale for pupils near the middle of the distribution.

Figure 9-13 shows a similar graph with smoothed lines drawn for each of seven social-class categories. As in Figure 9-11, the lines for each social-class category were truncated at the 10th and 90th percentiles of the P7 reading scores. The figure shows the size of gap between social-class groups after controlling for levels of P7 reading ability. The gap between pupils with parents in professional occupations and those with parents in partly skilled or unskilled occupations is about one-half of a standard deviation. This means that two pupils with similar reading scores on intake, but with differing social-class backgrounds, would likely differ substantially in their English O-grade scores four years later.

Concluding Remarks

Most of the analyses presented in this chapter pertain mainly to a district-level report. However, the same types of analyses are relevant for analyzing data collected by individual schools. For example, box plots, histograms, and dot plots can be used to show the distributions of pupils' scores within and between classes within a school. Line graphs are useful for charting a school's progress on a number of indicators. Individual schools can use pie charts to examine the extent of racial and ethnic segregation between classes or between instructional programs. Smoothed scatterplots are useful for examining the intake-outcome relationships within classes. Many of these types of analyses are useful also at higher levels of the schooling system.

The analyses in this chapter emphasized schooling outcomes, or the relationships between inputs and outcomes. Many of the analyses are useful also for summarizing data describing school processes. For example, one can use a dot plot similar to Figure 9-5 to summarize the scores of several schools on a set of indicators of schooling processes. A graph similar to Figure 9-13 showing the relationships between pupils' attitudes towards school and their sense of efficacy would provide useful feedback for both teachers and administrators.

The next chapter presents a model for a research program for a school district or EA. As a monitoring system matures, many of the analyses for an annual report become part of the research program, and *vice versa*.

Chapter 10

A Research Program

This chapter demonstrates how a monitoring system can be used to establish an ongoing research program at the district level. A research program is a systematic inquiry into a set of related questions. Researchers and practitioners adopting a research program usually share assumptions about the underlying theory, methods, and styles of inquiry. They tend to agree about the starting points for inquiry, the key topics, the implicit definitions, the unit of analysis, and the methods of investigation (Shulman, 1986). Hammersley (1985) contends that successful research programs are based on a theory that promises to be true. A central concern is to specify the conditions under which the theory does or does not hold. A successful program is also productive: it generates findings relevant to policy or to the development of theory. This chapter sets out four basic questions that can be addressed with indicator data, describes some proto-typical designs that can be used with the first three years of indicator data, and provides examples of the types of findings that a district research program can generate.

Research Questions Based on the Input-Process-Output Model

Nearly all research on school effectiveness has been directed at answering four principal questions:

- To what extent do schools vary in their outcomes?
- To what extent do outcomes vary for pupils of differing status?
- What school policies and practices improve levels of schooling outcomes?
- What school policies and practices reduce inequalities in outcomes between high- and low-status groups?

The first two questions concern *quality* and *equity*; the last two concern their causes. The same set of questions can be asked of other organizational units, such as the school district or classroom. Indeed, the large body of research on teacher effectiveness attempts to address these questions as they pertain to teachers' effects on children's outcomes in the classroom (see Gage and Needels, 1989; Linn, 1986).

The four questions are based on a theory of schooling derived from the input-process-output model. The model, which was discussed in Chapter 3, presumes that pupil outcomes are largely determined by family influences and pupils' experiences at school, and that the latter are shaped by the practices, policies, organizational structures, and norms of the classroom, school, and school district. The model is multilevel: it maintains that actions by educators at one level of the system affect policy and practice at other levels. This perspective is consistent with recent thinking about 'how schools work': Barr and Dreeben (1983) contend that educators decide how scarce resources are allocated within organizational units, and these decisions have differential effects on pupils of differing status.

The input-process-output model and the attendant questions suggest a quantitative approach, and because the goal here is to discuss the use of monitoring data for research on school effectiveness, I discuss only quantitative approaches. However, qualitative study is not inconsistent with the theory or the questions. Moreover, I view it is a necessary complement to quantitative work in this area. Qualitative studies can help the evaluator understand the particularities and complexity of processes operating at the local level. These understandings can serve to generate new hypotheses relevant to the theory. Indeed, much of the progress in addressing the 'why' questions about school effectiveness has come through qualitative research.

The four questions are intended as a structure to help one think about issues pertaining to the impact of schooling on pupils' learning. The first question asks only for description. Generally, the researcher wants to discern whether some schools have higher scores than others on the outcome measure of interest. Often the question is extended to ask how much schools vary in their outcomes after adjusting for pupil-intake characteristics, and for other factors exogenous to the schooling process. Usually the extent of variance between schools is expressed as a percentage of the total variance in the outcome measure.

The second question also requires only description. The interest is in the gap in outcomes between low- and high-status groups both within and between schools. For example, one could ask what the achievement gap between blacks and whites was across all schools in a district, and what the average achievement gap was within each school. The distinction is important because there may be a substantial achievement gap for a district as a whole, but a negligible achievement gap within every school in the district. This could occur, for example, if whites were over-represented in high-performing schools and blacks were over-represented in low-performing schools. Such results would suggest that within schools, policies and practices were equitable, but between schools they were not. District administrators might strive to reduce inequalities by implementing policies that altered the between-school distribution of pupils. Conversely, results might show a substantial achievement gap within schools, but a negligible gap for the entire district. This would call for an examination of within-school policies related to equity in achievement.

The third and fourth questions ask what *causes* differences between schools. Causal inferences require analyses beyond simple description. Researchers and philosophers debate whether the concept of causation should be used in social scientific research (Ennis, 1973; Travers, 1981), because even the most tightly controlled experiments are based on empirical assumptions and do not eliminate all alternative explanations (Linn, 1986). However, I use the term deliberately because it is the validity of causal statements that is at the heart of criticisms of research on school effects. This is because nearly all of the research in this area has been quasi-experimental, and as such, the validity of findings can be easily challenged — usually there are a number of plausible alternative interpretations.

Designs in which subjects are randomly assigned to treatments are referred to as 'true' experiments; designs without random assignment are called 'quasi-experiments'. Cook and Campbell (1979) describe a variety of quasi-experimental designs used in the social sciences, and discuss the threats to their validity. The major threats in most studies of school effectiveness are selection bias and confounding factors. Selection bias occurs when the schools being compared differ in their intakes, such that what may appear to be the effect of some policy may be due to intake composition. Also, what may appear to be the effect of some policy may actually be the effect of other (confounding) factors that are related to the policy, but not part of it. This does not mean that all quasi-experimentation should be abandoned, or that researchers should be content with sidestepping the issue of causation. Researchers studying teacher effects on pupils' learning made considerable progress with quasi-experimental (correlational) designs, before embarking on 'true' experiments (Gage and Needels, 1989). Also, amongst different types of quasi-experimental designs, some have fewer threats to validity than others (Cook and Campbell, 1979). The discussion below is aimed at describing designs that can be readily adapted to monitoring programs, and yet are stronger than the correlational designs that have characterized research on school effects.

One final point about the four research questions: they do not serve as a substitute for the skills and knowledge that are a part of the craft of educational research. For example, suppose a district wanted to investigate the effects of 'whole language' approaches to the instruction of reading. The first two questions would ask, to what extent do schools (or classrooms) vary in their reading outcomes, and do reading outcomes vary across different groups? Even at this stage the researcher is faced with the challenging task of identifying the appropriate outcome measures. Advocates of whole language maintain that the popular norm-referenced tests are inadequate because they decontextualize reading skills and do not adequately reflect current conceptualizations of the reading process or other aspects of literacy (McKenna, Robinson, and Miller, 1990; see also the response by Edelsky, 1990, and the McKenna *et al.* rejoinder). The third and fourth questions would ask whether whole language brings about superior levels of reading ability, and if so, is whole language effective for differing types of pupils? Here the researcher must determine what constitutes whole language and its implementation in the school. The task is difficult because in some respects whole language is a philosophical approach to language and learning, which differs amongst researchers and educators (Newman, 1985; Watson, 1989).

Multilevel Cross-Sectional Designs without Random Assignment

Multilevel designs employ data describing individuals and the organizational units in which they are grouped. Cross-sectional designs employ data collected at the same time. This section discusses multilevel, cross-sectional designs that could be based on a single wave of data collected as part of a monitoring program. In these designs schools (or classrooms) are considered the 'treatments' of a quasi-experiment. Because pupils are not randomly assigned to treatments, data describing pupils' characteristics are used to adjust statistically for 'pre-treatment' differences.

The basic cross-sectional design commonly used in the study of school effectiveness is the 'posttest-only design with nonequivalent groups' (Cook and Campbell, 1979). Pupils receive different treatments in their respective schools and the researcher observes pupil outcomes after the treatments. Differences between groups of pupils are presumed to be 'treatment' or 'school' effects. Typically the researcher attempts to collect the observations at the same time; thus it is a cross-sectional design.[1]

In the multilevel cross-sectional design, the researcher also collects data describing various aspects of the schooling process, and attempts to relate differences in the 'school effects' to differences in school policies and practices. For example, we could ask whether the schools with the highest achievement scores had the smallest class sizes.

The obvious shortcoming of this design is that differences between pupils' outcome scores may be due to differences in school policies or practices or due to differences between pupils upon intake into the schools. The researcher attempts to control for initial differences by collecting data on pupils' background (see Chapter 5) and making a statistical adjustment for intake characteristics.

The analysis of multilevel cross-sectional data employs multilevel regression techniques. The Technical Appendix describes the statistical model used in the examples below; Raudenbush and Bryk (1986) provide a more technical description. The idea underlying these techniques is that there are two or more levels of analysis. For the two-level case, the analysis first estimates relationships between pupils' outcomes and background characteristics within each school. The results of the separate analyses for each school become the outcome variables in a school-level analysis that examines the relationships between the within-school results and certain school policies and practices. In practice the relationships at the two levels are estimated simultaneously, but I find it easier to think about them as separate analyses.

The four basic questions set out at the beginning of the chapter are addressed as follows. Each within-school regression estimates how well a pupil with certain characteristics would be expected to perform in a given school. The estimate is based on data describing pupils' outcomes and

---

[1] Usually not all the data describing pupils' outcomes can be collected at exactly the same time; often certain schools cannot participate on a particular date, and typically some pupils are absent and are surveyed within a week or two of the survey date. But generally researchers attempt to collect the indicator data at the same time.

background characteristics for the pupils in that school. The estimate is the Type A effect for that school (see Chapter 4). One can compute separate estimates for pupils with differing background characteristics. Thus we could talk about Type A effects for an 'average' pupil, a high-SES pupil, a low-SES pupil, or a pupil with a certain racial and ethnic background. The estimates for the first level of analysis address the first two research questions. We are interested in whether schools vary significantly in their Type A school effects, and whether Type A effects vary for pupils with differing backgrounds. The multilevel programs provide estimates of each school's Type A effect, an estimate of the variance in these effects, and a statistical test of whether the variance differs significantly from chance variation. The within-school regression analysis also provides estimates of the relationships between pupils' background characteristics and schooling outcomes, and an estimate of the extent that these relationships vary across schools.

The second level of the multilevel analysis uses the results of the first-level regressions as the outcome measure. The second-level regression examines whether the estimated Type A effects are related to variables describing school policy and practice. For example, are Type A effects related to average per-pupil expenditures? This analysis therefore attempts to address the third basic research question — what school policies and practices improve levels of schooling outcomes? In addressing this question the model can also provide estimates of Type B effects. The analyst includes variables describing the school composition (e.g., school mean SES) and the social and economic context, in addition to the relevant policy and practice variables. The analysis provides estimates of how much of the variation between schools in their intake-adjusted outcomes is attributable to school policy and practices, independent of the school composition and the social and economic context.

The second-level analysis can also examine whether the estimated relationships between background and outcomes vary as a function of school policy and practice. For example, we could ask whether the employment of teacher aides affects the achievement of low-SES pupils more than it affects the achievement of high-SES pupils. If it does, we would expect to observe a weaker relationship between SES and outcomes in schools with lower pupil-aide ratios. (A low ratio means more aides per pupil.) The multilevel analysis would provide an estimate of the relationship between SES-outcome relationships and pupil-aide ratios for the schools in the sample. In this way the multilevel analysis attempts to address the fourth basic research question — what school policies and practices reduce inequalities in outcomes between high- and low-status groups?

In cross-sectional designs the data collected contemporaneously with the outcome measures often include SES or cognitive ability. These data are used to account for the 'pre-treatment' characteristics of pupils. The assumption is that these characteristics have not changed during the course of schooling. This assumption may not be valid, and can result in biased estimates of the differences between schools. Measures of cognitive ability are particularly problematic because the skills measured by the tests to some extent can be learned at school. Therefore, in removing statistically the effects of cognitive ability, one can inadvertently remove some of the effects of schooling.

A similar problem pertains to school-level data. Data describing school policy and practices might best be collected at several times while the 'treatment' (schooling) is being implemented. But typically data are collected at only one time point. Some school-level characteristics may be relatively stable, such as the appearance of the school building, but other factors, especially climate factors such as academic press or norms for academic success, might vary substantially over time. If the data on school-level characteristics are unreliable, then the corresponding estimates of Type B effects will be unreliable.

The multilevel model described above is a two-level (pupils and schools) model. This can be extended easily to a three-level (pupils, schools, and districts or EAs) model. In a three-level model, the results of the second-level analysis become the outcome variables in a district-level analysis. The first of the examples presented below employs a simple three-level model with no explanatory variables at the third level.

Example I: Differences between Schools and EAs in Scotland

In earlier work I estimated differences between schools and Scottish Education Authorities in their examination attainment for pupils who left school in 1976, 1980, and 1984 (Willms, 1986). The data were at the individual level, derived from the Scottish School-Leavers' Survey. Both private and state-funded schools were included. Comparisons between schools and EAs were made using a three-level (pupils, schools, EAs) hierarchical linear model. The outcome measures were the O-grade examination results in English and arithmetic, and an overall measure of SCE examination attainment. Controls for pupil background included gender and three indicators of SES: father's occupation, mother's education, and number of siblings.

One of the principal findings of the study was that much of the variability between EAs in their performance was attributable to differences between them in their pupil intakes. After controlling statistically for pupil intake, the variability between EAs in their performance was small compared with the variability between schools. In statistical terms, the results suggested that, of the variance in pupil outcomes remaining after controlling statistically for pupil intake, nearly 90 per cent was between pupils, about 10 per cent was between schools, and less than one-tenth of 1 per cent was between EAs.

Figure 10-1 portrays these findings for the 1980 estimates of Type A school and EA effects on overall attainment. The circles denote estimates of school effects, the squares denote estimates of EA effects. (The horizontal lines are estimates of the 95 per cent confidence intervals of the EA estimates based on conventional OLS regression techniques.) The figure shows that all EAs had schools that were well above or well below the national average in attainment. Although the differences between some EAs were large in educational terms — as much as two O-grade passes for the average child — they were small in comparison with the large variation

Figure 10-1   School and EA effects on overall attainment for Scotland, 1980

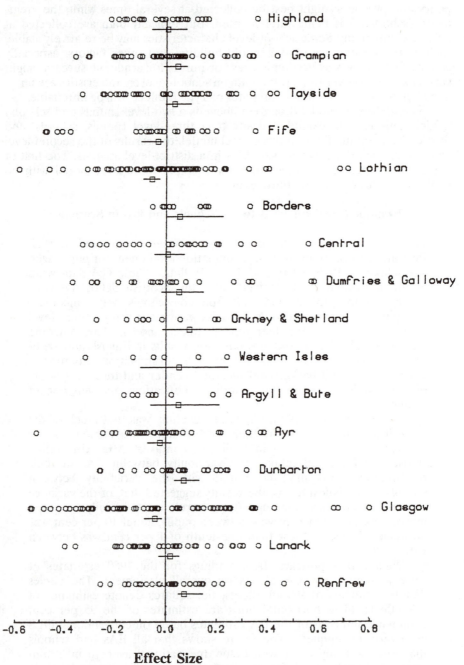

Effect Size

between schools. The study found also that the effects of some EAs changed dramatically after the effects of school context had been removed.

The analysis included both private and state-funded schools. For some purposes a comparison of EAs that excluded private schools would be preferable. The problem is that private schools to some extent 'cream' the most able pupils from the state sector (Echols *et al.*, 1990). Therefore, EAs with private schools are at a disadvantage in a comparison of EA performance that excludes private schools.

Although the model includes control for pupils' background characteristics, the estimates of school effects may be somewhat biased because the control measures do not capture all of the variables associated with attendance at a particular school. The estimates of EA effects shown by Figure 10-1 include the cumulative effects of both primary and secondary schooling. To isolate the effects of secondary schooling, a measure of entry-level achievement (taken at the end of P7 or the beginning of S1) is required. If data on pupils' entry-level achievement had been available for this analysis, the estimates of Type A effects for most EAs would likely have been smaller.

The differences between the best- and worst-performing EAs in this analysis are large in substantive terms; however, most of the variation in pupil performance is between pupils within schools, and between schools within EAs. Therefore, an analysis that attempted to relate EA effectiveness to specific policy variables, such as per-pupil expenditures, would lack the necessary controls and statistical power to accurately estimate the relationships. This kind of question requires either a 'true' experiment in which schools are randomly assigned to different treatment conditions, or a longitudinal design whereby changes in the effectiveness of each EA are related to changes in EA policies. These types of designs are discussed later in this chapter.

Example II: The Effects of Ability Grouping on the Ethnic Achievement Gap in Israeli Elementary Schools

A major concern of Israeli educators is the wide achievement gap between Jews of European and North American extraction (Ashkenazi) and Jews from Asian, Middle Eastern, or African origins (Sephardi) (Peleg and Adler, 1977). Some of the disparity may stem from the extent to which these groups are segregated in the schooling system (Yogev, 1981). The two groups are segregated not only between schools, but also between classes within schools, because some schools assign pupils to classes on the basis of their ability.

Chen and I used a two-level model to examine the effects of ability grouping on pupils' arithmetic and verbal proficiency in twenty-four elementary schools serving an industrial city in Israel (Willms and Chen, 1989). The pupil-level model in our study included measures of minority status, sex, SES, and pretest scores.[2] The school-level model included three variables: school sector (public or religious), average levels of grade 4 achievement, and a measure of the extent of between-class segregation. These variables were included in models that attempted to explain variation amongst schools in background-adjusted school means, and variation amongst schools in the ethnic achievement gap. Our results addressed each of the four questions set out at the beginning of this chapter.

To what extent do schools vary in their outcomes? The outcome scores were standardized to have a mean of zero and a standard deviation of one. Thus the results were expressed as 'effect sizes'. There were statistically significant differences between schools in their achievement test scores in both arithmetic and verbal proficiency. The variance in arithmetic was greatest: .1086. The range in adjusted achievement levels for the twenty-four schools, after adjusting for sampling error, was −.48 to .56. This suggests that a pupil who was of average SES and had average grade 4 test scores, would score more than one full standard deviation higher if he or she attended the top-performing school instead of the lowest-performing school. One full standard deviation is a substantial advantage; it is enough to alter a child's position from the 31st to the 69th percentile. The range in school effects was smaller for verbal proficiency — only about three-fifths of a standard deviation.

To what extent do outcomes vary for pupils of differing status? The study reported a significant achievement gap between Sephardi and Ashkenazi pupils, even with SES and grade 4 achievement in the model. The average gap within schools was about 12 per cent of a standard deviation in arithmetic, and about 15 per cent in verbal proficiency, favouring Ashkenazi pupils. The study found also that the gap varied significantly amongst schools: in three schools the achievement gap in arithmetic slightly favoured Sephardi pupils, and in three other schools the gap exceeded one-quarter of a standard deviation. The achievement gap in verbal proficiency varied significantly amongst schools, but the variance was small in substantive terms.

What school policies and practices improve levels of schooling outcomes? The analysis examined the effects of three school-level variables on the background-adjusted mean scores in arithmetic and verbal proficiency. (The multilevel model for this analysis is similar to that represented by Equations 3, 8, 9, and 10 in the Technical Appendix.) The estimated effects for school sector, mean pretest scores (a proxy for school context), and between-class segregation were not statistically significant.

---

[2] Our study could be classified as a longitudinal study because the data included pretest scores. However, I included it in this section because the approach to analysis is the same as that of the cross-sectional design. Throughout the book I reserve the term 'longitudinal' for growth studies where pupils' scores were measured on three or more occasions, or studies where the interest is in examining the effects of school-level measures collected on two or more occasions.

What school policies and practices reduce inequalities in outcomes between high- and low-status groups? The multilevel model also included terms representing the relationships between the ethnic achievement gap and the three school-level variables. The level of between-class segregation was significantly related to the size of the achievement gap between Sephardi and Ashkenazi pupils, but school sector and mean pretest scores were not significantly related to the ethnic achievement gap. The effect of between-class segregation was large and statistically significant for arithmetic, but for verbal proficiency it was not statistically significant. The findings suggest that schools that segregate their pupils between classes may have larger discrepancies between ethnic groups in their achievement.

One of the disappointing aspects of the study is that the tests of hypotheses about the effects of the school-level variables on the background-adjusted mean levels of achievement, or on the ethnic achievement gaps, were not very powerful. Thus the school-level variables may have had significant effects, but the quasi-experiment was not sensitive enough to detect them. The power of tests of hypotheses about school-level variables depends mainly on the number of schools, not the number of pupils. Our study examined only twenty-four schools and thus was not very powerful.

Cross-sectional Designs with Random Assignment

When researchers observe a relationship between two variables, say A and B, they want to know whether there is a *causal* relationship between them; that is, 'Does A cause B?'. For example, suppose monitoring data showed that pupils who received reading instruction based on a whole language approach outperformed those who received traditional instruction. Can we presume whole language causes better achievement scores? Perhaps whole language programs were implemented only in high-SES schools. The validity of the findings would be threatened by selection bias. Or maybe the most enthusiastic and energetic teachers in the district opted to undertake training in the new method, and once trained, their interest in developing children's reading ability inspired them to spend more time on reading than teachers using traditional approaches. The effects of whole language would then be 'confounded' with better teaching and time spent on instruction. The purpose of random assignment is to ensure that groups are probabilistically equivalent. The use of random assignment, combined with efforts to ensure that the treatment and outcomes mean what they are intended to mean, greatly enhances the validity of a researcher's claim of a causal relationship.

The purpose of research design is to enhance a researcher's ability to make causal inferences. In the example about the effects of whole language *versus* traditional instruction, a quasi-experimental design is inadequate because the comparison of test scores for the two groups probably suffers from selection bias. The researcher could strengthen the design by collecting measures of pupil intake (e.g., sex, SES, race, and ethnicity), teachers' attitudes, and time on instruction, and then applying the regression techniques described in the previous section. A dummy variable denoting whole language *versus* traditional would be added to the school-level model (Equations 8, 9, and 10 in the Technical Appendix). The estimate of the regression coefficient for this variable would be an estimate of the treatment effect. The problem with the quasi-experimental design, however, is that the model may not include all of the factors relevant to selection into whole language programs. If the model were incorrectly specified, the results would still be biased.

A much stronger design would entail the random assignment of some schools to whole language programs, leaving the remaining schools to continue with traditional programs. Random assignment of schools to whole language and traditional programs would provide control for *all* of the factors relevant to selection, because on average factors such as pupil ability and SES would be distributed equally in the two groups. However, even with random assignment, the two groups might differ initially simply because of sampling variation (i.e., 'luck of the draw'). The likelihood that the groups are unequal decreases as sample size increases. Thus another way to strengthen the design is to increase the number of schools and pupils participating in the experiment.

The design could be strengthened also by controlling for some of the selection factors in conjunction with random assignment. One way to do this is to 'block' the schools into sets, such that the schools in each set are similar in terms of variables related to progress in reading. For example, twenty schools might be blocked into five sets of four schools according to their mean SES and mean reading scores. Random assignment to the whole language and traditional groups would then be done within each set. This procedure dramatically increases the likelihood that the resulting groups are comparable at the outset of the experiment. Another way to control for selection factors is to measure them directly, and use statistical control in the same manner as in a design without random assignment. In this example, pupils' initial reading ability would be an important control variable.

Although random assignment controls for selection factors, there can be other factors confounding a causal interpretation. Sometimes there are operations that are closely associated with the treatment, but not really a part of it. The 'Hawthorne effect' in industrial relations research is an example: the validity of the inference that better illumination improved workers' performance was threatened by the possibility that workers were actually responding to increased supervision or to the novelty of being studied. In the example pertaining to reading methods, teachers' training in whole language might be associated with greater enthusiasm for teaching. If this attitudinal component were short-lived, one would not want it included as part of the estimated treatment effect. Similarly, one program might have markedly better teaching materials. If so, a rival interpretation would be that the use of the materials affected reading performance more than the instructional approach *per se*. Confounding can be associated also with the outcome measures. If they measure something other than what they purport to measure, or are dominated by irrelevant factors, the validity of causal inferences is threatened.

Cook and Campbell (1979) refer to these concerns as threats to *construct validity*. They suggest that such threats can be ameliorated by careful definition and explication of the constructs of interest, and through subsidiary analyses that examine the extent to which the independent and dependent measures represent the intended constructs.

There have been few true experiments of the effects of large-scale educational interventions, because most often political considerations override the desire for valid and reliable assessment. This does not mean they are impossible, particularly at the district or EA level. Random assignment would be possible, for example, to address a number of questions concerning classroom practices, curriculum innovations, teaching strategies, or special programs. Random assignment could involve the random assignment of either pupils, classrooms or schools to treatment groups.

Example III: The Tennessee Study of Class Size (Finn and Achilles, 1990)

The State of Tennessee funded a major longitudinal study of the effects of class size on achievement, self-concept, and academic motivation for pupils in kindergarten through grade 3 (Achilles, Bain, Bellott, Folger, Johnston, and Lintz, 1988; Finn and Achilles, 1990). The study is important because it is one of the few 'true experiments' of the benefits of reduction in class size. The sample comprised seventy-six elementary schools that were large enough to have at least three kindergarten classes, and were situated in districts willing to participate. The state covered costs of extra teachers and aides required for the experiment. Pupils entering kindergarten were assigned at random to one of three types of classes: small (thirteen–seventeen pupils), regular (twenty-two–twenty-five pupils), and regular with a teacher aide. Every class was to remain as the same type during the four years of the study. Teachers were also assigned at random to one of three class types. This design controls for the differential selection of pupils and teachers that would threaten the validity of an observed relationship between class size and schooling outcomes in a non-randomized experiment.

The researchers considered threats to construct validity. In particular, they paid attention to the construct of 'class size', making sure that discrepancies between the number registered and the number attending were negligible. They employed a range of outcome measures, including both standardized and curriculum-referenced achievement tests. They told schools not to make any significant operational changes, and did not offer teachers any special training relevant to their experimental setting.

The decision to randomly assign pupils to classes within schools meant that school effects were not confounded with the effects of class size. There was a tradeoff, however: the validity of their findings may have been threatened by such factors as compensatory rivalry or 'resentful demoralization' (Cook and Campbell, 1979, pp. 54–55). Teachers receiving the least desirable setting (regular class size) may not have given their best to the job, or conversely, tried to compete with teachers in the more advantaged settings. Parents may also have confounded results. In fact, the researchers found that parents had some concerns which required the reassignment of about half of the regular-class pupils to teacher-aide classes, and *vice-versa*. As the authors pointed out, the intake composition of regular and teacher-aide classes may have been confounded with the effects of class type.

Cross-sectional analyses of the grade 1 results found large and statistically significant effects of class size on academic achievement: pupils attending smaller classes had achievement scores that were about 25 per cent of a standard deviation higher than pupils attending regular classes or regular classes with aides. The study also examined whether the effects of reduced class sizes differed for white and minority pupils. The study reported a large, statistically significant minority-status-by-class-size interaction: the effect sizes for minority pupils ranged from 16 to 35 per cent of a standard deviation across the achievement tests, whereas for whites it ranged from 9 to 22 per cent of a standard deviation. The study found no statistically significant effects of class size on self-concept or academic motivation. The authors also examined the growth in achievement for the subset of pupils that had attended both kindergarten and grade 1 in project schools. The longitudinal results generally supported the cross-sectional findings.

Longitudinal Designs with Repeated Measures on Schools

Chapter 4 presented definitions of Type A and Type B school effects, and discussed the data requirements for their accurate estimation. After a monitoring system has been in place for a few years, each schools' Type A and B effects for a particular outcome can be estimated separately for successive cohorts of pupils. One can examine the trend, either positive or negative, of each school's effects over time. The logic of the longitudinal design with repeated measures on schools is to determine whether schools' trends in performance are related to changes in some policy variable, or to the presence or absence of some intervention. In other words, the researcher asks whether changes in school performance are related to changes in school policy. The design is powerful because, in essence, each school serves as its own control.

Raudenbush and I describe a hierarchical linear model (HLM) that can be used for analyzing this kind of longitudinal data, and provide an example based on data describing Fife's schools in 1980 and 1984 (Willms and Raudenbush, 1989). The model provides a means for estimating each school's trend, with adjustment for measurement and sampling error. Estimates of school effects based on longitudinal data are more reliable than estimates based on cross-sectional data.

Example IV. The Stability of School Effects in Fife Regional Education Authority

Figure 10-2 displays the estimates of school effects for our study of Fife's secondary schools. The first set of lines shows estimates of Type

Figure 10-2   Pre–post estimates of school effects for three different models

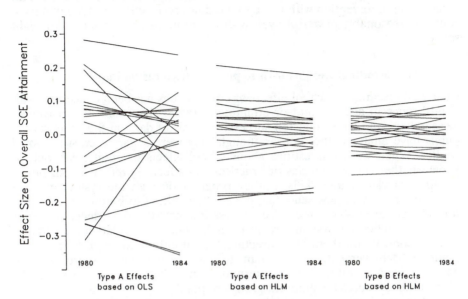

A effects based on separate analyses of each cross-sectional data set (1980 and 1984) using conventional regression techniques (Ordinary Least Squares). The estimates of effects were based on a model that included pupil-level controls for P7 verbal reasoning quotients, sex, father's occupation, and number of siblings. The second set shows estimates based on the HLM longitudinal model, using the same set of controls for pupils' background characteristics. The HLM results present a more accurate and stable picture of each school's effect. The third set are HLM estimates of Type B effects, which are smaller than the Type A effects for most schools.

The analysis also examined whether the schools' trends in adjusted performance, which are shown by the slopes of the lines in the latter two sets of Figure 10-2, were related to changes in the schools' mean SES between 1980 and 1984. During this period the authority made an effort to reduce differences between schools in their average SES. The analysis showed that changes in school performance were related to changes in school mean SES. The results suggest that as a result of the authority's policies, variation between pupils in their examination performance was reduced.

With monitoring data collected on an annual basis, a more powerful design is possible by employing data for three or more time points. The design described by Willms and Raudenbush (1989) allows for this possibility. After a trend has been established for a set of schools, one could introduce an intervention in some of the district schools. The design provides a powerful test of the effects of the intervention because it compares each school's effects with its own baseline data, and compares the average effect of schools that received the intervention with those that did not receive it. This type of design could be reasonably powerful even with a sample of only about six or eight schools.

Longitudinal Designs with Repeated Measures on Pupils

Nearly all research on school effects or equity issues has been concerned with pupils' *status* in achievement or attainment, rather than their *rate of growth*. Researchers who have collected successive waves of data on the same sets of pupils have analyzed the data as though they were separate cross-sectional studies. When we ask questions about school effects or equity, we want to know whether certain policies or practices can affect the *rate* at which pupils acquire knowledge and skills as they progress through the system; we are interested mainly in how schooling *per se* affects the distribution of outcomes for different groups of pupils. We are less interested in the effects of factors outside the schooling system, except to understand their relative importance, and to control for them. By directing our attention to pupils' growth in academic achievement, rather than to their achievement score on one occasion, we are better able to determine how policy and practice affect the distribution of scores for different groups of pupils.

A longitudinal design with repeated measures on pupils can best be accomplished when data have been collected on the same set of pupils on at least three occasions. The multilevel model includes a separate *within-pupil* model describing the relationship between pupils' scores and time. The within-pupil model specifies a separate regression for each pupil, which is simply the line through a child's outcome scores plotted against time. The intercept of the line is their 'initial status'; the slope is their 'rate of growth'. The 'initial status' and 'rate of growth' become the dependent variables in the next level of the model. The two higher levels of the multilevel model — between-pupils-within-schools and between-schools — are identical to the cross-sectional model described above (see Equations 3, 8, 9, and 10 in the Technical Appendix). The logic of the design is similar to that of the cross-sectional design, except that the interest is primarily in pupils' rates of growth.

The chief advantage of this design is that selection bias stemming from initial differences between pupils is less of a threat. In the same way that a pretest serves to control for selection differences between groups in a pretest-posttest design, growth rates control for initial differences in achievement or attainment. Selection bias at the pupil-level is therefore less of a threat. The validity of quasi-experimental designs which employ growth measures as the outcome can be threatened by other pupil-level intake factors, such as SES or initial ability, but to a large extent this threat is minimized. Shim (1991) found, for example, that without data on initial ability, estimates of Type A school effects for a sample of thirty-two elementary schools were substantially biased. However, the inclusion of data on initial ability had a negligible effect on estimates of Type A effects based on growth scores.

Another advantage of growth scores is that they allow the researcher to determine whether variation in pupils' achievement scores is changing over time. If the variation increases as pupils proceed through school, the growth pattern is called 'fan spread'; if it decreases it is called 'fan close' (Bryk, 1980). An examination of growth patterns for different groups provides a means to examine differences in distributions at different stages of their schooling careers. The programs used for estimating multilevel models provide estimates of the correlations between initial status and rates of growth. Positive correlations between initial status and growth indicate 'fan-spread' growth; negative correlations indicate 'fan-close' growth. Unbiased estimates of these correlations require at least three time points. Estimates of growth rates based on two time points — difference scores — are unbiased, but estimates of their correlation with initial status are biased because of measurement error (Rogosa, Brandt, and Zimowski, 1982). In many educational studies it is common to see a negative correlation between initial status and growth, suggesting a fan-close growth pattern, even though the true underlying correlation is positive (e.g., Willms, 1985). This is an important point with regard to the use of performance indicators for addressing questions about equity. Because of measurement error, growth measures based on only two time points can suggest that those with low initial scores are making better progress than those with high initial scores. Difference scores would therefore incorrectly favour low-status groups, and under-estimate the extent of inequality between groups.

Example V: Growth in Mathematics Achievement (Willms and Jacobsen, 1990).

A simple model for pupils' growth in mathematics is illustrated with Figure 10-3 and Table 10-1, which are based on earlier work that examined sex differences in mathematics growth (Willms and Jacobsen, 1990). The data were collected from a Canadian school district's records of pupils' scores on the Canadian Test of Basic Skills (CTBS) (King, 1982), the Canadian Cognitive Abilities Test (CCAT) (Thorndike and Hagan, 1982), and other data that were part of its performance indicator system. The CTBS is a modified version of the Iowa Test of Basic Skills designed for the 'continuous and comprehensive measurement of growth in fundamental skills'; the CCAT is a test of general cognitive abilities with verbal and non-verbal components. Our sample included all pupils born in 1974 who were tested on both the CTBS and CCAT in grade 3, and tested on at least two occasions thereafter between grades 4 and 7. Also, selected pupils had completed the grade 6 CTBS vocabulary subtest. The achieved sample included 469 pupils.

Figure 10-3 shows the growth scores on the mathematics concepts test for a random subsample of fifty pupils. The school year in Canada is ten months long, and pupils were tested in May of each year. At the end of grade 3, therefore, they had completed thirty-nine months of schooling, including kindergarten. Time is coded in months of schooling, and centred on thirty-nine; thus, estimated intercepts of the within pupil regressions ($\hat{\pi}_{0i}$ in Equation 11 of the Technical Appendix)

Figure 10-3   Growth scores on the CTBS subtest of mathematical concepts

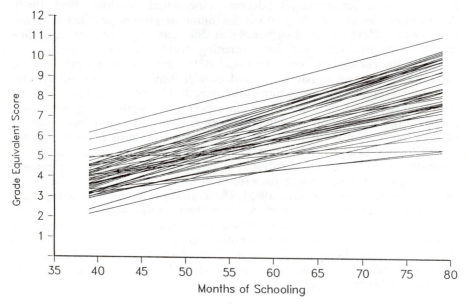

refer to pupils' status at the end of grade 3. Estimates of rates of growth ($\hat{\pi}_{1i}$ in Equation 11 of the Technical Appendix) are in units of months per month (or years per year) of schooling. A child proceeding in line with national norms would be expected to grow at a rate of 1.00.

The growth pattern displayed by Figure 10-3 suggests there is wide variation in pupils' scores at the end of grade 3: excluding a few outliers, the range extends from grade equivalent scores of 3.0 to 5.0. This variation increases as the pupils proceed through the intermediate years. By the end of grade 7, the range encompasses about four grade levels. Also, it appears that pupils generally maintain their initial position in the distribution.

Table 10-1 shows the results of the two-level growth model fitted separately for males and females to the data for each of the three subtests. The first two rows show, respectively, the estimates of the average status on these tests at the end of grade 3 and the average rates of growth between grades 3 and 7. [These are β_{00} and β_{01} (sample averages of π_{0i} and π_{1i}) in Equations 12 and 13 of the Technical Appendix.] The standard errors of these estimates are shown also. The estimates suggest that sex differences were small at the end of grade 3 across all three domains of mathematics skills, and that rates of growth were comparable on the concepts and problem-solving subtests. On the computation subtest, however, females had a substantially faster rate of growth than males: 1.065 compared with .999.

The bottom portion of the table shows estimates of the observed and 'true' variance in pupils' initial status and rates of growth, and

Table 10-1 HLM Results for CTBS Mathematics Tests: Grade 3 Status and Rate of Growth

| | Computation | | | | Concepts | | | | Problem-solving | | | |
| | Females | | Males | | Females | | Males | | Females | | Males | |
	Effect	(SE)	Effect	(SE)	Effect	(SE)	Effect	(SE)	Effect	(SE)	Effect	(SE)
Average within-student equation												
Grade 3 status	40.290**	(.535)	40.261**	(.514)	40.177**	(.516)	40.651**	(.521)	39.559**	(.590)	39.320**	(.578)
Rate of growth	1.065**	(.017)	.999**	(.018)	1.109**	(.018)	1.121**	(.019)	.939**	(.015)	.953**	(.017)
Estimated variance components (Random effects)	Estimate	(X^2)	Estimate	(X^2)	Estimate	(X^2)	Estimate	(X^2)	Estimate	(X^2)	Estimate	(X^2)
Observed parameter variance												
Grade 3 status	65.109		64.449		60.598		66.003		79.215		81.160	
Rate of growth	.068		.079		.072		.092		.056		.071	
True parameter variance												
Grade 3 status	29.364**	(396.3)	30.033**	(443.9)	30.299**	(439.2)	31.880**	(464.6)	49.826**	(610.9)	48.858**	(607.7)
Rate of growth	.013**	(268.3)	.021**	(329.0)	.026**	(339.9)	.034**	(389.4)	.011**	(283.2)	.016**	(319.1)
Reliability of estimates												
Grade 3 status	.451		.466		.500		.483		.629		.602	
Rate of growth	.188		.261		.355		.373		.189		.232	
Correlation between grade 3 Status and Growth	.793		.620		.838		.807		.407		.309	

Note: The degrees of freedom for the X² tests are 226 for females and 241 for males.
  ** Significant at the .01 level.

estimates of the reliability with which these could be determined. Reliability estimates are the ratio of true to observed parameter variance (Raudenbush and Bryk, 1986). The relatively low estimates of the reliability of grade 3 (initial status) scores are an artifact of the way the data were scaled. When the test measures were centred on fifty-nine instead of thirty-nine, the estimates of reliability were in fact higher than the reported estimates of (split-half) reliability for these subtests.[3]

Reliabilities of the growth rates also seem disappointingly low; they range from .19 to .37. But 'low reliability does not necessarily mean lack of precision' (Rogosa *et al.*, 1982, p. 744). Estimates of pupil growth might be very precise, but pupils might be growing at more or less the same rate. The reliability of growth scores would then be low, because reliability of a set of scores is simply the ratio of the variance in true scores to the variance in observed scores for the particular sample (see Willett, 1988).

The results show considerable sex differences in growth rates: males varied in their growth rates more than females. This means there were more males with very high growth rates and more males with very low growth rates. Given similar relationships between initial status and rates of growth, these results suggest that males spread out more in their scores as they progress through the intermediate grades. Because sex differences are small at the end of grade 3, the consequence of differential growth rates is that in the later grades males dominate the upper and lower ends of the distribution.

The correlations between initial status and rate of growth ranged from .31 to .84, indicating considerable fan-spread growth. Pupils who had higher scores at the end of grade 3 tended to make bigger gains between then and the end of grade 7. This tendency was particularly pronounced for the concepts test. For these data, the correlation between difference scores (grade 7 minus grade 3 scores) and grade 3 scores ranged from −.11 to −.24, even though the unbiased estimates provided by the multilevel model were large and positive. This demonstrates the point pertaining to the use of performance indicators for addressing questions about equity. If difference scores had been used as measures of growth, the findings would have suggested that

---

[3] The estimates of observed parameter variance in initial status are comparable to estimates of the observed variance in grade 3 test scores (which were approximately 61 for computation and concepts, and 84 for problem-solving). Estimates of reliability for initial status (.45 to .63) are lower than the reported split-half reliabilities of these tests, which ranged from .79 to .87 across grades 3 through 7. This is because the data were centred such that $(Time)_{it}$ was zero at the first testing occasion (see Equation 11 in the Technical Appendix). Estimates of status at the extremes of the data are less reliable in HLM regressions, as they are with OLS regression. When $(Time)_{it}$ was centred on fifty-nine months instead of thirty-nine months, such that the initial status was an estimate of status at the end of grade 5, the reliabilities were considerably higher; in fact, slightly higher than reported split-half reliabilities.

Table 10-2 HLM Results for CTBS Mathematics Tests: Models Explaining Variation between Pupils in their Grade 3 Status and Rates of Growth

	Computation				Concepts				Problem-solving			
	Females		Males		Females		Males		Females		Males	
	Effect	(SE)	Effect	(SE)	Effect	(SE)	Effect	(SE)	Effect	(SE)	Effect	(SE)
Average within-student equation												
Grade 3 status	39.368**	(.463)	39.698***	(.447)	38.925**	(.374)	39.876**	(.385)	38.231**	(.433)	38.584**	(.433)
Rate of growth	1.052**	(.018)	.969**	(.018)	1.072**	(.018)	1.083**	(.019)	.920**	(.016)	.924**	(.016)
Effects of between-student covariates on grade 3 status												
Ability (CCAT)	.224**	(.042)	.196**	(.035)	.314**	(.033)	.289**	(.030)	.337**	(.038)	.251**	(.055)
Vocabulary	.277***	(.060)	.280**	(.061)	.343**	(.046)	.388**	(.050)	.354**	(.052)	.491**	(.055)
Age			.309**	(.125)								
Effects of between-student covariates on rates of growth												
Ability (CCAT)	.001	(.001)	.001	(.001)	.004**	(.001)	.005**	(.001)	.002	(.001)	.001	(.001)
Vocabulary	.022**	(.006)	.029**	(.006)	.037***	(.006)	.029**	(.006)	.022**	(.005)	.028**	(.005)
Age			.012**	(.005)			.013**	(.004)			.013**	(.001)
R^2: Percentage of parameter variance explained												
Grade 3 status	60.1		61.0		93.8		91.8		76.9		75.1	
Rate of growth	—		39.5		7.6		26.3		4.2		60.8	

* Significant at the .05 level.
** Significant at the .01 level.

pupils with low initial scores were progressing faster than those with high initial scores, which is incorrect. Estimates of the extent of inequality between groups would have been negatively biased.

Control for Pupil-Level Factors Table 10-2 shows estimates of a two-level growth model with three pupil-level control variables: CCAT, vocabulary, and age-at-entry. Grade 3 vocabulary scores were used in the model to explain variation in initial status, and the difference between grade 6 and grade 3 vocabulary scores were used to explain rate of mathematics growth. Age-at-entry was coded in unit increments from −5.5 to 5.5, such that those who were young for the cohort (e.g., birthdates in November and December) received negative values, and those who were old for the cohort received positive values. The covariates were centred on values which I refer to as a 'typical' child: a child with a CCAT score of 100, a vocabulary score of 3.9 at the end of grade 3, vocabulary growth of three years between grade 3 and grade 6, and an age-at-entry score of zero (neither old or young for the grade).

As one might expect, children with above average CCAT and vocabulary scores had higher levels of initial status, and pupils who showed greater improvement in their vocabulary scores between grades 3 and 6 tended to have higher rates of growth. CCAT was significantly related to growth rates for the concepts subtest, but not for the other two. Age-at-entry was a statistically significant predictor of grade 3 computation scores for males, and of growth rates on all three subtests for males. It was not a statistically significant predictor of females' initial status or rate of growth (see Willms and Jacobsen, 1990, for a description of other models tested.)

The analysis demonstrates the power of multilevel methods for indicator data. The top row of Table 2 shows estimates of the expected score at the end of grade 3 of a 'typical' child attending a school in this district. These estimates are slightly lower than those in Table 1 because they include adjustment for vocabulary scores, which were above national norms in this district. Even with this downward adjustment, the adjusted estimates of grade 3 mathematics scores for this district were within one month of national norms. (Expected score of a typical child was thirty-nine months at the time of testing). Growth rates, however, varied across the three subtests: the district had above-average rates of learning new mathematical concepts (approximately 1.08 years of growth per school year), average rates of growth in computation skills (approximately 1.01 years per school year), and below-average rates of growth in problem-solving (approximately 0.92 years per school year).

There were no significant sex differences in concepts or problem-solving, but females acquired computation skills at a faster rate than did males (1.05 years per school year compared with .97). These differences are comparable to those in Table 10-1, which suggests that differing levels of cognitive ability or rates of vocabulary development do not account for sex differences in rate of growth on the computation subtest.

A Three-Level Model for Assessing Differences Amongst Schools

The two-level growth model described above can be extended to a three-level model with schools or classrooms as the third level (see Raudenbush and Bryk, 1988). The interest is in whether school policies and practices are significantly related to rates of growth in certain domains. For the example describing growth in mathematics, we were unable to obtain school-level data describing policies and practices. Our findings did suggest, however, that schools varied significantly in their initial statuses and rates of growth, but sex differences did not vary significantly across schools, nor did the relationships between achievement and CCAT (see Willms and Jacobsen, 1990, Table 4). Variation between schools in their average levels of initial status and in their rates of growth was significantly related to the average CCAT of the school.

In a review of research on sex differences in mathematics, Fennema (1981) argued that:

> [t]he most important place to look to see if change is taking place is in the schools themselves ... some schools have been remarkably successful in helping females learn mathematics and feel good about themselves as learners of mathematics. Other schools have not. (p. 93)

The beauty of a multilevel approach is that it allows the researcher to test propositions such as these. The model provides estimates of the differences between different groups of pupils in their outcomes for each school (or classroom); it provides an estimate of the variance of those differences across schools, and a test of the statistical significance of that variance. If there is significant variation, one can test whether specific school policies or practices explain it. Thus multilevel modelling provides a means for testing whether variables at one level of the system are significantly related to the achievement gap between different groups of pupils.

A Research Program for the First Three Years

The analyses suggested below correspond with the time line presented at the end of Chapter 8. I have not specified particular grade levels because these would vary depending on a district's priorities.

End of Year One
- Conduct analyses that establish generalizability: compare estimates of mean SES and cognitive ability for schools and the district to state or national norms.
- Estimate Type A and Type B school effects using cross-sectional data (Examples I and II).
- Estimate the effects of school policies and practices based on cross-sectional data (Example II).
- Examine the extent of between and within-school segregation (see Chapter 9).

End of Year Two
- Estimate the stability of school effects using the first two years of data (Example IV).
- Estimate the effects of changes in policies and practices on changes in school performance (Example IV).
- Plan interventions and design of an experiment employing random assignment of schools (Example III).

End of Year Three
- Estimate Type A and Type B effects based on analyses of pupil growth (Example V).
- Implement study employing random assignment (Example III).
- Estimate stability of school effects based on three time points.

Chapter 11

Conclusions

Executive Summary

In 1990, President Bush announced the Government's national goals for education in the nineties. One of these goals stated:

> By the year 2000, American students will leave grades four, eight, and twelve having demonstrated competency in challenging subject matter including English, mathematics, science, history, and geography; and every school in America will ensure that all students learn to use their minds well, so that they may be prepared for responsible citizenship, further learning, and productive employment in our modern economy. (See Walker, 1990, p. 16)

A 'national report card' is currently being produced to monitor progress towards these goals (Lewis, 1991; Pipho, 1991), Nearly every state has developed some form of monitoring system, as have many school districts and individual schools. Several other countries have developed or are in the process of developing national educational goals, national tests, and systems to monitor progress towards the national goals.

Some of the impetus for monitoring stemmed from a belief by legislators and policy-makers that taxpayers were dissatisfied with the nation's schools. Reports in the early 1980s on the condition of education in the US such as *A Nation at Risk* (National Commission on Excellence in Education, 1983) and *Making the Grade* (Twentieth Century Fund, 1983), suggested that the public was concerned about the quality of its schools and wanted school reform. Monitoring systems were to provide 'indicators' of the health of the educational system, and provide direction for school reform (Selden, 1988; Smith, 1988).

The Impetus for Monitoring and its Social and Political Context

Some administrators and educators view monitoring as a means to systematically introduce market mechanisms into education. The idea is that the estimation and publication of differences between schools in their test results will induce schools to achieve better results. This concept has been

143

embodied in recent legislation in the UK, which granted parents the statutory right to choose schools outside their catchment area, and required schools to publish their results on the national certificate examinations. The number of parents exercising their right to choose has been substantial in some areas, and as a result, some unpopular schools have become candidates for closure. Choice of schooling is not the only mechanism with which market forces are brought to bear on teachers and administrators. In some schooling systems, test results are used to make decisions about promotions, merit pay, or dismissals.

Data from monitoring systems can also provide useful information for teachers and administrators. In some states in the US, the goal of monitoring is to provide diagnostic information to teachers about which curricular objectives have been learned by a majority of pupils, and which topics require more attention. Monitoring data have been used also for determining how best to allocate resources at the federal, state, and district levels, and for assessing the impact of reforms initiated at each of these levels. Monitoring data are used to examine long-term trends in performance, and to estimate the extent of inequities between high- and low-status groups.

Many educators oppose monitoring. Their principal argument is that there is not an uncontested model of what constitutes effective teaching or an effective school, nor is there consensus about the goals of education. They feel monitoring is a means of steering education towards ends that are not justified or widely accepted by pupils, parents, and educators. The opponents to monitoring fear that once these means are institutionalized, critical dialogue about means and ends will be stifled. They also fear that monitoring restricts what is taught in schools to a narrow set of objectives covered by the tests. The result is a loss of teacher autonomy. Some teachers find monitoring unduly stressful on themselves and their pupils (Smith, 1991), and that it is too costly, especially in terms of displaced teaching time.

Even if one accepts monitoring as a worthwhile enterprise, there are many tensions inherent in its implementation. Concerns about accountability, teacher autonomy, and costs affect decisions about who designs the monitoring system, the kind of data to be collected, how the data are to be analyzed and reported, and who will have access to data and reports of findings. The kind of data collected is a contentious issue because the data useful to district- or state-level administrators generally are not useful to teachers, and *vice-versa*. The collection of monitoring data also creates tensions about whether findings will be used implicitly or explicitly to apply rewards or sanctions, or to apply political or psychological pressure. Questions about costs are also worrisome. Monitoring is expensive. Besides the direct costs of developing and administering a monitoring system, there are indirect costs associated with the time teachers and principals spend administering tests and questionnaires, and with the time pupils spend completing them. For a monitoring system to be successful, these considerations need to be taken into account.

The Input-Process-Output Model

Monitoring systems are based on a theory that schooling 'outputs', such as academic achievement, attitudes, and aspirations, are predominantly determined by pupil 'inputs', including sex, race, ability upon entering school, and family background, and by the many school-related 'processes' that determine a school's context and its inner workings. The goal of research in this area has been to estimate the effects of school-related factors on pupils' schooling outcomes by removing statistically the effects of pupil inputs. The progress of research in this vein has been slow, mainly because variation in pupils' outcomes between schools is small compared with the variation within schools, and because it is difficult to identify and measure most of the factors associated with schooling processes.

Monitoring systems can be classified into three types, according to their underlying assumptions about what motivates educational improvement (Richards, 1988). Compliance monitoring emphasizes schooling inputs, such as pupil-teacher ratio, teacher credentials, or size of the library. Administrators exact compliance to predetermined standards, based on the assumption that schools meeting the standards are providing a quality education. Diagnostic monitoring systems examine only schooling outcomes. Their goal is to determine whether specific aspects of the curriculum are being mastered by the majority of pupils. The assumption is that feedback to teachers about the academic strengths and weaknesses of their pupils will help them improve instruction and make better use of resources. Performance monitoring systems include measures of schooling inputs and outputs. The data are used to make comparisons between schools or districts in their outcomes, with adjustment for pupil inputs. The assumption is that inter-school or inter-district comparisons will stimulate market forces and motivate educators to provide a quality education.

Stronger models for monitoring schools can be achieved in at least three ways. One is to incorporate data on schooling processes. Some monitoring systems include measures of school processes, but usually they are not well explicated and are not incorporated into analyses aimed at determining why some schools produce better outcomes. Monitoring systems can be improved also by emphasizing pupil growth in achievement, rather than achievement at one particular time. Longitudinal analyses of growth provide a better estimate of the contribution to pupil learning that is associated with schooling *per se*, and provide a means to determine more accurately the effects of certain school policies and practices. The third way to improve monitoring results is to emphasize analyses that track each school's results over time. The goal of the analyses is to determine whether changes in school policy and practice are related to changes in schooling outcomes.

The Estimation of School Effects

The term 'school effect' is used in a number of ways. Some use it to mean the effect of a particular school policy or practice, such as the effect of reducing class size, or the effect of increasing teachers' salaries. The term is also used to refer to the difference between a school's average level of performance and some standard, after adjusting statistically for the intake characteristics of the school. Thus the 'school effect' is the effect associated with membership in a particular school instead of other schools. Sometimes researchers have used the term to refer to the variation between schools in their outcomes, or to the effect of attending school *versus* not attending school. I use the term to refer to the effect associated with attendance at a particular school, but distinguish between two types of school effects, one that includes the effects of school policies and practices as well as wider social and economic contextual factors, and one that includes only the effects of school policy and practice.

The estimation of school effects is based on the following model (see also Willms and Raudenbush, 1989):

Pupil's Outcome Score =
> the average score for all pupils in the schooling system (e.g., school district, region, country)
> + the effects of pupil background (e.g., pre-entry ability, SES, sex)
> + the effects of school policies and practices (e.g., school resources, organizational structures)
> + the effects of school characteristics (e.g., class size, per-pupil expenditures)
> + the effects of school composition (e.g., average SES of the school)
> + the effects of social and economic factors (e.g., local unemployment rate)
> + any unmeasured effects unique to the child's school
> + random error (e.g., error in measurement due to unreliability of the test).

A Type A school effect includes the effects of school policy and practices, the effects of school characteristics and composition, the effects of social and economic factors, and any unmeasured effects associated with the child's school. It excludes the effects of pupil background and random error. Thus it is the effect of attendance at a particular school net of pupil intake. Parents would be more interested in estimates of Type A effects, because they include all factors that might affect their child's performance, not just those that can be influenced by administrators and teachers.

A Type B school effect includes only the effects of school policies and practices, and unmeasured effects unique to the school. Teachers and administrators would be more interested in estimates of Type B effects because they address the question, 'How well does a school perform relative to other schools with similar compositions and social and economic contexts?' Type B effects include the effects of policy and practice, and exclude factors outside the control of school staff.

The distinction between Type A and Type B effects is important, because a number of research studies have shown that the composition of a school's intake has an effect on pupil outcomes over and above the effects associated with pupils' individual backgrounds. Also, factors outside the influence of the school, such as local employment opportunities, can affect schooling outcomes. If comparisons of Type A effects were used for accountability purposes, they would be unfair in that they would include factors beyond the control of teachers and administrators.

The estimation of school effects is far from being an exact science. The accuracy of estimates depends on the extent to which relevant factors have been included in the analysis, the reliability and validity of the input, process, and outcome measures, and the number of schools and pupils in the sample. Both types of estimate require pupil-level data; aggregate data produce biased estimates. Type B estimates, which would be the most useful for accountability purposes, have more stringent data requirements for their estimation than do Type A effects. The next three sections provide suggestions for the kind of data that might be included in a monitoring program.

Schooling Inputs

Measures of schooling inputs can serve several functions in a monitoring system. One is that they can act as control variables in the estimation of school effects. In most school districts, schools vary in the types of pupils entering them. Measures of pupil ability and prior academic achievement, and measures of socioeconomic status (SES), such as parental education and occupation, are related to most schooling outcomes. They can be used to make statistical adjustments for differences between schools in their intakes, and to increase the precision and statistical power of analyses aimed at determining the effects of particular school policies and practices. The input measures explain some of the variance in pupil outcomes, which makes it easier to determine whether particular policies and practices have an effect. Another function of input measures is to assess whether educational interventions have a differential impact on differing types of pupils. For example, a new approach to teaching mathematics may have a positive effect on the achievement of low-SES pupils, but a negative effect on the achievement of high-SES pupils. Input measures can be used to describe the extent of segregation between racial and ethnic groups in their allocation to classes and schools. Finally, input measures can be used to establish the generalizability of findings generated by monitoring systems.

When the goal of analysis is to estimate school effects or the effects of some school policy or practice, measures of prior performance are essential. Measures of family background, such as parental education and occupation, add little to the degree of statistical control. Amongst measures of prior performance, a pretest on the same measure to be used as the outcome measure has some advantages. Such pretests tend to have slightly better predictive power than other measures of prior performance, and enable the analyst to frame the questions in terms of pupil growth. Although measures of prior performance generally overshadow measures of SES and other pupil characteristics, the latter measures are important for the analysis of interactions, for use as descriptive measures, and for making inferences about generalizability.

Schooling Processes

Although researchers have found statistically significant differences between schools in their outcomes, they have made little progress in identifying the processes related to successful schooling. I use the term 'schooling processes' to describe the many factors that affect schooling outcomes, such as those associated with a school's context and setting, and the less tangible factors related to the inner workings or climate of a school. Identifying a key set of schooling processes is difficult. The literature on school effects offers some guidance, but many of the factors are complex and multifaceted, and have differing effects for different types of pupils and across levels of the schooling system. Factors describing school processes are also difficult to define and measure: their meaning depends in part on the level at which they are measured, and their measurement requires subjective interpretation and judgement.

To distil a set of key indicators of school process, I reviewed the last ten years of literature on schooling processes, relying heavily on the work of Anderson (1982, 1985), Oakes (1989), and Rosenholtz (1989a, 1989b). The most important constructs were classified by level of the schooling system, and by categories used by Tagiuri (1968) for depicting organizational climate. From the extensive list of constructs (see Figure 6-1), I used four criteria for selecting a key set of indicators:

- Which indicators provide a *balanced picture* of schooling processes across levels of the system, and across types of (Tagiuri) constructs?
- Which indicators facilitate self-examination and the process of school renewal?
- Which indicators are seen as tractable variables by school staff and administrators?
- Which indicators are easy and inexpensive to measure?

Based on these criteria, I recommend collecting data on the following aspects of schooling:

I **Ecology and Milieu Constructs** (variables describing the physical and material environment, characteristics of teachers and principals, and intake composition of the school)

II **Segregation** (measures of the extent to which pupils are separated according to social class, ability, academic achievement, gender, race, and ethnicity)

III **Disciplinary Climate** (the extent to which there is a clear set of rules, how rules are perceived and enforced, and the extent to which pupils comply with them)

IV **Academic Press** (the extent to which pupils, parents, and school staff value academic achievement, and hold high expectations for academic success)

V **Intended *versus* Enacted Curriculum** (the strength and intent of curriculum policy instruments, coverage of instructional topics)

VI **Pupil Attitudes**
Sense of efficacy *versus* futility (the extent to which pupils feel they have control over their school successes and failures, whether teachers care about their progress, and whether other pupils punish them if they do succeed)
Attitudes towards school (pupils' satisfaction with their schooling)

Quality of school life (pupils' general sense of well-being, quality of pupil-pupil and pupil-teacher relationships, academic behavior and life plans)

VII **Teacher Attitudes**

Sense of efficacy *versus* **futility** (teachers' confidence that they can affect pupil learning, and manage pupil behavior)

Commitment and morale (the extent to which teachers believe their work is meaningful, and the extent to which they accept organizational goals and values)

Working Conditions (autonomy in accomplishing school goals, opportunities for professional growth, type and frequency of evaluation, salaries, class size, time available for non-instructional activities, extent of collegial decision-making)

VIII **Instructional Leadership of Principals** (the extent to which principals: (a) set high standards and create incentives for pupil learning, and transmit the belief that all pupils can achieve at a high level; (b) set clearly-defined goals and priorities for pupil learning, and prescribe means to achieve them; (c) enhance teacher commitment by involving teachers in making decisions, by providing opportunities for teachers to improve their skills and by evaluating teachers consistently and fairly; and (d) minimize extraneous and disruptive influences that keep teachers from teaching and pupils from learning)

This list of schooling processes could be supplemented with two or three measures that were of particular interest to teachers and administrators in the district. To measure all of these constructs well, on an annual basis, would be costly. Costs could be reduced by measuring half of them one year and the remainder the following year, or by targeting different versions of the questionnaire for each grade level.

Schooling Outcomes

The most difficult issue pertaining to the measurement of schooling outcomes is the identification of school goals. Most monitoring systems limit the measurement of outcomes to achievement tests of basic skills in reading and mathematics. Yet nearly all schools see their mandate as more than teaching the basics; their goals generally include personal and social development, and vocational training. Schools vary in the relative emphasis they place on different types of goals, and in the emphasis they place on different academic subjects. Thus, monitoring systems that measure only a few aspects of academic achievement are likely to misrepresent the performance of some schools.

A related problem is whether monitoring systems emphasize excellence or equity. Schools vary also in their allocation of resources to different types of pupils. Some schools may do well at bringing all pupils up to a minimum standard, but not as well at helping their most talented pupils excel. Care

must be taken to ensure that indicators describe a range of levels of performance, and that analyses of data describe the distribution of scores in a school
or district, not just the average scores.

Two of the critical issues in selecting outcome measures for monitoring
purposes are their validity and reliability. Validity refers to whether a test
measures what it is supposed to measure, which is determined largely by
the purposes for which the test scores are to be used. Reliability refers to the
consistency of measurement — consistency over time, over different forms of
the test, and across raters. It is affected by the homogeneity of the group
being tested, the degree that the test is of suitable difficulty, the number of
items requiring subjective scoring, and the length of the test. Reliability also
depends on the level at which scores are used: a test can yield scores that are
reliable at the individual level but not the group level, or *vice versa*. The
choice of outcome measures must also consider the costs associated with test
construction, administration, scoring, and displaced teaching time.

Design of a District or Education Authority (EA) Monitoring System

Chapter 8 presents a design for a district or EA monitoring system. The purpose of the chapter is to provide some starting points for a district or EA that
is in the early stages of developing a monitoring system. There are several
features of the design which distinguish it from other district or EA monitoring systems:

- **The use of entire age cohorts rather than grade cohorts.** Age cohorts
  provide a more accurate means for assessing schools and the effects of
  interventions.
- **Measurement of personal, vocational, social, and academic outcomes.**
- **Measurement of pupil growth.** Estimates of the effects of schools on
  academic achievement are based, in part, on pupils' rates of growth,
  rather than on a cross-section of scores for one occasion. Although
  educational researchers strongly advocate the use of growth scores,
  few monitoring systems use them.
- **Estimates of school effects adjusted for family background.** Most
  monitoring systems compare schools without controlling for pupils'
  family backgrounds, or with crude techniques based on data
  aggregated to the school level. The proposed system entails the
  collection of individual-level data, which enable the use of the
  recently-developed multilevel modelling techniques. These techniques
  allow the researcher to more accurately take account of pupil background, and adjust for measurement and sampling error.
- **Measurement and analysis of data on school policies and processes.**
  The system will be capable not only of assessing how much schools
  vary in their performance, but also of addressing questions about why
  they vary. The analytical approach assesses how much of the variation
  in school performance is attributable to differences between schools
  in their policies and practices.
- **Complements monitoring efforts at higher and lower levels.** The

proposed district system uses data collected at higher levels of the system to provide a wider context for data collected at the district and school levels. The district system also enhances the information systems of individual schools.

Analyses for an Annual Report

Chapter 9 describes several types of analyses that are useful for summarizing and displaying indicator data. The chapter also shows how most of these analyses can be displayed graphically. I strived to include analyses that display distributions of scores, are easily interpreted, can be contextualized in terms of norms at higher levels, and are easy to compute and display. The analyses are relatively simple — they can be accomplished with most statistical software packages.

A Research Program Based on Performance Monitoring

Chapter 10 makes suggestions for the use of indicator data in an ongoing research program at the district level. The program strives to answer four questions that are basic to most educational research:

- To what extent do schools vary in their outcomes?
- To what extent do outcomes vary for pupils of differing status?
- What school policies and practices improve levels of schooling outcomes?
- What school policies and practices reduce inequalities in outcomes between high-and low-status groups?

The chapter presents four types of designs that could be used to address these questions: multilevel cross-sectional designs without random assignment, multi-level cross-sectional designs with random assignment, longitudinal designs with repeated measures on schools, and longitudinal designs with repeated measures on pupils. Examples are provided for each type of design. The chapter discusses the role that research design plays in being able to make causal statements about observed relationships. One of the chief advantages of ongoing monitoring programs is that they provide longitudinal data which enable researchers to examine the effects of particular policies and practices with much stronger designs than those used previously.

Towards the Authentic Assessment of Schools

If monitoring programs are to be successful, administrators must grapple with the tensions regarding accountability, reduction of the curriculum, and teacher autonomy. In the UK there has been widespread resistance to national testing and the associated efforts to make schools and teachers accountable. The resistance has come from teachers and their unions, from parents, and from EA administrators. The chief objection is that the UK Government has not made explicit how data will be analyzed and reported, or how the results will be used. In the US there is resistance to district- and state-level efforts to monitor schools. The professional journals are replete with articles criticizing what has been called 'high-stakes' testing (Madaus, 1988). The stakes are high because in some cases, pupils' performance on the tests is linked with teachers' salaries, merit increases, and employment. The pressure to raise scores has resulted in practices such as teaching to the test, coaching, and the dismissal of potentially low-achieving pupils on the day of the test. These and other practices 'pollute' the inferences made from test results (Haladyna, Nolen, and Haas, 1991).

Without the support of teachers and parents, monitoring efforts will probably have little utility, and their costs will not be justifiable. One reason is that most of the data on schooling inputs and processes must be collected with questionnaires completed by teachers and pupils. These data are essential for estimating school effects, and for most other kinds of analyses. Successful monitoring depends also on pupils' willingness to give their genuine effort on standardized tests. Yet in Canada and the US, standardized test results do not usually contribute substantially to pupils' grades. A series of surveys in the US indicated that pupils are disillusioned about the validity of standardized tests, are not motivated to excel on them, and sometimes use inappropriate test-taking strategies (Paris, Lawton, Turner, and Roth, 1991). If teachers and pupils do not see the value in monitoring, they can easily sabotage it, and without their cooperation, monitoring programs will be reduced to the administration of only a few outcome measures of questionable validity. Ironically, it is under these circumstances that educators' worst fears about monitoring are likely to be legitimate.

To alleviate the tensions concerning monitoring we could apply some of the principles of the authentic assessment of pupils to the assessment of schools. At the end of Chapter 2, I stressed the importance of teacher involvement in designing and implementing monitoring programs. Teacher involvement in monitoring can potentially enhance the autonomy of teachers. It can afford them the opportunity to construct tests and questionnaires that better represent what is taught and learned in school, and can yield the kind of information that informs classroom practice. Also, teachers are more likely to value information derived from a monitoring system designed by expert teachers. I contend that teacher involvement is a requisite condition for monitoring school performance. There are also some strategies that may increase the likelihood that monitoring efforts are successful. These are discussed below.

Locus of Control

As far as possible, the control of monitoring activities should reside at the school level. This principle applies to decisions concerning the kind of data collected, who has access to data, the types of analyses conducted, and the content and distribution of reports. Consortia of teachers from schools across a district could collectively set standards for their subject area, develop new forms of assessment, and appraise the work of pupils. Monitoring activities aimed at determining whether pupils have mastered certain aspects of the curriculum can easily be conducted at the school level. School staff can also conduct relevant analyses and report their findings.

The district's role in these efforts would be to offer technical assistance, and to provide the resources necessary for successful monitoring at the school level. The district could assist teachers in the construction of criterion-referenced tests and other forms of assessment. It could also provide assistance in conducting analyses and writing reports, and could enable teachers to participate in district research activities. For example, the district could sponsor workshops and conferences on new assessment procedures, fund sabbatical leaves for teachers to pursue research questions relevant to district needs, and establish university-school partnerships.

Ideally, district-level monitoring activities should support school-level monitoring activities, and *vice-versa*. For example, items from norm-referenced tests that were deemed relevant to the curriculum could be included as part of a school's assessment. District-level analyses of these 'thin' data would provide an external criterion against which local standards could be compared. Similarly, data on schooling processes could be collected and analyzed at the school level, but district-level aggregates of these data would provide a backdrop against which schools could place their own findings.

Intrinsic Validity

The intrinsic validity of indicators refers to whether they represent the qualities that educators and policy-makers want to influence, and whether improvements in policies and practices are reflected in better scores (Haertle, 1986). Indicators have low intrinsic validity if they encourage other, less desirable practices, such as restricting classroom instruction to topics covered by examinations. A critical test for the validity of a set of schooling indicators, then, is whether they measure those aspects of schooling we want to change, and whether scores are sensitive to the changes we make. The intrinsic validity of indicators is not embodied solely in the measures themselves; it entails the entire process of monitoring from data collection to analysis and reporting.

Frequently, monitoring activities have low intrinsic validity because those designing the system do not ask teachers and administrators what they want to know, what would serve as evidence, and how they might use the information. One administrator told me he disapproved of making comparisons between schools in their test scores because he could not decide whether extra district resources should be allocated to schools doing well on the tests, or to those doing poorly. Sproull and Zubrow (1981) found that although administrators made little use of test scores, most wanted to have them. Research on performance monitoring could examine what kind of information is useful to educators, and how they can use that information.

The criticisms of current monitoring efforts have provided some direction on how to increase the intrinsic validity of performance indicators. Educators want to extend evaluation beyond the testing of basic skills in reading and mathematics with standardized tests. They want alternative means of assessment that cover a broad array of schooling outcomes, including non-cognitive outcomes. They want diagnostic information about whether specific aspects of the curriculum are being mastered by the majority of pupils. They want indicators of schooling processes and information about equity issues. Analyses need to address whether new programs are having their intended effect, and whether certain school policies and practices improve schooling outcomes and reduce inequities. Educators want information they can use to demonstrate to the public that their schools are teaching their children well.

Authentic Forms of Assessment

One of the principles of authentic assessment of pupil learning is that it should describe the degree of learning in terms of external criteria, rather than norm-referenced criteria. Monitoring activities could apply this principle by emphasizing *criterion-related performance* for schools. Instead of emphasizing the relative ranking of schools on a few standardized tests, assessment could strive to present profiles of schools on a wide range of performance criteria. These could include a number of indicators of school process as well as pupil outcomes. For example, a report might state that:

- average daily attendance at classes for the year was 97.3 per cent;
- 92 per cent of the grade 8 pupils completed science projects requiring ...;
- 84 per cent of the pupils in the school achieved mastery on the level 6 computer literacy exam; or
- 34 per cent of the teachers successfully completed a three-week summer course on reading methods.

The list could be extensive covering several aspects of schooling processes, such as disciplinary climate, academic press, and pupil and teacher attitudes. Many of the criteria would vary across schools in a district, depending on the schools' goals, but some criteria would be common to all schools.

Authentic assessment for schools would also embrace alternate means of assessment. One approach would be to assemble cross-school review teams made up of teachers, principals, and subject-area specialists. The teams would conduct 'external reviews' of other schools in the district. Their reviews might entail observations of classroom instruction, critiques of teaching materials and textbooks, and interviews with pupils, parents, and teachers. The reviews would be conducted on a regular basis with the goal of providing formative feedback about the operation of the school. Similarly, teachers might conduct assessments of other teachers in their disciplines. Currently new forms of teacher assessment are being developed, such as the high-inference observation system used in Connecticut (see Haertle, 1991).

Accountability

One of the initial premises of the book was that if monitoring data were available, they would inevitably be used, either formally or informally, in decisions concerning accountability. Another premise was that monitoring data should be used in conjunction with data collected from discussions with staff and pupils, and through detailed observations of school and teacher practice. In British Columbia, the government's reform package of the 1990s requires schools to abolish norm-referenced testing at the primary level. This move was made partly in response to calls from the teachers' federation for a ban on norm-referenced testing at all levels. I contend the elimination of norm-referenced testing would be a mistake. Norm-referenced testing provides a means to ensure that assessments of schools are not unduly affected by variation in teachers' judgements, the history of a school, and parents' and pupils' expectations. Much of the criticism of norm-referenced testing pertains to their use at the individual level; however, it also has many uses at the school and district levels for which most of the criticisms do not apply. For example, norm-referenced testing is better suited than other approaches for evaluating the impact of district, state, and national reforms, and for assessing inequities in achievement.

This book has pointed out the many limitations of the technology for estimating school effects. But despite these limitations I would not call for a ban on comparisons of schools or districts. One reason is that there is considerable room to improve the standards with which monitoring data are collected, analyzed, and reported. The limitations of school comparisons lie more in their interpretation and use than in the technology used to obtain them. School comparisons can serve as an early warning system to identify schools that require attention. In this role they should be used in the same way that wide-range screening tests are used to identify individuals requiring further testing. For most purposes of accountability, school comparisons are inadequate by themselves. They need to be supplemented with other data based on observations of teaching and discussions with school staff. One district administrator likened reports of school test results to her children's report cards: 'I am not interested in rank-ordering my children, nor do I disown them if they are not doing well. But the report cards tell me the areas where more work is required'.

Concluding Remarks

At the outset I stated that I believed the benefits of monitoring can outweigh any negative consequences. We are in an era when there are new demands placed on teachers and principals to manage school affairs, adopt new teaching strategies, and institute school reforms. Yet at the same time they are being held accountable for their results under new terms. The recommendations in this book are offered in the hope that monitoring does not become an activity that divides district administrators and school staff. For some teachers and principals the book may serve to defend them against inappropriate monitoring practices. But I hope the book will also guide educators towards the development of better monitoring systems. The intention of assessment for administrators and teachers alike is to provide better opportunities for children to learn. I believe monitoring systems can provide corrective feedback and facilitate self-examination. They can enable us to examine questions about inequities between high- and low-status groups, and can induce debate about school policy and practice. Monitoring systems can contribute to our understanding about how schools work.

Technical Appendix

Multilevel Cross-Sectional Designs

The general multilevel cross-sectional design can be described with two sets of regression equations.[1] The first is a set of within-school equations, one for each school. Suppose, for example, we had an outcome measure of mathematics achievement, and two variables describing pupils' background: minority status (0 = non-minority, 1 = minority) and SES (measured on a continuous scale). The regression equation for each school would be given by:

$$(Mathematics)_i = \beta_0 + \beta_1 \, (Minority)_i + \beta_2 \, (SES)_i + \epsilon_i \qquad (1)$$

where $(Mathematics)_i$, $(Minority)_i$, and $(SES)_i$ are the scores for the ith pupil on those variables. β_0, β_1, β_2, and ϵ_i are parameters estimated from the data. β_0 is the intercept or 'constant'. β_1 is the minority effect; that is, the size of the achievement gap between non-minority and minority pupils. β_2 is the effect of SES, which represents the change in mathematics scores for each 1-point increase in SES. ϵ_i are the 'residual' or error terms associated with pupils' scores.

After estimating each of the parameters in equation 1, we could estimate an expected value for a pupil with a particular minority status and SES:

$$(\widehat{Mathematics})_0 = \hat{\beta}_0 + \hat{\beta}_1 \, (Minority)_0 + \hat{\beta}_2 \, (SES)_0 \qquad (2)$$

The 'hat' on the parameters denotes that they are estimates derived from the data. The subscript 'zero' (called 'not') indicates that we are considering a particular pupil with specific values of minority status and SES.

Usually the results can be more easily interpreted if the independent variables are rescaled by centring them on the sample means. In many applications, the sample means are estimates of the district, state, or national means (e.g., see Willms, 1987; Rumberger and Willms, 1991). For this

---

[1] See Raudenbush & Bryk (1986) for a more technical description. Raudenbush and Willms (1991) discuss the model in detail as it pertains to the estimation of school effects.

discussion, I presume the independent variables are centred on the district means (i.e., the district mean of each independent variable is subtracted from each pupil's score on that variable). With this scaling, $\hat{\beta}_0$ in equation 2 is the predicted value for an 'average' pupil (i.e., one with district average characteristics). The latter two terms in equation 2 are zero because $(Minority)_0$ and $(SES)_0$ are zero for the hypothetical 'average' pupil.

If there were j schools in the district, we would have j equations like equation 1. These can be represented by adding a second subscript to each of the elements of equation 1:

$$(Mathematics)_{ij} = \beta_{0j} + \beta_{1j} (Minority)_{ij} + \beta_{2j} (SES)_{ij} + \epsilon_{ij}. \tag{3}$$

Notice that we now have j different β_0's, β_1's, and β_2's to describe the relationships in the j schools.

We can write a between-school regression model for each of the sets of j regression coefficients:

$$\beta_{0j} = \theta_{00} + u_{0j} \tag{4}$$

$$\beta_{1j} = \theta_{01} + u_{1j} \tag{5}$$

$$\beta_{2j} = \theta_{02} + u_{2j} \tag{6}$$

where θ_{00} is the mean district mathematics score, θ_{01} is the mean within-school achievement gap between non-minority and minority pupils, and θ_{02} is the mean within-school achievement-SES relationship. The discrepancies between each school's parameters from the district mean for those parameters are given by the residuals, u_{0j}, u_{1j}, and u_{2j}. Equations 4, 5, and 6 can be substituted into Equation 3 to form a combined multilevel model. The parameters for multilevel models of this type can be estimated with the computer programs developed by Bryk, Raudenbush, Seltzer, and Congdon (1986), Longford (1986), and Rasbash, Prosser, and Goldstein (1991).

With the estimation of the multilevel model described by equations 3 through 6, we are in a position to address the first two of the four basic research questions specified in Chapter 10. Estimates of β_{0j} are estimates of each school's mean mathematics score, after adjusting for minority status and SES. The deviations of these scores from the district mean, which can be positive or negative, are given by u_{0j}. If we assume the within-school model is correctly specified, then estimates of these residuals are Type A effects (see Chapter 4). The first research question in Chapter 10 asked about the extent to which schools varied in their outcomes, and therefore we are interested in the variance of the adjusted mean scores; that is, $Var(\beta_{0j})$ or $Var(u_{0j})$. The variance of the *observed* β_{0j}'s can be partitioned into two components: sampling variance, v_j, and parameter variance, τ (Raudenbush and Bryk, 1986):

$$Var(\hat{\beta}_0) = v_j + \tau. \tag{7}$$

The multilevel programs provide estimates of v_j and τ for each of the within-school parameters β_0, β_1, and β_2. The estimate of τ for β_0 is an estimate of the differences between schools in their outcomes, after account has been taken of the independent variables in the within-school model. To estimate the variance in school means without any adjustment for pupils' background characteristics, one can simply estimate the multilevel model without any control variables in the model. This is referred to as a 'null' model.

The second research question in Chapter 10 asked 'To what extent do outcomes vary for pupils of differing status?'. Estimates of β_{1j} are estimates of the minority achievement gap, after account has been taken of pupils' SES. The average within-school achievement gap is given by θ_{01}. Variance in the observed estimates of within-school achievement gaps is partitioned into sampling variance and parameter variance. The estimate of the parameter variance (i.e., τ for u_{1j}) is an indication of the extent to which the achievement gaps vary across schools. One could ask a similar question about the relationship between mathematics scores and SES, within and between schools.

To address the last two of the four research questions specified in Chapter 10, we extend the between-school model to include variables describing school context, policy, and practice:

$$\beta_{0j} = \theta_{00} + \theta_{10}C_j + \theta_{20}P_j + u_{0j} \tag{8}$$

$$\beta_{1j} = \theta_{01} + \theta_{11}C_j + \theta_{21}P_j + u_{1j} \tag{9}$$

$$\beta_{2j} = \theta_{02} + u_{2j} \tag{10}$$

where C_j is a variable denoting school context, such as the mean level of SES of a school, and P_j is some variable representing school policy or practice, such as size of the school or whether the school tracks its pupils. In most cases there are several school policy and practice variables, but to simplify the model, I included the single variable P_j. Also, I did not include C_j or P_j in Equation 10, but they could be included there as well to determine the effects of context and policy on SES slopes.

Our interest is in the magnitude and statistical significance of estimates of θ_{10}, θ_{20}, θ_{11}, and θ_{21} (e.g., $\hat{\theta}_{10}$, $\hat{\theta}_{20}$, $\hat{\theta}_{11}$, and $\hat{\theta}_{20}$). $\hat{\theta}_{10}$ and $\hat{\theta}_{20}$ are estimates of the effects of school context and school policy, respectively, on the adjusted mean outcome scores. Similarly, $\hat{\theta}_{11}$ and $\hat{\theta}_{21}$ are estimates of the effects of school context and school policy, respectively, on the within-school achievement gaps. In term of the multilevel model, then, the third and fourth questions are tantamount to asking whether policy and practice variables have an effect on adjusted mean outcome scores, or on the adjusted achievement gap, after account is taken of school context. The multilevel programs provide estimates of these effects and their standard errors.

Type B effects include the effects of school policies and any unmeasured effects associated with the school (see Chapter 4). In terms of this model, then, Type B effects are given by $\theta_{20}P_j + u_{0j}$. Notice that unbiased estimation of Type B effects depends on correct specification of both the within- and between-school models.

The multilevel models described above are two-level (pupils and schools) models. These can be extended easily to three-level (pupils, schools, and districts or EAs) models. In a three-level model the parameters of the second level (i.e., the θ's) become the dependent variables in district-level models. The first example in Chapter 10 employs a simple three-level model with no independent variables at the third level.

Longitudinal Designs with Repeated Measures on Pupils

Null Model

The simplest form of a multilevel growth model describes a linear growth pattern for each pupil. It comprises two levels described by a within-pupil equation and two between-pupil equations. The within-pupil equation describes a simple linear regression model for each pupil:

$$Y_{it} = \pi_{0i} + \pi_{1i}(Time)_{it} + R_{it} \qquad (11)$$

where Y_{it} is the achievement score for pupil i ($i = 1 \ldots$ n) at occasion t ($t = 1 \ldots$ T_i), and $(Time)_{it}$ is the amount of schooling the pupil has received by occasion t. $(Time)_{it}$ can be represented in months of schooling, years of schooling, or some other time-related metric. Notice that the number of occasions T is subscripted with an i; this means that all pupils do not necessarily have to be tested at the same time, or on the same number of occasions. The parameters π_{0i} and π_{1i} represent each pupil's *true* initial status and *true* rate of growth, respectively. R_{it} is a random error term assumed normally distributed with mean zero and a covariance structure Σ_i. (Σ_i is a square matrix with dimensions equal to the number of testing occasions.) This is the simplest form of a more general model provided by Bryk and Raudenbush (1987, Equation 1). More complex forms allow for non-linear growth; these would be appropriate, for example, in situations where pupils initially make rapid gains in learning, but then level off.

The second level of the model describes variation between pupils in their initial status and rates of growth:

$$\pi_{0i} = \beta_{00} + \epsilon_{0i} \qquad (12)$$

$$\pi_{1i} = \beta_{01} + \epsilon_{1i} \qquad (13)$$

where β_{00} and β_{01} are the sample averages of pupils' true initial status and true rates of growth, respectively. The ϵ_{0i} and ϵ_{1i} are pupil-level error terms with mean zero and variances σ_0^2 and σ_1^2 respectively. Estimates of σ_0^2 and σ_1^2 are of interest because they describe the extent of variation between sample members in their initial status and rates of growth. The three equations above can be combined into a single equation by substituting Equations 2 and 3 into Equation 1.

Control for Pupil-Level Factors

The simple two-level model can be extended to include sex, minority status, or other pupil-level variables. These are added to the second-level equations (Equations 2 and 3); for example:

$$\pi_{0i} = \beta_{00} + \beta_{10}(Sex)_i + \beta_{20}(Minority)_i + \beta_{30}(SES)_i + \epsilon_{0i} \qquad (14)$$

$$\pi_{1i} = \beta_{01} + \beta_{11}(Sex)_i + \beta_{21}(Minority)_i + \beta_{31}(SES)_i + \epsilon_{1i} \qquad (15)$$

If the variable $(Sex)_i$ is coded 0 for males and 1 for females, then β_{10} represents the difference between females and males in their initial levels of achievement, after adjusting for *minority* status and *SES*. Similarly, β_{11} represents the adjusted sex difference in rates of growth, after adjusting for *minority* status and *SES*. β_{20} and β_{21}, the coefficients for *minority status*, are estimated in the same way. β_{30} and β_{31} denote the effects of SES.

If one were interested primarily in sex inequities, one could fit the model obtained with Equations 1, 4, and 5, and ask whether the estimates of β_{10} and β_{11} were substantively and statistically significant. Alternatively, one could drop the variable *Sex* from Equations 4 and 5, and fit the resulting model separately for males and females. The advantage of this approach is that one obtains separate coefficients describing the effects of *SES* and *Minority* status for each sex. Thus the analysis directly allows for interactions between *Sex* and the other pupil-level variables. One also obtains separate estimates of the variance in initial status and growth rates for each sex. The disadvantage of two separate models is that the analysis has slightly less statistical power, although this is not an issue with the large sample sizes typical of data collected for monitoring school and district performance. Also, the use of separate models does not provide directly a test for the statistical significance of interactions between sex and the other pupil-level variables, whereas these can be added to the single-equation model. If interactions are statistically insignificant, one can constrain the relationships to be identical for the sexes. This yields a biased but more precise estimate of sex differences. The single-equation model can be adapted so that there are separate variance terms for males and females in Equations 4 and 5 (Goldstein, 1987), which would be useful also if sample sizes were small.

A Three-Level Model

The two-level growth model described above can be extended into a three-level model with schools (or classrooms) as the next higher level (see Raudenbush and Bryk, 1988). The first two levels are described by Equations 1, 4, and 5. They are repeated here with a third subscript j which denotes membership in school j ($j = 1 \dots n_j$):

$$Y_{ijt} = \pi_{0ij} + \pi_{1ij}(Time)_{ijt} + R_{ijt} \qquad (16)$$

$$\pi_{0ij} = \beta_{00j} + \beta_{10j}(Sex)_{ij} + \beta_{20j}(Minority)_{ij} + \beta_{30j}(SES)_{ij} + \epsilon_{0ij} \qquad (17)$$

$$\pi_{1ij} = \beta_{01j} + \beta_{11j}(Sex)_{ij} + \beta_{21j}(Minority)_{ij} + \beta_{31j}(SES)_{ij} + \epsilon_{1ij} \qquad (18)$$

Notice that we have j sets of between-pupil parameters, one set for each school. We want to know whether these parameters vary significantly between schools, and if so, whether their variance can be explained by particular school policies or practices. For example, we might want to know whether differences between schools in sex differences in mathematics are related to whether a school practised ability grouping, or to the type of mathematics program they employed (e.g., new *vs.* old curriculum). The school-level equations regress parameters from the second level on school-level variables describing policy or practice:

Differences between schools in their average levels of initial status:

$$\beta_{00j} = \theta_{000} + \theta_{001}(Ability\ Grouping)_j + \theta_{002}(New\ Program)_j + u_{00j} \qquad (19)$$

Differences between schools in sex differences in levels of initial status:

$$\beta_{10j} = \theta_{100} + \theta_{101}(Ability\ Grouping)_j + \theta_{102}(New\ Program)_j + u_{10j} \qquad (20)$$

Differences between schools in their average rates of growth:

$$\beta_{01j} = \theta_{010} + \theta_{011}(Ability\ Grouping)_j + \theta_{012}(New\ Program)_j + u_{01j} \qquad (21)$$

Differences between schools in sex differences in rates of growth:

$$\beta_{11j} = \theta_{110} + \theta_{111}(Ability\ Grouping)_j + \theta_{112}(New\ Program)_j + u_{11j} \qquad (22)$$

One could write similar pairs of equations for *Minority* status and *SES*; however, to simplify I have assumed that the effects of these variables do not vary significantly across schools. (This assumption could be tested with a multilevel model.) The subscript j could therefore be dropped from these variables in equations 7 and 8. The full three-level model could be described with a single equation by substituting Equations 9 through 12 into 7 and 8, and the resulting equations into Equation 6.

References

ACHILLES, C.M., BAIN, H.P., BELLOTT, F., FOLGER, J., JOHNSTON, J., and LINTZ, M.N. (March, 1988) *Project STAR Technical Report. Year One. (1985–86): Kindergarten Results.* Nashville, TN: State Education Department.

ADLER, M., PETCH, A., and TWEEDIE, J. (1989) *Parental Choice and Educational Policy.* Edinburgh: Edinburgh University Press.

ADLER, M., and RAAB, G.M. (1988) Exit, choice and loyalty: The impact of parental choice on admissions to secondary schools in Edinburgh and Dundee. *Journal of Education Policy,* 3(2), 155–179.

AITKIN, M., and LONGFORD, N. (1986) Statistical modelling issues in school effectiveness studies. *Journal of the Royal Statistical Society, Series A,* **149**(1), 1–26.

ALEXANDER, K.L., NATRIELLO, G., and PALLAS, A. (1985) For whom the bell tolls: The impact of dropping out on cognitive performance. *American Sociological Review,* **50**, 409–420.

ALEXANDER, K.L., PALLAS, A.M., and COOK, M.A. (1981) Measure for measure: On the use of endogenous ability data in school-process research. *American Sociological Review,* **46**(5), 619–631.

ANDERSON, C.S. (1982) The search for school climate: A review of the research. *Review of Educational Research,* **52**(3), 368–420.

ANDERSON, C.S. (1985) The investigation of school climate. In AUSTIN, G.R. and GARBER, H. (Eds.), *Research on Exemplary Schools.* Orlando: Academic Press.

ANDERSON, S., AUQUIER, A., HAUCK, W.W., OAKES, D., VANDAELE, W., and WEISBERG, H.I. (1980) *Statistical Methods for Comparative Studies.* New York: John Wiley and Sons.

AVERCH, H.A., CARROLL, S.J., DONALDSON, T.S., KIESLING, H.J., and PINCAS, J. (1974) *How Effective is Schooling? A Critical Review and Synthesis of Research Findings.* Englewood Cliffs: Educational Technology Publications.

BALL, S.J. (1984) Introduction: Comprehensives in crisis? In BALL, S.J. (Ed.), *Comprehensive Schooling: A Reader.* Lewes: Falmer Press (pp. 1–26).

BARR, R., and DREEBEN, R. (1983) *How Schools Work.* Chicago: University of Chicago Press.

BEALE, E.M., and LITTLE, R.J.A. (1975) Missing values in multivariate analysis. *Journal of the Royal Statistical Society,* 37(1), 129–145.

BECHER, T., ERAUT, M., and KNIGHT, J. (1981) *Policies for Educational Accountability.* London: Heinemann Educational Books.

BLASE, J.L. (1986) A qualitative analysis of teacher stress: Consequences for performance. *American Educational Research Journal,* **23**, 13–40.

BOARDMAN, A.E., and MURNANE, R.J. (1980) Using panel data to improve estimates of the determinants of educational achievement. *Sociology of Education,* **53**, 113–21.

References

BOCK, R.D., and MISLEVY, R.J. (1988) Comprehensive educational assessment for the states: The duplex design. *Educational Evaluation and Policy Analysis*, **10**(2), 89–105.

BOSSERT, S., DWYER, D., ROWAN, B., and LEE, G. (1982) The instructional management role of the principal. *Educational Administration Quarterly*, **18**(3), 34–64.

BOYD, W.L. (1983) What school administrators do and don't do: Implications for effective schools. *The Canadian Administrator*, **22**(6), 1–4.

BRIDGE, R.G., JUDD, C.M., and MOOCK, P.R. (1979) *The Determinants of Educational Outcomes*. Cambridge, MA: Ballinger.

BRIMER, A., MADAUS, G.F., CHAPMAN, B., KELLAGHAN, T., and WOOD, R. (1978) *Sources of Difference in School Achievement*. Slough: NFER.

BROOKOVER, W.B., BEADY, C.H., FLOOD, P., SCHWEITZER, J., and WISENBAKER, J. (1979) *School Social Systems and Student Achievement*. New York: Praeger.

BROOKOVER, W.B., SCHWEITZER, J.H., SCHNEIDER, J.M., BEADY, C.H., FLOOD, P.K., and WISENBAKER, J.M. (1978) Elementary school social climate and school achievement. *American Educational Research Journal*, **15**(2), 301–318.

BRYK, A.S. (1980) Analyzing data from premeasure/postmeasure designs. In ANDERSON, S., AUQUIER, A., HAUCK, W.W., OAKES, D., VANDAELE, W. and WEISBERG, H.I. *Statistical Methods for Comparative Studies* New York: Wiley. (pp. 235–260).

BRYK, A.S., and RAUDENBUSH, S.W. (1987) Application of hierarchical linear models to assessing change. *Psychological Bulletin*, **101**(1), 147–158.

BRYK, A.S., and RAUDENBUSH, S.W. (1988) Toward a more appropriate conceptualization of research on school effects: A three-level hierarchical linear model. *American Journal of Education*, **97**(1), 65–108.

BRYK, A.S., RAUDENBUSH, S.W., SELTZER, M., and CONGDON, R.T. (1986) *An Introduction to HLM: Computer Program and User's Guide*. Chicago: University of Chicago.

BURSTEIN, L. (1980) Issues in the aggregation of data. In BERLINER, D.C. (Ed.), *Review of Research in Education* Washington, DC: American Educational Research Association. (pp. 158–233).

BURSTEIN, L. (1984) The use of existing data bases in program evaluation and school improvement. *Educational Evaluation and Policy Analysis*, **6**(3), 307–318.

BURSTEIN, L., and MILLER, M.D. (1979, April) *The use of within-group slopes as indices of group outcomes*. Paper presented at the annual meeting of the American Educational Research Association, San Francisco, CA.

CARR, W., and KEMMIS, S. (1986) *Becoming Critical: Education, Knowledge and Action Research*. London: Falmer Press.

CARTER, L.F. (1984) The sustaining effects study of compensatory and elementary education. *Educational Researcher*, **13**(7), 4–13.

CHARTERED INSTITUTE OF PUBLIC FINANCE ACCOUNTS (1986) *Performance indicators in the education service*. London: Chartered Institute of Public Finance Accounts.

CLARK, D.L., LOTTO, L.S., and ASTUTO, T.A. (1984) Effective schools and school improvement: A comparative analysis of two lines of inquiry. *Educational Administration Quarterly*, **20**(3), 41–68.

CLEVELAND, W.S. (1979) Robust locally weighted regression and smoothed scatterplots. *Journal of the American Statistical Association*, **74**(368), 829–836.

CLINCHY, E. (1989) Public school choice: Absolutely necessary but not wholly sufficient. *Phi Delta Kappan*, **71**(4), 289–294.

COHEN, D.K., and WEISS, J.A. (1977) Social science and social policy: Schools and race. In WEISS, C.H. (Ed.), *Using Social Research in Public Policy Making* Lexington, MA: Lexington Books. (pp. 67–83).

COHEN, M. (1981) Effective schools: What the research says. *Today's Education*, *April/May*, 46G–49G.

COLEMAN, J.S., CAMPBELL, E.Q., HOBSON, C.F., MCPARTLAND, A.M., MOOD, A.M., WEINFELD, F.D., and YORK, R.L. (1966) *Equality of Educational Opportunity*. Washington, D.C.: Department of Health, Education, and Welfare.

COLLINS, A. (1988) Reformulating testing to measure learning and thinking. In FREDRIKSEN, N., GLASER, R., LESGOLD, A., and SHAFTO, M. (Eds.), *Diagnostic monitoring of skills and knowledge acquisition* Hillsdale, NJ: Erlbaum. (pp. 75–87).

COOK, T.D., AND CAMPBELL, D.T. (1979) *Quasi-experimentation: Design and Analysis for Field Settings*. Chicago: Rand McNally.

COOPERS and LYBRAND (1988) *Local Management of Schools*. A report to the Department of Education and Science. London: HMSO.

CRONBACH, L.J., AMBRON, S.R., DORNBUSCH, S.M., HESS, R.D., HORNIK, R.C., PHILLIPS, D.C., WALKER, D.F., and WEINER, S.S. (1980) *Toward Reform of Program Evaluation*. San Francisco, CA: Jossey-Bass.

CRONBACH, L.J., DEKEN, J.E., and WEBB, N. (1976) *Research on Classrooms and Schools: Formulation of Questions, Design, and Analysis*. Occasional Paper of the Stanford Evaluation Consortium. Stanford University.

CUBAN, L. (1983) Effective schools: A friendly but cautionary note. *Phi Delta Kappan, June*, 695–696.

DAVID, J.L. (1988) The use of indicators by school districts: Aid or threat to improvement? *Phi Delta Kappan*, **69**(7), 499–502.

DENSCOMBE, M. (1985) *Classroom Control: A Sociological Perspective*. London: Allen and Unwin.

DEPARTMENT OF EDUCATION AND SCIENCE (1983) *School Standards and Spending: Statistical Analysis*. Statistical Bulletin No. 16–83. London: HMSO.

DEPARTMENT OF EDUCATION AND SCIENCE (1984) *School Standards and Spending: Statistical Analysis: A Further Appreciation*. Statistical Bulletin No. 13–84. London: HMSO.

DEPARTMENT OF EDUCATION AND SCIENCE (1988) *Education Statistics for the UK*. London: HMSO.

DEPARTMENT OF EDUCATION AND SCIENCE AND THE WELSH OFFICE (1987) *National Curriculum: Task Group on Assessment and Testing*. London: HMSO.

DEPARTMENT OF EDUCATION FOR NORTHERN IRELAND (1988) *Statistical Bulletin No. 1/1988*. Bangor, Northern Ireland: HMSO.

DIPRETE, T.A. (1981) *Discipline, Order, and Student Behavior in American High Schools*. National Center for Education Statistics, US Department of Education.

DORNBUSCH, S.M., RITTER, P.L., LEIDERMAN, P.H., ROBERTS, D.F., and FRALEIGH, M.J. (1987) The relation of parenting style to adolescent school performance. *Child Development*, **58**, 1244–1257.

DORNBUSCH, S.M., and SCOTT, W.R. (1975) *Evaluation and the Exercise of Authority: A Theory of Control Applied to Diverse Organizations*. San Francisco: Jossey-Bass.

DREEBEN, R., and GAMORAN, A. (1986) Race, instruction, and learning. *American Sociological Review*, **51**, 660–669.

DUKE, D.L. (1982) What can principals do? Leadership functions and instructional effectiveness. *NASSP Bulletin*, **66**(456), 1–12.

DUKE, D.L., and PERRY, C. (1978) Can alternative schools succeed where BENJAMIN SPOCK, SPIRO AGNEW, and SKINNER, B.F. have failed? *Adolescence*, **8**(51), 375–392.

ECHOLS, F., MCPHERSON, A.F., and WILLMS, J.D. (1990) Choice among state and private schools in Scotland. *Journal of Education Policy*, **5**(3), 207–222.

EDELSKY, C. (1990) Whose agenda is this anyway? A response to McKenna, Robinson, and Miller. *Educational Researcher*, **19**(8), 7–11.

EISNER, E. (1985) *Educational Imagination: On the Design and Evaluation of School Programs* (2nd ed.). New York: Macmillan.

ELAM, S.M., and GALLUP, A.M. (1989) The 21st annual Gallup poll of the attitudes toward the public schools. *Phi Delta Kappan*, **71**(1), 41–56.

References

ENNIS, R.H. (1973) On causality. *Educational Researcher*, **2**, 4–11.

EPSTEIN, J.L., and MCPARTLAND, J.M. (1976) The concept and measurement of the quality of school life. *American Educational Research Journal*, **13**, 15–30.

FENNEMA, E. (1981) The sex factor. In FENNEMA, E. (Ed.), *Mathematics Education Research: Implications for the 80s*. Reston, VA: National Council of Teachers of Mathematics. (pp. 92–105).

FETTERMAN, D.M. (1988) Qualitative approaches to evaluating education. *Educational Researcher*, **11**, 17–23.

FINN, J.D., and ACHILLES, C.M. (1990) Answers and questions about class size: A statewide experiment. *American Educational Research Journal*, **27**(3), 557–575.

FUTRELL, M.H. (April, 1986) *Restructuring Education: A Call for Research*. Address presented at the annual meeting of the American Educational Research Association, San Francisco.

FUTRELL, M.H. (1989) Mission not accomplished: Education reform in retrospect. *Phi Delta Kappan*, **71**(1), 8–14.

GAGE, N.L., and NEEDELS, M.C. (1989) Process-product research on teaching: A review of criticisms. *The Elementary School Journal*, **89**(3), 253–300.

GAMORAN, A. (1990) *The Variable Effects of Tracking: Inequality and Productivity in American High Schools*. Madison, WI: University of Wisconsin, National Center on Effective Secondary Schools.

GARNER, C., and RAUDENBUSH, S.W. (1991) Neighbourhood effects on educational attainment: a multilevel analysis. *Sociology of Education*, **64**(4), 251–262.

GASKELL, J. (1988) Policy research and politics. *Alberta Journal of Educational Research*, **34**(4), 403–417.

GLASMAN, N.S., and BINIAMINOV, I. (1981) Input-output analysis of schools. *Review of Education Research*, **51**(4), 509–539.

GLENN, C.L. (1989) Putting school choice in place. *Phi Delta Kappan*, **71**(4), 295–300.

GOLDSTEIN, H. (1987) *Multilevel Models in Educational and Social Research*. New York: Oxford University Press.

GOOD, T.L., and BROPHY, J.E. (1986) School effects. In WITTROCK, M.C. (Ed.), *Handbook of Research on Teaching*. New York, Macmillan. (3rd ed., pp. 570–602).

GOODLAD, J.I. (1984) *A Place Called School: Prospects for the Future*. New York: McGraw Hill.

GRAY, J. (1989) Multilevel models: Issues and problems emerging from their recent application in British studies of school effectiveness. In BOCK, D.R. (Ed.), *Multi-level Analyses of Educational Data*. University of Chicago Press. (pp. 127–145).

GRAY, J., JESSON, D., and JONES, B. (1984) Predicting differences in examination results between local education authorities: Does school organisation matter? *Oxford Review of Education*, **10**(1), 45–68.

GRONLUND, N.E. (1985) *Measurement in Evaluation and Teaching* (5th ed.). New York: Macmillan.

HAERTLE, E.H. (1986) Measuring school performance to improve school practice. *Education and Urban Society*, **18**(3), 312–325.

HAERTLE, E.H. (1991) New forms of teacher assessment. In GRANT, G. (Ed.), *Review of Research in Education* (Vol. 17, pp. 3–29). Washington, DC: American Educational Research Association.

HAERTLE, E.H., JAMES, T. and LEVIN, H.M. (1987) *Comparing Public and Private Schools: School Achievement* (Vol. 2). London: Falmer Press.

HALADYNA, T.M., NOLEN, S.B., and HAAS, N.S. (1991) Raising standardized achievement test scores and the origins of test score pollution. *Educational Researcher*, **20**(5), 2–7.

HALLINGER, P., and MURPHY, J. (1985) Assessing the instructional management behavior of principals. *Elementary School Journal*, **86**(2), 217–247.

HAMMERSLEY, M. (1985) From ethnography to theory: A programme and paradigm in sociology of education. *Sociology*, **19**(2), 244–259.

HAMMERSLEY, M., and ATKINSON, P. (1983) *Ethnography: Principles into Practice*. London: Tavistock.

HANNAN, M.T., FREEMAN, J.H., and MEYER, J.W. (1976) Specification of models for organizational effectiveness. *American Sociological Review*, **41**(1), 136–143.

HEATH, A. (1984) In defence of comprehensive schools. *Oxford Review of Education*, **10**(1), 115–123.

HEATH, A. (1987, July 17) Class in the classroom. *New Society*, pp. 13–15.

HEATH, A. (1990) Class inequalities in education in the twentieth century. *Journal of the Royal Statistical Society, Series A*, **153**(1), 1–16.

HENDERSON, V., MIESZKOWSKI, P., and SAUVAGEAU, Y. (1978) Peer group effects and educational production functions. *Journal of Public Economics*, **10**, 97–106.

HOPKINS, K.D., and GLASS, G.V. (1978) *Basic Statistics for the Behavioral Sciences*. Englewood Cliffs, NJ: Prentice-Hall.

HOWE, J.G. (1977) Group climate: An exploratory analysis of construct validity. *Organizational Behavior and Human Performance*, **19**, 106–125.

HOY, W.K., and FERGUSON, J. (1985) A theoretical framework and exploration of organizational effectiveness in schools. *Education Administration Quarterly*, **21**, 117–134.

HUSEN, T., and KOGAN, M. (Eds.) (1984) *Educational Research and Policy: How Do They Relate?* Oxford: Pergamon.

HUTTENLOCHER, J.E., HAIGHT, W., BRYK, A.S., and SELTZER, M. (1988) Parental Speech and Early Vocabulary Development. Unpublished manuscript, University of Chicago, Department of Education, Chicago.

JACOBSEN, S. (1990) *Identifying Children at Risk: The Predictive Validity of Kindergarten Screening Measures*. Unpublished doctoral dissertation, University of British Columbia, Vancouver.

JENCKS, C.S., SMITH, M., ACLAND, H., BANE, M.J., COHEN, D., GINTIS, H., HEYNS, B., and MICHELSON, S. (1972) *Inequality: A Reassessment of the Effect of Family and Schooling in America*. New York: Basic Books.

KELLY, A. (1976) A study of the comparability of external examinations in different subjects. *Research in Education*, **16**, 37–63.

KERCKHOFF, A.C. (1986) Effects of ability grouping. *American Sociological Review*, **51**(6), 842–58.

KIM, J., and CURRY, J. (1977) The treatment of missing data in multivariate analysis. *Sociological Methods and Research*, **6**(2), 215–240.

KING, E.M. (1982) *Canadian Test of Basic Skills (Teachers Guide)*. Canada: Nelson Canada Limited.

KOGAN, M. (1986) *Educational Accountability: An Analytic Overview*. London: Hutchison Education.

KORETZ, D. (1986) *Trends in Educational Achievement*. Washington, D.C.: Congressional Budget Office.

KORNHAUSER, R.R. (1978) *Social Sources of Delinquency*. Chicago: University of Chicago Press.

KULIK, C.-L., and KULIK, J.A. (1982) Effects of ability grouping on secondary school students: A meta-analysis of evaluation findings. *American Educational Research Journal*, **19**, 415–428.

KULIK, C.-L., and KULIK, J.A. (1984, August) *Effects of Ability Grouping on Elementary School Pupils: A Meta-analysis*. Paper presented at the annual meeting of the American Psychological Association, Toronto.

KUSHMAN, J.W. (1990, April) *The Role of Teacher Commitment in Urban School Effectiveness: A Study of Elementary and Middle Schools*. Paper presented at the annual meeting of the American Educational Research Association, Boston, MA.

References

LANDSBERGER, H.A., CARLSON, J.R., and CAMPBELL, R.T. (1988) Education policy in comparative perspective: similarities in the underlying issues in debate among educational elites in Britain, the Federal Republic of Germany and the USA. *Research Papers in Education*, **3**(6), 103–130.

LAU, L.J. (1979) Educational production functions. In WINDHAM, D.M. (Ed.), *Economic Dimensions of Education*. Washington, D.C.: National Academy of Education. (pp. 33–69).

LEE, V.E., and BRYK, A.S. (1988) Curriculum tracking as mediating the social distribution of high school achievement. *Sociology of Education*, **61**(2), 78–94.

LEE, V.E., and BRYK, A.S. (1989) A multilevel model of the social distribution of high school achievement. *Sociology of Education*, **62**(3), 172–192.

LEFCOURT, H.M. (1982) *Locus of Control: Current Trends in Theory and Research (Second Edition)*. Hillsdale, N.J.: Erlbaum Associates.

LEVIN, H.M. (1980) Education production theory and teacher inputs. In BIDWELL, C. E. and WINDHAM, D.M. (Eds), *The Analysis of Educational Productivity* Cambridge, MA: Ballinger: (pp. 203–231).

LEVIN, H.M., GLASS, G.V., and MEISTER, G.R. (1984) *Cost-effectiveness of Four Educational Interventions* (Project Report No. 84-A11). Stanford, CA: Stanford University, Institute for Research on Educational Finance and Governance.

LEWIS, A.C. (1991) National assessment: A reprise. *Phi Delta Kappan*, **72**(9), 654–655.

LIGHTFOOT, S.L. (1983) *The Good High School: Portraits of Character and Culture*. New York: Basic Books.

LINCOLN, Y.S., and GUBA, E.G. (1985) *Naturalistic Inquiry*. Newbury Park, CA: Sage.

LINN, R.L. (1986) Quantitative methods in research on teaching. In WITTROCK, M.C. (Ed.), *Handbook of Research on Teaching*. New York, Macmillan. (3rd ed., pp. 3–36).

LOCKHEED, M.E., and LONGFORD, N.T. (1991) School effects on mathematics achievement in Thailand. In RAUDENBUSH, S.W. and WILLMS, J.D. (Eds), *Schools, Classrooms, and Pupils: International Studies of Schooling from a Multilevel Perspective*. New York: Academic Press. (pp. 131–148).

LONGFORD, N.T. (1986) VARCL-Interactive software for variance components analysis. *The Professional Statistician*, **5**, 28–32.

LORD, R. (1984) *Value for Money in Education*. London: Chartered Institute of Public Finance and Accountancy (CIPFA).

LORTIE, D.C. (1973) Observations on teaching as work. In TRAVERS, R.M.W. (Ed.), *Second Handbook of Research on Teaching*. Chicago: Rand McNally. (pp. 474–497).

LORTIE, D.C. (1975) *Schoolteacher: A Sociological Study*. Chicago: University of Chicago Press.

MACLURE, S. (1988) *Education Reformed: A Guide to the Education Reform Act 1988*. Exeter: Hodder and Stoughton.

MADAUS, G.F. (1988) The influence of testing on curriculum. In TANNER, L.N. (Ed.), *Critical Issues in Curriculum: Eighty-seventh yearbook of the National Society for the Study of Education*. Chicago, IL: University of Chicago Press. (pp. 83–121).

MADAUS, G.F., KELLAGHAN, T., RAKOW, E.A., and KING, D.J. (1979) The sensitivity of measures of school effectiveness. *Harvard Educational Review*, **49**(2), 207–230.

MANDEVILLE, G.K., and ANDERSON, L.W. (1987) The stability of school effectiveness indices across grade levels and subject areas. *Journal of Educational Measurement*, **24**(3), 203–216.

MARCH, J.G., and OLSEN, J.P. (1976) *Ambiguity and Choice in Organizations*. Bergen, Norway: Universitetsforlaget.

MARKS, J., COX, C., and POMIAN-SRZEDNICKI, M. (1983) *Standards in English Schools*. London: National Council for Educational Standards.

MARSH, H.W., and O'NEILL, R. (1984) Self Description Questionnaire III (SDQ III):

The construct validity of multidimensional self-concept ratings by late adolescents. *Journal of Educational Measurement*, **21**, 153–174.

MARSH, H.W., and SHAVELSON, R.J. (1985) Self-concept: Its multifaceted, hierarchical structure. *Educational Psychologist*, **20**, 107–125.

MARTIN, D.J., and HOOVER, H.D. (1987) Sex differences in educational achievement: A longitudinal study. *Journal of Early Adolescence*, **7**(1), 65–83.

MASSEY, D.S., and DENTON, N.A. (1988) Suburbanization and segregation in US metropolitan areas. *American Journal of Sociology*, **94**(3), 592–626.

McDILL, E.L., and RIGSBY, L.C. (1973) *Structure and Process in Secondary Schools: The Academic Impact of Educational Climates*. Baltimore, Md: Johns Hopkins University Press.

McGILL, R., TUKEY, J.W., and LARSEN, W.A. (1978) Variations of box plots. *The American Statistician*, **32**(1), 12–16.

McKENNA, M.C., ROBINSON, R.D., and MILLER, J.W. (1990) Whole language: A research agenda for the nineties. *Educational Researcher*, **19**(8), 3–6.

McKNIGHT, C.C., CROSSWHITE, F.J., DOSSEY, J.A., KIFER, E., SWAFFORD, J.O., TRAVERS, K.J., and COONEY, T.J. (1987) *The Underachieving Curriculum: Assessing US School Mathematics from an International Perspective*. Champaign, IL: Stipes.

McNEIL, L.M. (1986) *Contradictions of Control: School Structure and School Knowledge*. New York: Methuen/Routledge and Kegan Paul.

McNEIL, L.M. (1988) Contradictions of control, Part 1: Administrators and teachers. *Phi Delta Kappan*, **69**(5), 333–339.

McPHERSON, A.F. and WILLMS, J.D. (1986) Certification, class conflict, religion and community: A socio-historical explanation of the effectiveness of contemporary schools. In KERCKHOFF, A.C. (Ed.), *Research in Sociology of Education and Socialization*. Greenwich, Connecticut: JAI Press. (Vol. 6, pp. 227–302).

McPHERSON, A.F., and WILLMS, J.D. (1987) Equalisation and improvement: Some effects of comprehensive reorganisation in Scotland. *Sociology*, **21**(4), 509–539.

McPHERSON, A.F., and WILLMS, J.D. (1989) Comprehensive schooling is better and fairer. In COSIN, B., FLUDE, M. and HALES, M. (Eds.), *School, Work, and Equality*. London: Hodder and Stoughton. (pp. 189–194).

MERCER, C.D., ALGOZZINE, B., and TRIFILETTI, J. (1988) Early identification — an analysis of the research. *Learning Disability Quarterly*, **11**, 176–188.

MEYER, J.W. (1980) Levels of the educational system and schooling effects. In BIDWELL, C. and WINDHAM, D. (Eds.), *The Analysis of Educational Productivity*. Cambridge, MA: Ballinger. (Vol. 2, pp. 15–63).

MEYER, J.W., and ROWAN, B. (1988) The structure of educational organizations. In WESTOBY, A. (Ed.), *Culture and Power in Educational Organizations*. Philadelphia: Open University Press. (pp. 87–112).

MITCHELL, J.V., JR. (1968). Dimensionality and differences in the environmental press of high schools. *American Educational Research Journal*, **5**(4), 513–530.

MOOS, R.H. (1979) *Evaluating Educational Environments*. San Francisco: Jossey-Bass.

MOSTELLER, F., and TUKEY, J.W. (1977) *Data Analysis and Regression*. Reading, MA: Addison-Wesley.

MOWDAY, R., STEERS, R., and PORTER, L. (1979) The measurement of organizational commitment. *Journal of Vocational Behavior*, **14**, 224–247.

MUELLER, C.W., and PARCEL, T.L. (1981) Measures of socioeconomic status: Alternatives and recommendations. *Child Development*, **52**, 13–30.

MURNANE, R.J. (1975) *The Impact of School Resources on the Learning of Inner City Children*. Cambridge: Ballinger.

MURNANE, R.J. (1981) Interpreting the evidence on school effectiveness. *Teachers College Record*, **83**, 19–35.

References

MURNANE, R.J. (1987) Improving education indicators and economic indicators: The same problems? *Educational Evaluation and Policy Analysis*, 9(2), 101–116.

MURNANE, R.J., and PAULY, E.W. (1988) Lessons from comparing educational and economic indicators. *Phi Delta Kappan, March*, 509–513.

MURPHY, J. (1988) Methodological, measurement, and conceptual problems in the study of instructional leadership. *Educational Evaluation and Policy Analysis*, 10(2), 117–139.

MURPHY, J., HALLINGER, P., and MESA, R.P. (1985) School effectiveness: Checking progress and assumptions and developing a role for state and federal government. *Teachers College Record*, 86(4), 615–641.

NATIONAL COMMISSION ON EXCELLENCE IN EDUCATION (1983) *A Nation at Risk: The Imperative for Educational Reform*. Washington, DC: US Government Printing Office.

NEWMAN, J.M. (1985) Introduction. In NEWMAN, J.M. (Ed.), *Whole Language: Theory in Use*. Portsmouth, NH: Heinemann. (pp. 1–6).

OAKES, J. (1986) *Educational Indicators: A Guide for Policymakers* (New Brunswick, N.J.: Center for Policy Research in Education, Rutgers University).

OAKES, J. (1989) What educational indicators? The case for assessing school context. *Educational Evaluation and Policy Analysis*, 11, 181–199.

ODDEN, A. (1982) Schools can improve: Local strategies need state backing. *State Education Leader, Summer*, 1–3.

PALLAS, A. (1988) School climate in American high schools. *Teachers College Record*, 89, 541–553.

PARIS, S.G., LAWTON, T.A., TURNER, J.C., and ROTH, J.L. (1991) A developmental perspective on standardized achievement testing. *Educational Researcher*, 20(5), 12–20.

PATERSON, L. (1989) *Socio-economic Status and Educational Attainment: A Multidimensional and Multi-level Study* (Report No. 8962). Edinburgh: University of Edinburgh, Center for Educational Sociology.

PATTON, M.Q. (1980) *Qualitative Evaluation Methods*. Newbury Park, CA: Sage.

PELEG, R., and ADLER, C. (1977) Compensatory education in Israel: Conceptions, attitudes, and trends. *American Psychologist*, 32, 945–958.

PETCH, A.C. (1986) Parental choice at entry to primary school. *Research papers in education*, 1(1), 26–47.

PIPHO, C. (1991) The unbridled, undebated national test. *Phi Delta Kappan*, 72(8), 574–575.

PORTER, A.C. (1988) Indicators: Objective data or political tool? *Phi Delta Kappan*, 69(7), 503–508.

PORTER, A.C. (1991) Creating a system of school process indicators. *Educational Evaluation and Policy Analysis*, 13(1), 13–29.

PORTER, A.C., FLODEN, R., FREEMAN, D., SCHMIDT, W., and SCHWILLE, J. (1988) Content determinants in elementary school mathematics. In GROUWS, D.A. and COONEY, T.J. (Eds.), *Perspectives of Research on Effective Mathematics Teaching*. New York: Longman. (pp. 370–391).

POWELL, A., FARRAR, E., and COHEN, D. (1985) *The Shopping Mall High School: Winners and Losers in the Educational Marketplace*. Boston: Houghton Mifflin.

POWELL, B., and STEELMAN, L.C. (1984) Variations in SAT performance: Meaningful or misleading? *Harvard Educational Review*, 54(4), 389–412.

PURKEY, S.C., and SMITH, M.S. (1983) Effective schools: a review. *The Elementary School Journal*, 83, 427–452.

RAFFE, D. (1984) School attainment and the labour market. In RAFFE, D. (Ed.), *Fourteen to Eighteen. The Changing Pattern of Schooling in Scotland*. Aberdeen: Aberdeen University Press. (pp. 174–193).

RAFFE, D. (1991) Assessing the impact of a decentralised initiative: The British

Technical and Vocational Education Initiative. In RAUDENBUSH, S.W. and WILLMS, J.D. (Eds.), *Schools, Classrooms, and Pupils: International Studies of Schooling from a Multilevel Perspective.* San Diego: Academic Press. (pp. 149–166).

RAFFE, D., and WILLMS, J.D. (1989) Schooling the discouraged worker: Local-labour-market effects on educational participation. *Sociology*, **23**(4), 559–581.

RALPH, J.H., and FENNESSEY, J. (1983) Science or reform: Some questions about the effective schools model. *Phi Delta Kappan, June*, 689–694.

RASBASH, J., PROSSER, R., and GOLDSTEIN, H.I. (1991) *ML3: Software for Three-level Analysis.* London: Institute of Education, London University.

RAUDENBUSH, S.W. (1989) Educational applications of hierarchical linear models: A review. *Journal of Educational Statistics*, **13**(2), 85–116.

RAUDENBUSH, S.W., and BRYK, A.S. (1986) A hierarchical model for studying school effects. *Sociology of Education*, **59**, 1–17.

RAUDENBUSH, S.W., and BRYK, A.S. (1988) Methodological advances in analyzing the effects of schools and classrooms on student learning. In ROTHKOPF, E.Z. (Ed.), *Review of Research in Education.* Washington, DC: American Educational Research Association. (Vol. 15, pp. 423–475).

RAUDENBUSH, S.W., and WILLMS, J.D. (1988) *Sources of Bias in the Estimation of School Effects.* Edinburgh University: Centre for Educational Sociology, and University of British Columbia: Center for Policy Studies in Education.

RAUDENBUSH, S.W., and WILLMS, J.D. (1991) The organization of schooling and its methodological implications. In RAUDENBUSH, S.W. and WILLMS, J.D. (Eds.), *Schools, Classrooms, and Pupils: International Studies of Schooling from a Multilevel Perspective.* San Diego: Academic Press. (pp. 1–12).

RESEARCH FOR BETTER SCHOOLS (1990, July) Plea: Eschew school comparisons. *Educational Assessment-Policy and Use*, p. 1.

RESNICK, D.P.R., and RESNICK, L.B. (1988) Understanding achievement and acting to produce it: Some recommendations for the NAEP. *Phi Delta Kappan, April*, 576–579.

RESNICK, L.B. (1987) Learning in school and out. *Educational Researcher*, **16**(9), 13–20.

RICHARDS, C.E. (1988) Indicators and three types of educational monitoring systems: Implications for design. *Phi Delta Kappan*, **69**(2), 495–499.

ROBERTSON, C. (1988) *Scaling Attainment in S5.* CES Working Paper. Centre for Educational Sociology, Edinburgh University.

ROGOSA, D.R., BRANDT, D., and ZIMOWSKI, M. (1982) A growth curve approach to the measurement of educational change. *Psychological Bulletin*, **90**, 726–748.

ROGOSA, D.R., and WILLETT, J.B. (1983) Demonstrating the reliability of the difference score in the measurement of change. *Journal of Educational Measurement*, **20**, 335–343.

ROGOSA, D.R., and WILLETT, J.B. (1985) Understanding correlates of change by modelling individual differences in growth. *Psychometrika*, **50**, 203–228.

ROSENBAUM, J.E. (1976) *Making Inequality.* New York: Wiley.

ROSENBAUM, J.E. (1984) Track misperceptions and frustrated college plans: An analysis of the effects of tracks and track perceptions in the National Longitudinal Survey. *Sociology of Education*, **53**, 74–88.

ROSENHOLTZ, S.J. (1985) Effective schools: Interpreting the evidence. *American Journal of Education*, **93**, 352–387.

ROSENHOLTZ, S.J. (1989a) *Teachers' Workplace: The Social Organization of Schools* (Research on Teaching Monograph Series). New York: Longman.

ROSENHOLTZ, S.J. (1989b) Workplace conditions that affect teacher quality and commitment: Implications for teacher induction programs. *The Elementary School Journal*, **89**(4), 421–439.

ROSENSHINE, B., and STEVENS, R. (1986) Teaching Functions. In WITTROCK, M.C.

(Ed.), *Handbook of Research on Teaching*, New York, Macmillan. (3rd ed., pp. 376–391).

ROWAN, B., and MIRACLE, A.W. JR. (1983) Systems of ability grouping and the stratification of achievement in elementary schools. *Sociology of Education*, **56**(2), 133–144.

ROWAN, B., RAUDENBUSH, S.W., and KANG, S.J. (1991) School climate in secondary schools. In RAUDENBUSH, S.W. and WILLMS, J.D. (Eds), *Schools, Classrooms, and Pupils: International Studies of Schooling from a Multilevel Perspective*. New York: Academic Press. (pp. 203–223).

RUMBERGER, R.W., and WILLMS, J.D. (1991, April) *The Impact of Racial and Ethnic Segregation on the Achievement Gap in California High Schools.* Paper presented at the Annual Meeting of the American Educational Research Association, Chicago.

RUTTER, M. (1983) School effects on pupil progress: Research findings and policy implications. *Child Development*, **54**(1), 1–29.

SALVIA, J., CLARK, G., and YSSLEDYKE, J. (1973) Teacher retention of stereotypes of exceptionality. *Exceptional Children*, **39**, 651–652.

SCHOOL BOARDS (SCOTLAND) BILL, S125, No. 950 (1982).

SCOTTISH EDUCATION DEPARTMENT (1965) *Reorganisation of Secondary Education on Comprehensive Lines.* Circular No. 600. Edinburgh: HMSO.

SELDEN, R.W. (1988) Missing Data: A Progress Report from the States. *Phi Delta Kappan*, **69**(7), 492–494.

SHAVELSON, R.J., HUBNER, J.J., and STANTON, G.C. (1976) Validation of construct interpretations. *Review of Educational Research*, **46**, 407–441.

SHAVELSON, R.J., MCDONNELL, L., OAKES, J., CAREY, N., and PICUS, L. (1987, August) *Indicators Systems for Monitoring Mathematics and Science Education* (Report No. R-3570-NSF). Santa Monica: Rand Corporation.

SHAVIT, Y., and WILLIAMS R.A. (1985) Ability grouping and contextual determinants of educational expectations in Israel. *American Sociological Review*, **50**, 62–73.

SHEPARD, L. (1991) Interview on assessment issues with Lorrie Shepard. *Educational Researcher*, **20**(2), 21–23, 27.

SHIM, M. (1991) Models Comparing Estimates of School Effectiveness Based on Cross-sectional and Longitudinal Designs. Unpublished master's thesis, University of British Columbia, Vancouver, BC.

SHULMAN, L.S. (1986) Paradigms and research programs in the study of teaching: A contemporary perspective. In WITTROCK, M.C. (Ed.), *Handbook of Research on Teaching*. New York, Macmillan. (3rd ed., pp. 3–36).

SIROTNIK, K.A. (1980) Psychometric implications of the unit-of-analysis problem (with examples from the measurement of organizational climate). *Journal of Educational Measurement*, **17**(4), 245–282.

SIROTNIK, K.A. (1984) An outcome-free conception of schooling: Implications for school-based inquiry and information systems. *Educational Evaluation and Policy Analysis*, **6**(3), 227–239.

SIROTNIK, K.A. (1987) Evaluation in the ecology of schooling: The process of school renewal. In GOODLAD, J.I. (Ed.), *The Ecology of school Renewal: Eighty-sixth Yearbook of the National Society of Education*. Chicago: University of Chicago Press. (pp. 41–61).

SIROTNIK, K.A., and BURSTEIN, L. (1987) Making sense out of comprehensive school-based information systems: An exploratory investigation. In BANK, A. and WILLIAMS, R.C. (Eds.), *Information Systems and School Improvement: Inventing the Future*. New York: Teachers College Press. (pp. 185–209).

SLAVIN, R.E. (1987) Ability grouping and student achievement in elementary schools: A best-evidence synthesis. *Review of Educational Research*, **57**(3), 293–336.

SMITH, M.L. (1991) Put to the test: The effects of external testing on teachers. *Educational Researcher*, **20**(5), 8–11.

SMITH, M.S. (1988) Educational indicators. *Phi Delta Kappan*, **69**(7), 487–491.

SORENSEN, A.B. (1970) Organizational differentiation of students and educational opportunity. *Sociology of Education*, **43**, 355–376.

SPENCER, B.D. (1983) On interpreting test scores as social indicators: Statistical considerations. *Journal of Educational Measurement*, **20**, 317–333.

SPROULL, L.S., and ZUBROW, D. (1981) Performance information in school systems: Perspectives from organization theory. *Educational Administration Quarterly*, **17**(3), 61–79.

STAHL, S.A., and MILLER, P.D. (1989) Whole language experience approaches for beginning reading: A quantitative research synthesis. *Review of Educational Research*, **59**(1), 87–116.

STEEDMAN, J. (1983) *Examination Results in Selective and Non-selective Schools.* London: National Children's Bureau.

STERN, J.D. (1986, April) *The Education Indicators Project on the US Department of Education.* Paper presented at the Annual Meeting of the American Educational Research Association, San Francisco, CA.

STERN, J.D., and WILLIAMS, M. (Eds.) (1986) *The Condition of Education.* Washington, DC: US Government Printing Office.

STILLMAN, A. and MAYCHELL, K. (1986) *Choosing schools: Parents, LEAs and the 1980 Education Reform Act.* Windsor: NFER-Nelson.

SUMMERS, A.A., and WOLFE, B.L. (1977) Do schools make a difference? *American Economic Review*, **67**, 639–652.

TAGIURI, R. (1968) The concept of organizational climate. In TAGIURI, R. and LITWIN, G.H. (Eds.), *Organizational Climate: Exploration of A Concept.* Boston: Harvard University, Graduate School of Business Administration. (pp. 11–32).

THOMPSON, J.D. (1967) *Organizations in Action.* New York: Mcgraw Hill.

THORNDIKE, R.L., and HAGEN, E. (1982) *Canadian Cognitive Abilities Test: Examiner's Manual.* Canada: Nelson Canada.

TIMAR, B., and KIRP, D.L. (1989) Education reform in the 1980s: Lessons from the States. *Phi Delta Kappan*, **70**(7), 504–511.

TORGERSON, D. (1986) Between knowledge and politics: Three faces of policy analysis. *Policy Sciences*, **19**, 33–59.

TRAVERS, R.M.W. (1981) Letter to the editor. *Educational Researcher*, **10**, 32.

TWENTIETH CENTURY FUND TASK FORCE ON FEDERAL ELEMENTARY AND SECONDARY EDUCATION POLICY (1983) *Making the Grade.* New York: Twentieth Century Fund, Inc.

US DEPARTMENT OF EDUCATION (1988) *Measuring Up: Questions and Answers About State Roles in Educational Accountability.* Washington, DC: Office of Educational Research and Improvement.

US DEPARTMENT OF EDUCATION (1989) *National Education Longitudinal Study, User's Manual.* Washington, DC: Office of Educational Research and Improvement.

WALKER, R. (1990, February 28) Governors set to adopt national education goals. *Education Week*, (p. 16).

WATSON, D.J. (1989) Defining and describing whole language. *The Elementary School Journal*, **90**, 129–141.

WEICK, K.E. (1976) Educational organizations as loosely coupled systems. *Administrative Science Quarterly*, **21**, 1–19.

WELCH, F. (1987) A reconsideration of the impact of school desegregation programs on public school enrolment of white pupils, 1968–76. *Sociology of Education*, **60**(4), 215–221.

WHITE, K.R. (1982) The relation between socioeconomic status and academic achievement. *Psychological Bulletin*, **91**(3), 461–481.

WHITE, K.R. (1986) The efficacy of early identification. *The Journal of Special Education*, **19**, 401–415.

References

WILLETT, J.B. (1988) Questions and answers in the measurement of change. In ROTHKOPF, E.Z. (Ed.), *Review of Research in Education*, Washington, DC: American Educational Research Association. (Vol. 15, pp. 345–422).

WILLIAMS, R.C., and BANK, A. (1984) Assessing instructional information systems in two districts: The search for impact. *Educational Evaluation and Policy Analysis*, 6(3), 267–282.

WILLMS, J.D. (1983) *Achievement Outcomes in Public and Private High Schools*. Doctoral dissertation, Stanford University.

WILLMS, J.D. (1985a) Catholic-school effects on academic achievement: New evidence from the High School and Beyond Follow-Up Study. *Sociology of Education*, 58(2), 98–114.

WILLMS, J.D. (1985b) The balance thesis: contextual effects of ability on pupils' O-grade examination results. *Oxford Review of Education*, 11(1), 33–41.

WILLMS, J.D. (1986) Social class segregation and its relationship to pupils' examination results in Scotland. *American Sociological Review*, 51(2), 224–241.

WILLMS, J.D. (1987) Differences between Scottish Education Authorities in their examination attainment. *Oxford Review of Education*, 13(2), 211–232.

WILLMS, J.D., and CHEN, M. (1989) The effects of ability grouping on the ethnic achievement gap in Israeli schools. *American Journal of Education*, 97(3), 237–257.

WILLMS, J.D., and JACOBSEN, S. (1990) Growth in mathematics skills during the intermediate years: Sex differences and school effects. *International Journal of Educational Research*, 14, 157–174.

WILLMS, J.D., and RAUDENBUSH, S.W. (1989) A longitudinal hierarchical linear model for estimating school effects and their stability. *Journal of Educational Measurement*, 26(3), 209–232.

WISE, A.E. (1988) The two conflicting trends in school reform: Legislated learning revisited. *Phi Delta Kappan*, 69(5), 328–332.

WOLF, D., BIXBY, J., GLENN, III, J., and GARDNER, H. (1991) To use their minds well: Investigating new forms of student assessment. In GRANT, G. (Ed.), *Review of Research in Education*. Washington, DC: American Educational Research Association. (Vol. 17, pp. 31–74).

WOODHOUSE, G., and GOLDSTEIN, H. (1988) Educational performance indicators and LEA league tables. *Oxford Review of Education*, 14(3), 301–320.

WYNNE, E.A. (1980) *Looking at Schools: Good, Bad, and Indifferent*. Lexington, MA: Heath.

WYNNE, E.A. (1984) School award programs: Evaluation as a component of incentive systems. *Educational Evaluation and Policy Analysis*, 6, 85–93.

YOGEV, A. (1981) Determinants of early educational career in Israel: Further evidence for the sponsorship thesis. *Sociology of Education*, 54, 181–95.

ZOLOTH, B.S. (1976) Alternative measures of school segregation. *Land Economics*, 52(3), 278–298.

Index

ability
  composition of 39–40, 48
  grouping 33, 68, 72–3, 84, 127, 130, 162
  intake 28, 99
  level 5–6, 10, 33–4, 36, 41–2, 44–6, 50, 54–5, 63, 65, 84, 89–90, 95, 124, 134–5, 140–1, 145, 148
  selective schooling 18–20
academic press 68, 71, 74, 80, 93, 96, 125, 148, 150, 154
access to data 6, 8, 24, 27, 97, 144, 152
accountability 4, 8–9, 11, 13–15, 17, 21, 23–4, 27, 30–1, 33, 35, 41, 48, 144, 146–7, 151, 155
accuracy 6, 35–6, 44–9, 53–4, 62–3, 75, 102, 145, 150
achievement
  educational 4, 7, 10, 13, 17, 28, 43, 53, 65, 67, 69, 72, 74–6, 78, 80, 82, 87–8, 93–5, 124, 131–2, 134, 144, 148, 150, 157–60
  gap 121, 128–9, 141
  input 38
  prior 6, 33–5, 45, 48–50, 52, 54, 56–63, 84, 127–8, 134, 146–7
  range 5–6
  rate of growth 34–7, 45, 90, 95–6, 102, 104
  SES and 50–2
  status 34–6
  targets 16, 35
  tests 30–1, 92, 95–6
  time 74–5
Achilles, C.M. 53, 131–2
Acland, H. 38
adjusted results 104, 115–17, 123, 128, 140, 145, 147, 158–9, 161
Adler, C. 127
Adler, M. 14
administration of tests 89–90, 95, 144, 150

affective measurement 92, 95
age v. grade 100, 102, 140, 150
aggregation 15, 18, 24, 31, 44, 49, 52–4, 63, 65, 72, 75, 80–1, 87–8, 90, 102, 147, 150, 153
Aitkin, M. 31, 39, 44
Alexander, K.L. 33, 38, 39, 54
Algozzine, B. 93
Ambron, S.R. 8
analysis
  achievement growth 34, 37
  annual report 103–19
    adjusted results 115–17
    segregation 113–15
    variation between schools 107–9
    variation in scores between groups 117–19
    year-to-year performance 109–13
  of covariance (ANCOVA) 53, 114
  data 5–6, 8, 10, 12, 24, 26–7, 30, 55, 94, 96, 100–1, 144, 151–5
  level 80–1
  policy 102
  regression 31, 46, 56, 61–3, 104, 116, 123–5, 129–30, 133–4, 138, 157–62
  techniques of statistical 10
Anderson, C.S. 32, 66, 67, 74, 79, 148
Anderson, L.W. 4, 23
Anderson, S. 53
assignment, random 52–3, 122, 129–31, 142, 151
Astuto, T.A. 667
Atkinson, P. 5
attainment 22, 24, 28, 42–3, 54, 56–7, 60, 95, 98, 125, 133
  selective schooling 18–20
attitude 66–8, 79, 144
  pupil 33, 71, 75–6, 78, 80–1, 93, 95, 119, 148–9, 154
  teacher 71, 76–8, 93, 129–30, 149, 154
Auquier, A. 53